GOOD

GOVERNMENT

in the

TROPICS

THE JOHNS HOPKINS STUDIES IN DEVELOPMENT

Vernon W. Ruttan and T. Paul Schultz, Consulting Editors

GOOD

GOVERNMENT

in the

TROPICS

• • •

Judith Tendler

THE JOHNS HOPKINS UNIVERSITY PRESS
BALTIMORE AND LONDON

The Johns Hopkins University Press
2715 North Charles Street
Baltimore, Maryland 21218-4319
The Johns Hopkins Press Ltd., London

Library of Congress Cataloging-in-Publication Data
will be found at the end of this book.
A catalog record for this book is available from the British Library.

ISBN 0-8018-5452-0

To Albert Hirschman,
with gratitude

Contents

Acknowledgments

THE RESEARCH behind this book could not have been done without the support of several people and institutions. For financial and other invaluable support, I thank the Institute of Planning of the state government of Ceará in Brazil (Fundação Instituto de Planejamento do Estado do Ceará/ IPLANCE), particularly its director, Antônio Cláudio Ferreira Lima, now Secretary of Planning. I also thank the Department of Urban Studies and Planning of the Massachusetts Institute of Technology for providing unstinting logistical support, funding, and leaves at the appropriate moment. I am grateful to Tasso Jereissati and Ciro Gomes, the two governors who brought good government to Northeast Brazil, for supporting the research and, at the same time, appreciating the academic freedom needed for research and publication. Jose Rosa Abreu Vale, who was Secretary of Social Action (and is again now), and Antônio Carlile Holanda Lavor, who was Secretary of Health, were important figures in the stories that follow. They showed enormous kindness to me and my students and passionate interest in talking about their work with us. Most of all, I thank Antônio Rocha Magalhães, colleague and friend, who was the Secretary of Planning of the state of Ceará when I first met him in 1988. He not only made this project possible in many ways, but he was strongly and silently behind some of the important achievements described herein.

For an opportunity to present my findings in Brazil on two separate occasions, I thank the Ceará state Department of Planning, the State University of Ceará, and the Development Bank of the Northeast in Brazil.

I also benefited immensely from the opportunity to get feedback on earlier versions of this manuscript in various seminars—in particular, the daylong workshop organized around the book by the Inter-American Dialogue and the Inter-American Development Bank at the latter institution in Washington. I thank Peter Hakim and Michael Shifter of the Dialogue for suggesting the event and making it happen, as well as a half-day session sponsored by the Dialogue at the Brookings Institution on an earlier occasion. I also received valuable feedback from colleagues at the workshop on "Social Capital, Government Action, and Economic Development" at the American Academy of Arts and Sciences, the UNDP workshop in Buenos Aires on New Generation Social Policies in Latin America, the LBJ School of Public Affairs in Austin, the Texas Industrial Areas Foundation of Austin, the Joint Harvard-MIT Political Development Seminar, the MIT workshop on the works of Albert Hirschman, the MIT Industrial Relations Seminar, and the U.S. Agency for International Development.

I am particularly grateful to the many colleagues who interacted with me about the ideas set forth here. For dedicating their time to reading one or another version of the manuscript—or parts of it—and giving me valuable comments and criticisms, I thank Gabrielle Watson, Jose Rosa Abreu Vale, Meenu Tewari, Paul Streeten, Elisabeth Stock, Paul Smoke, Herman Schwartz, Donald Schön, Bish Sanyal, Charles Sabel, Vernon Ruttan, Lloyd Rodwin, E. B. Rice, Dennis Purcell, Michael Piore, Robert Picciotto, Barbara Nunberg, Lynn McCormick, Antônio Rocha Magalhães, Albert Hirschman, Peter Hakim, Sara Freedheim, Silvia Dorado, Octavio Damiani, Alice Amsden, and Mônica Amorim. For invaluable research assistance, I thank Brandt Witte, Laura Tagle, Mônica Pinhanez, and John Frankenhoff.

For helping me put parts of a marked-up manuscript into neat hard copy on very short notice, I thank Janice Molloy and Grant Emmison. Maria den Boer of Nighthawk Designs was a superb and remarkably understanding copy editor. Kathy Hoag, senior secretary at MIT, helped me in myriad ways that made it possible for me to complete the book.

For tangling with me intensely over the ideas in the book, providing me with wonderful sources of reading, and marking up my prose from beginning to end with demanding questions, I am eternally grateful to Hubert Schmitz, Mick Moore, Richard Locke, Peter Evans, Susan Eckstein, and Rose Batt.

None of the persons or institutions named above, of course, is responsible for the ideas or interpretations within these pages, nor necessarily agrees with them.

This book was informed by several years of evaluation research that I carried out on government programs in Northeast Brazil, starting in the early 1980s. In addition, the project resulted from an unusual combination of research and teaching, starting in 1992, which I could not have done without the support of MIT and department heads Donald Schön, Phil Clay, and, particularly, Bish Sanyal. They all supported my integrating the training of graduate-student research assistants for this project and two subsequent ones into the teaching curriculum of the Department of Urban Studies and Planning. Much of the fieldwork on the four central cases was carried out under my supervision by five of these graduate students, with the collaboration of two more senior students in administrative and supervisory roles—Gabrielle Watson and Hugo Eduardo Beteta. We met together weekly for the semester preceding the fieldwork, which took place during the three summer months of 1992, and during the semester thereafter. I spent three weeks with them in Ceará and, since the 1992 fieldwork, returned there five times—most recently in August 1996—which allowed me to continue following developments there.

Two additional graduate students were an integral part of the group, although the cases they worked on ended up, for fortuitous reasons, not appearing in this book. Each of the seven went on to write a master's thesis on his or her particular case. The theses are listed in the references under their names—Sandra Zarur, Ruth Wade, Sara Freedheim, Silvia Dorado, Octavio Damiani, Julia Bucknall, and Mônica Amorim. They were a delight to work with—sharp, hard-working, intellectually challenging, passionate about their work, generous, and fun. The success of this venture with them made possible two subsequent projects of this nature—one in the state of Ceará again, in 1995, and another in the state of Maranhão in 1996—all of which earned the MIT Irwin Sizer Award in 1996 for Most Significant Improvement in Education at MIT.

Sara Freedheim worked on the preventive health case of chapter 2, Ruth Wade on the emergency employment-creating program of chapter 3, Octavio Damiani on the case of agricultural extension of chapter 4, and Mônica Amorim and Silvia Dorado on the small-firm public procurement program of chapter 5. (Sandra Zarur looked at innovative municipal governments, and Julia Bucknall at the history of a project to conserve a large area of mangroves in the capital city as an urban park.)

Earlier versions of parts of this manuscript appeared in Tendler and Freedheim (1994a,b) and Tendler and Amorim (1996). I thank *World Development* and the Brookings Institution for their permission to use these materials.

GOOD

GOVERNMENT

in the

TROPICS

· I ·

Introduction

THIS IS A book about good government in developing countries. We actually know much more about *bad* government in these places, and stories about it are by now a familiar litany. According to these accounts, public officials and their workers pursue their own private interests rather than those of the public good. Governments overextend themselves in hiring and spending. Clientelism runs rampant, with workers being hired and fired on the basis of kinship and political loyalty rather than merit. Workers are poorly trained and receive little on-the-job training. Badly conceived programs and policies create myriad opportunities for bribery, influence peddling, and other forms of malfeasance. All this adds up to the disappointing inability of many governments to deliver good public services and to cope with persistent problems of corruption, poverty, and macroeconomic mismanagement. In trying to explain this sad state of affairs, economists and political scientists have richly chronicled the bad behavior and used it to good advantage in the building of theory.[1]

This sorry experience, and the literature attempting to explain it, have given rise to the current body of advice proffered by bilateral and multilateral donor institutions, governments in North America and Western Europe, and even smaller nongovernment aid-giving organizations (NGOs). Much of the advice is directed at limiting the "damage" the public sector can do in developing countries, and falls into three categories: (1) reducing the size of government by getting rid of "excess" workers, contracting out for services, privatizing, and decentralizing; (2) terminating many of the policies and programs that inadvertently provide opportunities for bureaucrats to exert undue influence and for citizens to bribe them—such as the licensing of imports or exports, the subsidized provision of credit and other inputs to industry and agriculture, and the subsidized purchase of certain products; and (3) subjecting public agencies and their managers and workers to market-like pressures and incentives to perform, including exposing them to the wishes and dissatisfactions of users.[2]

I refer to the literature on which the advice is based as mainstream development thinking, and the advice-givers as the mainstream donor community. I purposely avoid the terms *neo-liberal* or *Washington consensus*[3] because the views summarized above, or some subset of them, are held by a larger and more disparate set of observers and practitioners than those terms imply. For example, both neo-liberals and their ardent critics, like the NGOs, believe that government in developing countries is overbearingly powerful, and that several of its functions would be better carried out or monitored by private entities, including NGOs. Again, both advocates and critics of state intervention stress the importance of incentives, pressures, and increased user voice in improving the performance of government. And a good number of development practitioners who feel perfectly comfortable using the language and concepts of the mainstream development community are not aware of the writings that gave rise to these views and, if asked, would disagree with them. Nevertheless, this set of ideas about the causes of poor performance and about how to improve it profoundly influences the way development practitioners interpret what they see, write reports, and give advice.

The explanations of poor performance summarized above, although in many ways accurate, have given rise to a consistently flawed body of advice about how to improve government. The flaws fall into the following categories.

First, the mainstream donor community's advice about public-sector reform arises from a literature that looked mainly at *poor* performance. Although this literature has advanced our understanding of why governments so often do badly,[4] it has provided nowhere near the same insights and case material on the circumstances under which governments perform well.[5] This means that countries and the experts that advise them have few models of good government that are grounded in these countries' own experiences.

Second, and insofar as the mainstream development community has shown more interest recently in analyzing good performance and "best practice," it has focused too much on recommending that developing countries import ideas and practices from the already industrialized countries or from some of the more recently industrialized countries, particularly those of East Asia. The exemplars of best practice for advice about public management are Australia, New Zealand, Britain, and, to a lesser extent, the United States—the so-called New Public Management or Managerialism;[6] the exemplars of best-practice macroeconomic policies and development strategies are, as everyone knows, the East Asian countries. Approaching inquiry in this way often leads to incorrect interpretations of why governments in developing countries sometimes perform well, as examples below and others throughout this book show, or completely misses instances of good performance that do not fit the mold.

Third, the development literature likes to label whole countries (or groups of them) as good or bad performers. This habit comes from the overwhelming preoccupation of the field in the 1980s with major macrolevel economic problems, as well as from the "national models" literature of the field of comparative politics and international political economy.[7] But it is difficult to be engaged in characterizing a whole country as good or bad, on the average, and at the same time to be curious about the variation between good and bad experiences within that same country and the lessons to be learned from it. For this reason, the donor community is not very adept at unearthing and explaining promising developments within countries that perform poorly on the average, or good performance by some government agencies as distinct from others in the same country. In giving advice to the bad performers, then, donors are best at telling them about the practices of good performers somewhere else and how to be more like them.

A good illustration is the set of studies explaining why Latin America did not do what East Asia did,[8] followed by a cottage industry of advice to Latin America on how to be more like East Asia. A recent World Bank publication criticizing the Latin American "populist state," for example, declares that "[r]elatively little is known about the process leading to massive institutional change" in Latin America (Burki and Edwards 1996:27). With respect to labor market and employment policies, it then suggests looking at "the lessons of East Asia's success"; with respect to ideas about how to create "a modern civil service," it suggests looking at East Asia's "efficient meritocracies" (pp. 23, 26). Once the seal of good (or bad) ap-

proval is stuck to a country, finally, observers interpret much of what is
going on there through that particular lens. For example, while Italy was
fabled for many years for its corruption and lack of political stability, significant developments in institutional dynamism, stability, and trust between major actors at the regional level remained, until recently, unchron-
icled (Locke 1995:chap. 1).

Fourth, the mainstream development community often filters what it
sees through the lens of a strong belief in the superiority of the market
mechanism for solving many problems of government, economic stagnation, and poverty. This also creates a propensity for misinterpretation of
good performance, the classic example coming from the successful growth
stories of the East Asian countries. Until the World Bank's publication of
The East Asian Miracle in 1993,[9] the donor community interpreted these
successes as representing minimal government intervention in markets,
despite substantial evidence to the contrary.[10] These governments used
highly interventionist policy instruments, all of which are considered by
the donor community to be wrong: they subsidized credit to agriculture
and industry, they fixed key prices, and they told firms what to produce.
Other instances of the development community's inattention to the evidence in interpreting success will be revealed in the course of this book.

Fifth, many of today's views on the roots of poor performance in developing countries simply ignore and even contradict an impressive body
of evidence on the causes of improved performance in large organizations
in the industrialized countries. This evidence, based partly on studies of
high-performing firms, appears in recent research on industrial performance
and workplace transformation, in an older literature on the sociology of
organizations, and even in the popular treatments of private-sector restructuring in the press. I refer to this body of research and advice as the literature of industrial performance and workplace transformation (IPWT).[11]
Although the earlier research on this subject involved mainly manufacturing firms, many of the same findings have emerged from later studies
of large service firms.[12] Although focused mainly on private firms rather
than public agencies, many of the IPWT findings are now being applied
to the public sector of the industrialized countries.[13]

IPWT researchers have pointed to the importance of worker dedication
to the job, among other things, in accounting for increases in productivity and other improvements in performance. This has caused the best-practice firms to pay close attention, even when downsizing, to a set of innovative practices that has increased worker dedication. These include what

is now popularly known as worker participation and self-managed worker teams, multiskilling of workers and multitask jobs, and flexibly organized or "specialized" production. Almost all these innovations involve greater worker discretion and autonomy, greater cooperation between labor and management, and greater trust between workers (or firms) and their customers, as well as between workers and managers.[14] Many of these practices were disseminated as a result of extensive research on Japanese "lean" production, which produced grounded models of how to change organizational practices and management.[15]

In analyzing governments and in issuing advice about how to reform them, the mainstream development community has shown remarkably little interest in the subject of worker dedication to the job. Guided by an almost religious belief in self-interest as an explanation of human behavior—what Charles Sabel so aptly calls "the science of suspicion"[16]—the attention of the development literature has been riveted on the *absence* of worker commitment. Whereas the IPWT research tries to understand the kinds of social norms and organizational cultures that foster dedication among workers, the donor community starts with the assumption that civil servants are self-interested, rent-seeking, and venal unless proven otherwise. Whereas the IPWT literature prescribes greater worker autonomy and discretion as a way of obtaining better performance, the development community prescribes just the opposite—namely, reducing the discretion of civil servants and, thereby, their opportunities to misbehave. Whereas downsizing is but one of many measures used by successfully restructuring firms to increase productivity and profits, the donor community has focused most of its attention on downsizing government to the exclusion of complementary measures required to increase performance.[17] This despite the clear evidence from the private sector that without measures to reorganize work in ways that increase worker commitment, downsizing does not lead to increased productivity and often makes performance worse.[18]

Sixth, and related, today's views on reforming the public sector place excessive faith in the actions of the "user" or "client" of public services. In an otherwise laudable advance, the development community now views consultations with and pressures from the client—the citizen, the villager, the grass roots—as key to fixing government. This new faith manifests itself in three ways: the proliferation of research on user behavior and preferences, the keen interest in decentralizing government in order that it be (among other things) closer to the user, and the enthusiasm over "associ-

ationalism" and civil society—particularly user associations and other
NGOs that demand accountability from government or provide services
themselves.[19]

This turn of attention toward users of public services and their local
setting represents a distinct improvement over the previous period of almost complete disinterest by planners in what citizens thought or wanted.
It is also quite consistent with the findings of the IPWT studies, which
show that the best-practice service firms try to be more responsive to customers and work closely with them. But the IPWT studies also show that
responsiveness to the client requires a larger context of relations of trust
between committed workers and their customers. This has translated into
research on, and enactment of, the kinds of changes in workplace conditions that enable trusting relations to develop. Although the mainstream
development community has now become as interested in the user as the
IPWT community, it has nevertheless shown little interest in the larger
setting of trust between workers and users that user involvement requires
in order to improve performance.

Seventh, IPWT researchers and practitioners have dwelled on the need
to change the existing system of centralized and highly defined labor-management relationships that have prevailed since the 1930s in the United
States and other Western countries. This system, in which big labor negotiated collective bargaining agreements with big management, worked
fairly well under the mid-twentieth-century system of stable consumer markets and mass production. The system is no longer compatible, however,
with the requirements of today's rapidly changing, more globalized, highly
competitive markets. The high-performance practices associated with adaptation to these changed conditions depend on greater consultation between
labor and management around daily problems, more cooperative and informal relations between the two parties, greater flexibility around the
definition of jobs, and decentralization of production, management, and
supervision. For this reason, IPWT researchers and practitioners have been
engaged in a profound debate over the past 10 years about how to change
a system of labor-management relations that no longer works.[20]

The mainstream development community has shown little appreciation
of the need for this kind of debate or research.[21] But its regular complaints
about public-sector unions—that stalemates between governments and
their public-sector unions have seriously jeopardized needed reforms—
suggest a dire need for such research. Similarly, the international donors
have displayed no interest in the important role that they, as third-party

institutions, could play in stimulating and mediating the difficult debates and supporting the research needed to face this challenge properly. Instead, the donor community has cast public-sector unions and professional associations as the villains in stories of attempted reform, particularly in the social sectors of education and health—to be avoided, circumvented, and undermined.[22] Ironically, this vilification of public-sector employee associations has occurred at a time when the donor community has been celebrating all other forms of associationalism and civil society, including business associations. Surely, associations of workers and professionals should number among this now-celebrated set of collective actors. But while the development community consistently describes public employee associations as the ultimate in *self*-interest, it views all other forms of associationalism—in a serious lapse of consistency—as wholesome expressions of the *public* interest. This amounts to a lopsided picture not only of worker associations, but of what is necessary to achieve reform in problem sectors.

Associations of public-sector workers and professionals have certainly made reform difficult on various occasions and continue to do so, creating a serious problem for improving government. But they have also presented more opportunities for constructive action in the public interest than the current vilification of them suggests. In a study of the responses of Latin American unions to proposed reforms of social service delivery, for example, Murillo notes that despite "the common assumption . . . that public sector unions opposed these reforms, union responses were diverse . . . [including] resistance, cooperation, negotiation and inaction" (1996:1). In research on significant recent advances made in the public management of India's forests, Joshi (forthcoming) discovered, to her surprise, that the public-sector workers' association—the West Bengal Subordinate Forest Employees Association—played a key role in advocating and implementing these reforms.

In a study of high performance in education by a municipal government in Northeast Brazil, Frankenhoff (forthcoming) found that the best teachers had spearheaded a long campaign to promote these reforms. Opponents to the reform, moreover, were not the usual suspects—teachers and teachers' unions—but elected local government officials who did not want to lose their power to use teacher appointments for patronage. This finding is actually quite consistent with those of a forthcoming book by Ames on Brazilian politics, particularly his analyses of governors who were modernizing and clientelistic at the same time.[23] Ames describes how certain developmental governors in Northeast Brazil—legendary for being one of the worst-performing regions of the world in primary education—devoted their "modernizing" attention mainly to certain initiatives and government agencies in the spheres of budgeting, planning, and economic development. They built those agencies up with technocratic expertise, endowed them with considerable power, and carefully protected them from clientelistic meddling. In order to meet their continuing needs to distribute patronage, these governors turned to the social sectors, particularly education—the very sectors whose problems are attributed to intransigent public-sector unions. Although politicians as opposed to public-sector unions are not mutually exclusive explanations for the difficulties of reforming the social sectors, Ames' analysis certainly suggests an important additional explanation unrelated to public-sector unions.

Studies of positive experiences involving worker associations like those cited above are rare and we therefore know very little about their dynamics. This represents a strange lack of research interest in a subject of great importance to the performance of the public sector—research that could impart strategic lessons for reform. Lessons like these are needed to help break the stalemate—just as the IPWT community, toward this very end, has been chronicling cases of union-management cooperation in the late twentieth century in both private and public sectors.[24] Although an outstanding example of reform led by public-sector professionals emerges in the course of this book—that of public health physicians and nurses—public-sector worker associations are not its main topic; instead, the book focuses on workers themselves—what they think, how they respond, and what makes them dedicated.

This book constructs an argument for thinking differently about public-sector reform and presents some examples of how to formulate advice by drawing on cases of good performance. In so doing, it reveals how some of the current advice goes wrong. The argument is developed through a set of four cases, each of which constitutes a chapter of the book. The cases involve programs in different sectors—rural preventive health, employment-creating works programs, agricultural extension, and assistance to small enterprises. The programs were carried out by a state government in Brazil whose performance turned rapidly from bad to good in the mid-1980s, and remained so until the time of this writing.

The Research

In the December 1991 issue of the *Economist* of London, the editors devoted three pages of a special supplement on Brazil to the remarkable accomplishments of one of the state governments in that country's poor Northeast region, Ceará. With almost seven million inhabitants and an area of 147,000 square kilometers, Ceará is one of Brazil's smaller states in terms of population, although it is still larger than a few dozen small countries.[25]

The *Economist* story told of how the state's payroll commitments were consuming 87 percent of the state's receipts (65% is the constitutional limit) when a newly elected reformist governor, Tasso Jereissati, took over in 1987 at the age of 36.[26] This left so little for nonpersonnel operating costs, public investment, and servicing of the debt that public servants had not been paid for three months. The new governor succeeded in solving the crisis with various bold measures, including the collection of taxes already on the books, reducing payroll obligations to 40,000 "ghost" workers (out of a total of 146,000 workers), slowing down the indexing of salaries to the cost-of-living index (inflation was more than 20% a month during that period), and insisting that new government employees be hired only through competitive exams.[27] Together, these measures reduced the share of salaries in total receipts from 87 percent of expected receipts in 1987 to 45 percent in 1991, all during a time when federal transfers were decreasing. This was the dream of every Brazilian governor in the 1980s, but only an idle one for most. Just as noteworthy, and also mentioned by the *Economist* article, the new government introduced some outstanding and innovative programs in preventive health, public procurement from informal-sector producers, and a large emergency employment-creating public works program. This last set of achievements is the subject of this book.

As a sign of the dramatic import and political difficulty of all these reforms, Jereissati lost 90 percent of his support in the state legislature soon after he started his term. His popularity among voters nevertheless remained high enough for him to elect his successor (Ciro Gomes) when his term expired, and then to win reelection himself four years later. Immediately following Jereissati's initial reforms, the leader of his party in the legislature—also Ciro Gomes at that time—frequently recounted publicly how he was booed for days every time he entered the chamber. Despite these setbacks, the advances were sustained throughout the subsequent four-year administration of Ciro Gomes (1991–94), also a reformer, and into the second administration of Jereissati, still unfolding (1995–). Clearly, this set of reforms represents a striking feat, unheard of among the state administrations of Northeast Brazil. Also interesting, but hardly noted in the various accounts of Ceará's story, none of these reforms or programs could be attributed to the presence or pressures of an outside donor. Indeed, the one sector in which donors had an appreciable presence—that of agriculture—was strangely absent from the list of both these governors' achievements.

The two reformist governors were also able to take credit for the fact that the economy of the state grew better during the late 1980s and early 1990s than that of the rest of the Northeast and even the more developed parts of Brazil—during a period when growth rates for Brazil were generally low or even negative. While Northeast output declined by an annual average of 0.04 percent during the 1987–93 period, and Brazil grew at only 0.87 percent, Ceará grew at 3.4 percent.[28] The *Economist* attributed the better growth record to the modernizing and probusiness policies of the state's new leadership, as did other laudatory articles that appeared elsewhere in the international and Brazilian press.[29] It should be pointed out, however, that the state grew at significantly higher rates in the earlier period before the two governors took over. To grow faster than Brazil and the rest of the Northeast during a time of stagnation, in any case, was quite an unusual accomplishment for a small state government in a poor and clientelistic region of a very large country.

To anyone who knows Brazil, the Ceará stories were surprising. Ceará and its eight neighbor states belong to the country's poorest region, Northeast Brazil, in which one-third of the population lives in absolute poverty. With a population of 45 million and an area of 1.6 million square kilometers, the Northeast holds almost one-third of Brazil's population. Its area is roughly equivalent to France, Germany, and Spain combined, and its population somewhat larger than that of Spain.[30] Like state governments in many chronically underdeveloped regions, the nine Northeast states are legendary for their clientelistic ways of governing and for the resulting poor quality of public administration.[31] They are exactly the kinds of governments that have fueled the despair about government with which this chapter started.

How could a state government that was part of a region with such a long and consistent history of mediocre performance "suddenly" do so well? How could it have become, as the news coverage reported, a "model" of public administration sought out by other states in Brazil and other countries of Latin America, and feted by international institutions like the World Bank? The press coverage and the international development community attributed the success to the leadership of the two successive reformist governors. They belonged to a new center-left political party of modernizing urban elites, the Brazilian Social Democratic Party, which had been formed in the late 1980s and went on to win the presidential elections in 1994. Granted the centrality of these leaders to the Ceará story, it was still not clear how they could have so rapidly overcome, as the press portrayed it, a long tradition of clientelism in the administration of public expenditures and political opposition to taking away such privileges. It was also not clear how reputedly mediocre state agencies could have delivered the sustained performance, over a period of more than eight years and including two changes in administration, that was necessary to make these reforms work.

These questions, and my dissatisfaction with the prevailing thinking of the mainstream development community, led me to formulate the research project that gave rise to this book. I worked together with seven research assistants looking into the four cases of good performance under the new Ceará governors. Three of these cases appeared in the *Economist* article, and the fourth entered the study for reasons explained below. I briefly summarize the accomplishments of these programs, presented in roughly descending order of the strength of their accomplishments. (This order is slightly different from the sequence of the four chapters, which follows the logic of the themes that unite them.)

The first program involved rural preventive health (chap. 2). Only a few years after the state Department of Health undertook a new preventive health program, vaccination coverage for measles and polio had tripled from a low of 25 percent to 90 percent of the child population, and infant deaths had fallen from the high rate of 102 per 1,000 to 65 per 1,000. Started in 1987 by the state Department of Health as part of an emergency program to create jobs during a drought, the program hired 7,300 workers (mostly women) as community health agents at the minimum wage, and 235 half-time nurses to supervise them. Before the program's inception, only 30 percent of the state's 178 municípios[32] had a nurse, let alone a doctor or health clinic. Four years later, the program operated in virtually all of the state's municípios.[33] For these accomplishments, Ceará became, in March 1993, the first Latin American government to win UNICEF's Maurice Pate prize for child support programs.

The second program involved business extension and public procurement from small firms, and also originated in the employment-creating concerns of the 1987 drought (chap. 5). The state Department of Industry and Commerce and the Brazilian Small Enterprise Service, a semiprivate agency, redirected 30 percent of the state's purchases of goods and services to firms operating mainly in the informal sector. In doing so, the state saved approximately 30 percent over its previous purchases of these items from fewer, larger, and more sophisticated suppliers. Along with these new contracts to small firms, the two agencies provided small firms with highly focused technical and other problem-solving assistance. Some of these contracts had lasting effects on the producers, helping to launch them into private markets to which they could never have otherwise aspired. Some of the contracts also resulted in striking developmental effects in the regions where the producers were located, which endured even when the contracts were not renewed. Alongside this successful "demand-driven" assistance to small firms, the same two agencies continued to carry out their less impressive, and more typical, "supply-driven" programs.

The third initiative involved employment-creating public works construction and other emergency relief (chap. 3). During the 1987 drought, which lasted almost a whole year, the state Department of Social Action gave work to one million unemployed rural farmers and other workers, mainly in public works construction. In the peak month, 240,000 were employed, roughly 50 percent of the economically active population in the state's rural area. Although the state government had succeeded in creating at least this number of temporary jobs in previous droughts (which occur roughly every seven years in the semiarid Northeast region), the 1987 program dramatically reduced the clientelism surrounding the awarding of jobs, the selection of works projects, and the allocation of relief. Insisting on more democratic decision making according to universal criteria, the Department of Social Action also succeeded in delivering jobs and relief supplies more rapidly than in previous droughts, and in creating more jobs per dollar spent than similar programs in other states and countries.

The fourth case revolved around agricultural extension and small farmers (chap. 4). Conspicuously absent from the *Economist* article on Ceará was the agricultural sector, where 33 percent of the labor force works. The state's lack of achievements in this traditionally important sector are perhaps not that surprising, given that agriculture has been afflicted by low productivity and declining output shares for many years. (Agriculture's share of state output fell from 14.7% to 8.5% between 1985 and 1994.)[34] Unlike the sectors in which the state could report significant accomplishments, ironically, Ceará's agricultural sector had received major infusions of funding and technical assistance over the preceding 15 years for agricultural and rural development programs jointly funded by international donors and the central government. These programs had targeted small farmers because they constituted a large percentage of the population and accounted for a major share of the state's production of staple foods and cash crops. A majority of them cultivated the land through insecure tenancy arrangements that stifled the adoption of productivity-increasing practices.

Given the significance of agriculture in the state and the sustained outside support from multilateral donors, I found the absence of any striking achievements in this sector to be puzzling. The rural development programs had worked mainly through the state's Agricultural Extension Service, and had encouraged small farmers to form associations through which they could receive the state's agricultural assistance. I therefore chose to look into the experiences of a few small-farmer associations that had done relatively well in terms of increased output or provision of services to their members, in order to see what lessons for state policy might emerge.

Each of these four cases represents a sector for which a self-contained literature and a corresponding body of advice exists—namely, preventive health care, employment-creating public works programs, agricultural extension to small farmers, and assistance to small and micro enterprises. Much of these four literatures and their advice is, understandably, specific to each particular sector. No one writes in the same breath about agricultural extension agents, barefoot doctors, small-enterprise assistance agents, and drought relief workers. While this book grounds each case in the debates of each of these sectors, its greater significance lies in the findings that run across the cases.

The Previews

My search for the explanations of good performance produced five central themes. Something happened in all of these programs—sometimes unintentionally—that structured the work environment differently from the normal and, in certain cases, from the way experts think such services should be organized.

First, government workers in all these cases demonstrated unusual dedication to their jobs. They reported feeling more appreciated and recognized, not necessarily by superiors but by their clients and the communities where they worked. This was remarkable in an era of public revulsion for the government bureaucrat. Only against the background of the IPWT literature did I come to understand the relation of these expressions of worker commitment to the achievements being studied, and the importance of looking into what caused them. This does not mean that I found worker-management teams or total quality management thriving in the backlands of Ceará where these programs unfolded. Rather, the explanations people gave for why they liked their jobs better, and of how their work was different from normal, had much in common with current explanations for the cases of better worker performance in the industrialized world. The way citizens spoke about the workers who served them in these programs, in turn, was reminiscent of the way this literature describes the relations of trust between customers and the firms they buy from, or between customer firms and their subcontractors.

Second, the state government contributed in an unusual and sometimes inadvertent way to the new sense of recognition. It created a strong sense of "calling" and mission around these particular programs and their workers. It did this through public information campaigns, prizes for good performance, public screening methods for new recruits, orientation programs, and sheer boasting through the media about its successes.

Third, workers carried out a larger variety of tasks than usual, and often voluntarily. They did this in response to their perception of what their clients needed, and out of a vision of the public good. Workers were able to provide this more customized service because they had greater autonomy and discretion than usual. On the one hand, this conflicts with the donor community's interest in reducing discretion as a way of minimizing the opportunities for rent-seeking behavior. On the other hand, it is perfectly consistent with the findings of the IPWT literature on the customization of work: multitask jobs, multiskilled workers, and greater discretion tend to be linked to better performance—in contrast to the more narrowly defined and standardized jobs of the mass production era.[35]

Fourth, the greater discretion and responsibilities inherent in the "self-enlarged" jobs, and their fuzzier job definitions, would seem to make supervision even more difficult than it already is in large public bureaucracies. Would this greater autonomy not simply provide even more opportunities for the rent-seeking misbehaviors that public-sector reformers worry about—graft, bribery, and other malfeasances? This did not happen in the Ceará cases because two other mechanisms—hemming civil servants in with new pressures to be accountable—worked in the opposite direction. These pressures did not come from supervisors or formal monitoring bodies.

On the one hand, workers wanted to perform better in order to live up to the new trust placed in them by their clients and citizens in general. The trust was a result of the more customized arrangements of their work and the public messages of respect from the state. On the other hand, the communities where these public servants worked watched over them more closely. The state's publicity campaigns and similar messages had armed citizens with new information about their rights to better government and about how public services were supposed to work. Government played a powerful role in monitoring, then, but it did so indirectly.

Fifth, a final set of findings emerged with respect to issues of decentralization, local government, and participation of civic associations and other NGOs. The enthusiasm about decentralization in the development community today portrays local government and civil society as locked in a healthy two-way dynamic of pressures for accountability that results in improved government. Central government, in this scenario, has retreated to the place of an enabling bystander. Civic associations and other NGOs, physically closer to local government than to central government, now become key independent actors in advocating for citizens, demanding greater accountability and "transparency" from government, and providing some services previously delivered by central or local government.[36] Numerous examples of this line of reasoning can be found in the narratives of donor organizations,[37] including the claims made for the social investment funds, one of the important new program approaches of the donor community in the 1990s.[38]

My cases did not confirm this scenario of a two-way dynamic and a diminishing central government. They revealed, rather, a three-way dynamic that included an activist "central government"—in this case, the state government—as well as local governments and civil society. (I use the terms *central government* and *state government* interchangeably in this text, because state governments are powerful actors vis-à-vis municipal governments in Brazil's federal system, and because to the extent that decentralization was involved in these programs, it was from state to municipal government.)[39] The state government took certain traditional powers away from municipal governments, while at the same time devolving others. It carried out some tasks, moreover, that are considered to be to its disadvantage in the standard portrayal of the most desirable division of labor between central and local governments—like outreach to the poor and the hiring and training of municipal workers. It was not that central government continued to do what it had done in the past, but that it was doing something different and quite actively so. Although these findings portray a different picture than that of the decentralization scenario outlined above, they are nevertheless consistent with the findings of some recent case studies of successful public-service bureaucracies in developing countries.[40]

The state government, in these cases, was also contributing in a major way to the creation of civil society by encouraging and assisting in the organizing of civic associations, including producer groups, and working through them. These groups then turned around and "independently" demanded better performance from government, both municipal and central, just as if they were the autonomous entities portrayed by students of civil society. This complicates the currently popular assumption of one-way causality, according to which good civil society leads to good government and, correspondingly, good government is dependent on the previous existence of a well-developed civil society.[41]

In contributing to the creation of civil society, it should be noted, the state government was doing something normally considered to fall within the domain of NGOs—advocacy for citizens and for the protection of their rights. Both the improvement of municipal government and the strengthening of civil society, in sum, were in many ways the result of a new activism by central government, rather than of its retreat. By no means a mere enabler, central government was doing more and not less than it had done before.

All this suggests a path to improved local government that is different, or at least more complex, than the current thinking about decentralization and civil society. Although I relate the decentralization findings only loosely to those about workplace transformation, the two are nevertheless intertwined throughout the stories in this book.

Clarifications

The intention of this book is to ground my critique and the alternative perspectives I outline above in the specifics of real cases. I do not develop the cases for their own intrinsic value, nor do I tell "the Ceará story." Those readers looking for that story should stop here and consult the interesting literature on the subject in Portuguese.[42] Not dwelling on the Ceará case as such will disappoint some readers and be appreciated by others, including the many Brazilians who are experiencing "Ceará fatigue." The approaches to better government reflected in these cases, moreover, should not be taken literally as "models" of good government. Those familiar with successful experiences in other countries may not find them especially unusual, and may well have observed variations on these particular solutions or even better ones elsewhere.

One of the most interesting facets of the achievements related below is their mixed nature. This is not, in other words, a story of unmitigated success. In this sense, however, it may be a more realistic portrayal of the typical development success story. Some of the achievements represented outstanding episodes embedded in otherwise quite pedestrian programs. Similarly, others were exceptions that took place only in certain local offices of statewide programs. As the years passed, moreover, some programs lost part of the ground they had gained. Most interesting, some of the achievements seemed inadvertent or, at least, not attributable to strongly intentioned leadership. This poses a particularly interesting challenge to researchers of good government: if good performance is unintentional, then is it not difficult to draw lessons from it? I return to this subject in the conclusion.

An additional clarification follows from the above. Although I was attracted to the study of Ceará by the glowing reports about two successive reformist governors there, this book does not give center stage to the issue of their leadership. It does not look into the interesting question of how and why they could be elected in a state with a long tradition of clientelism; and it does not analyze the difficult reforms for which they were most directly responsible—increasing revenues and controlling expenditures. The achievements of three of the programs outlined above, however, might be said to have indirectly resulted from these reforms, in that they were partly inspired by the desire of a new government to announce bold initiatives that would not exacerbate, or perhaps even reduce, the fiscal crisis.

My decision not to pay major attention to the subject of leadership merits some comment. Many observers of reforms like these stress the importance of good leadership and, correspondingly, point to the lack thereof in explaining failures to reform elsewhere. Ironically, moreover, they point to cases like Ceará as containing no generalizable lessons precisely *because* of their "unusually" good leadership. Although I do not question the importance of leadership, I do disagree with this kind of reasoning.

It is difficult to pursue the kinds of questions raised above about unintentional or unnoticed successes while, at the same time, trying to explain a case of "good leadership." The strong leader, after all, represents the ultimate in intentionality. An explanation of good performance that stresses outstanding leadership emphasizes, by its very focus on individuals, the singularity of certain experiences, namely, their unlikelihood of being repeated. Planners, however, need to search for the repeatable lessons contained in stories of achievement like these, even though they may not have the same appeal as stirring tales of individual endeavor by a charismatic leader. Those who are in the business of intervening in the development process, moreover, do not have much control over whether and when good leaders appear. When they do, the lesson for planners seems to be, if anything, that a good leader is hard to find. This does not add up to much of a guide for action.

In addition to the good leaders behind the successful programs, there are also many programs shepherded by outstanding leaders that have not done well or that simply passed out of existence. More than the question of leadership, then, I have been drawn toward the question of why some programs succeed and others do not, even when both kinds have good leaders. An equally challenging question is why some good programs are able to survive the departure of their "charismatic leader," while others do not. The most successful and sustained program described here, the preventive health program, poses precisely this question. Its architect and visionary leader left the program less than two years after he started it and, in the five years of sustained program success after his departure, no fewer than six replacements followed him as director of the state Department of Public Health. Why did this loss of leadership and subsequent high turnover in management not spell doom—as would have been predicted by those who see good leadership as paramount and, at the same time, hard to come by? I have chosen to address these particular kinds of questions and quandaries because their answers seem to hold more lessons than does an exploration of leadership for those thinking about how planners can intervene successfully.

This research, finally, looked mainly at good performance rather than bad. In this sense, is it not subject to the same criticism of lopsidedness that I made of the prevailing literature of failure and its corresponding policy advice? The answer is no, thanks to the very abundance of the literature on public-sector failures and the reasons for them, and also to my own 25 years of exposure to the shortcomings of government programs in developing countries.[43] This prior schooling in the dynamics of failure became the point of departure for my questions about success.

Why, for example, did nurses and doctors not resist a new preventive health program that relied on the hiring of 7,300 barely trained community health agents? After all, resistance to the use of paraprofessionals in health routinely blocks or undermines many such programs in other countries. Why, in turn, did the small firms that flourished with contracts from the new public procurement program not regress to their prior fragile state when the government did not renew the contracts? This, after all, is a typical scenario in such programs elsewhere. Why would mayors and other traditionally influential local notables simply give up the right to name constituents for local jobs, or relinquish their power to determine which works projects would be undertaken in their municipalities and where?

I asked these same kinds of questions about the variation within programs. Why, for example, did these programs work better in some municípios than in others? Why did the state government's support for small firms lead to a growth-pole success story with the furniture producers of São João do Aruaru but not with the footwear producers of Sobral? Why, again, was the state's campaign against the cotton boll weevil successful with small landowning farmers but not with large landowners or sharecroppers? Poor performance, in short, was always in my mind, and often lurking inside the very successes chosen for study.

A few closing words about the logic of the following chapters. In presenting evidence for the themes laid out above, the four chapters are not symmetrical. Some of the cases illustrate a particular theme more than the others. Although a case may clearly exemplify one or more of the themes noted above, moreover, I have sometimes devoted at least equal attention to the relevance of the case to larger debates about service delivery in that particular sector. The cases and their unfolding, then, are used more as a way of developing the argument than as equal blocks of evidence.

The first theme, that of higher productivity and worker dedication to the job, appears clearly in each case, although I dwell on it most in the first two cases of rural preventive health and emergency public works programs (chaps. 2 and 3). The second theme, that of multitask jobs and "customized" patterns of work, appears most clearly in the cases of agricultural extension and public procurement (chaps. 4 and 5). Evidence on the linked issues of decentralization, local government, participation, civil society, and nongovernment organizations runs throughout the cases. Partly for this reason, and partly because of the current importance of the social investment funds as instruments for targeting the poor, I fully develop these themes only in the conclusion (chap. 6), where examples can be drawn from the case material that went before.

I devote more attention throughout to the subjects of worker dedication to the job, the customization of work, and trust between workers and citizens, than to the matter of outside pressures to perform. The development literature has already brought to light the importance of these pressures, as reflected in the current recommendations to bring competition-like pressures to bear on government providers through partial privatization, decentralization, and performance contracting.[44] All these measures are expected to make service provision more demand-driven and client-friendly. Because I had extensively explored the role of outside pressures to perform in previous evaluation research,[45] I was somewhat less interested in the subject this time around. In the course of the research, moreover, I discovered that outside pressures were only half the story. When they were effective, that is, they were strongly reinforced by worker commitment, a different work environment, and trust.

I start with the health program because it was the most clear-cut success story. Given the sheer breadth and longevity of the program in comparison to the other achievements, the theme of dedication to work and its relation to performance was writ particularly large. Because the health program started with a whole new set of workers, moreover, it had more opportunity than the other programs to pay attention to what would induce its workers to perform well. Understanding how this worked in the case of health makes it easier to identify the variations on this theme that appeared in the three other cases.

• 2 •

Preventive Health: The Case
of the Unskilled Meritocracy

PRIOR TO THE initiation of the preventive health program in 1987, Ceará's indicators of health and access to health services were among the worst in Latin America. The rate of infant deaths, at 102 per 1,000, was double that for all of Brazil. Vaccination coverage for measles and polio was only 25 percent, and only 30 percent of the state's municípios had a nurse, let alone a doctor or health clinic. At best, mayors had an ambulance at their disposal and kept a small dispensary of prescription medicines in their homes. They typically doled out these medicines, as well as ambulance rides, to relatives and friends and to needy constituents in return for political loyalty. The new Brazilian constitution of 1988 augmented the mayors' access to revenues for health expenditures by increasing the share of federal transfers to the municípios, giving them greater taxing power, and mandating that 10 percent of these new revenues be spent on health (plus 25% on education).[1] Many mayors, however, continued spending less than the mandated amount on health, because enforcement mechanisms were not strong enough. If they did increase health expenditures, they often continued dispensing services in the traditional clientelistic way.

By 1992, after only five years in operation, the new preventive health program—named the Health Agent Program (Programa de Agentes de

Saúde/PAS) and designed and run by the state Department of Health (Secretaria de Saúde)—changed this dramatically. Infant deaths had declined by 36 percent to 65 per 1,000, vaccination coverage for measles and polio tripled to 90 percent of the population, and virtually all the state's 178 municípios had a nurse and a public health program.[2] The health agents were visiting 850,000 families in their homes every month—roughly 65 percent of the state's population. They provided assistance and advice with respect to oral rehydration therapy, vaccination, prenatal care, breastfeeding, and growth monitoring, and they collected data for the monitoring of health. The success of the program was widely noted throughout Brazil and internationally, and various state governments became interested in replicating it.[3] For all these accomplishments, Ceará won the UNICEF Maurice Pate prize for child support programs in 1993, the only Latin American government to do so since the prize's inception 27 years before.[4]

The health initiative started in 1987 as a minor part of an emergency employment-creating program responding to one of the periodic droughts that afflict Northeast Brazil twice each decade. Financed out of temporary disaster relief funds from the central and state governments, and accounting for only three percent of the employment created by that measure,[5] the program was nevertheless so successful that the state decided to fund it permanently in 1989, after the emergency funding ended. Program costs averaged US$1.50 per capita served—compared to the US$80 estimated per capita costs of Brazil's existing health care system[6]—and totaled approximately US$7 to $8 million a year. About 80 percent of costs represented payments to the health agents, who earned the minimum wage (US$60 per month) and worked under temporary contracts without job security or fringe benefits. Unlike the jobs offered to the unemployed during droughts and other critical times by temporary employment-creating programs, the health-agent jobs went mainly to women. Nurse-supervisors earned an average of five times the minimum wage (US$300 per month), often higher than they would have earned in urban clinics and hospitals.

In the eyes of the mainstream development literature, and given the long clientelistic history of Ceará's government, the hiring of thousands of fieldworkers by the new health program should have constituted the makings of a rent-seeking nightmare.[7] This chapter explains why the results were just the opposite, and why such a large force of low-paid, barely skilled public workers performed so well.

The Central in the Decentralized

Ceará's health program represented an important first step in the decentralization of health from state government to the municípios. It has been noted as such in Brazil,[8] and even appeared as a case study of successful decentralization in a World Bank sourcebook on decentralization.[9] But some of the lessons that emerge from the story do not receive much attention in the current literature of decentralization, or are even contrary to prevailing conceptions of what happens in decentralization.

When governments start to decentralize, according to widely held views on decentralization in developing countries, the central branch of government recedes and does less than it did before. The proper division of labor between the local and more centralized units of government follows the "comparative advantage" of each.[10] The more centralized part of government is best at tasks with economies of scale, those that draw on its superior finance-raising and regulatory powers (capital-intensive facilities, technical expertise, financing, oversight, training). These are the more sophisticated, more costly, or "harder" parts of the package.[11] Conversely, according to this portrayal, central governments are not very good at outreach and responsiveness to users of public services, particularly in programs providing the poor with access to public services. Local governments and, alternatively, nongovernment organizations, are better at outreach by dint of their greater accessibility and their vulnerability to citizens who are dissatisfied with service quality. Although some students of decentralization have questioned the view that local governments are "automatically 'closer to the people' than other levels of government," this assumption is nevertheless widely held and voiced in the writings and the meetings of the mainstream development community.[12]

Most decentralized programs, like the one described here, are obviously a mix of local and central. The lion's share of the development community's concern about decentralization, however, has been devoted to local governments and other local institutions—namely, civic associations and other NGOs—and to the new capacities and revenue sources they must acquire. It is understandable that less attention would be paid to what the tasks of the central arm of government should be in the new order. The agenda of decentralization, after all, is to reduce the over-centralization of government and to remedy the traditional weakness of local government, which is in relatively greater need of attention. Asking central governments to do less than they normally have done, moreover, would not seem that demanding or complex a task, albeit politically challenging. In this case of preventive health, however, the state government—the more "central" of the two units in these cases—was not simply doing less of what it had been doing in the health sector. It was doing more, and something quite different as well. The following two subsections show how and why.

Dividing the Labor

The planners of Ceará's new preventive health program knew that they had to work within the new mandates of decentralization, regardless of their concerns about the clientelism associated with municipal health spending. According to the formal division of labor between state and local governments, the state financed 85 percent of program costs (health-agent wages mainly, and supplies), and the município 15 percent (one to four nurse-supervisors, usually half-time and working the remaining time in curative care for the município). Financial support from the município for other items, such as bicycles, canoes, or donkeys for the agents to make their household visits, was not formally required but was usually forthcoming, for reasons explained below.[13]

The state quelled its fears about clientelism and the hiring of so many new public workers in three ways. First, it hired workers without the usual job tenure, giving them only temporary contracts. Second, during the program's early years, the state kept the funds for health-agent salaries not only out of the hands of the municípios, but away from the Department of Health itself; these funds remained in an account in the office of the governor. Third, and most relevant to the decentralization issue, the Department of Health appropriated to itself the responsibility for hiring the health agents, while leaving to each município the responsibility for hiring and paying one or two half-time nurse-supervisors. To administer all this, a nine-member coordinating team ran the program with an iron hand out of the Department of Health and traveled extensively throughout the interior to recruit the agents through a rigorous selection process (described in the next section) and later to supervise the program. The team gave the newly hired agents three months of training and substantial on-the-job training. The nurse-supervisors were given three days of orientation and attended numerous subsequent meetings with the coordinating team.

This way of dividing the labor between the state and municipal governments was the opposite of what one might expect. Instead of controlling the hiring of the more skilled nurse-supervisors, who usually had to be recruited from outside the community anyway, the state chose to control the hiring of the much more numerous unskilled workers, who resided in the communities where they worked. Given the ultimately felicitous results of this division of labor, moreover, it is important to note that the state saw it as "second-best." It would have preferred to have complete responsibility for the program and, particularly, to not cede control over the hiring of the nurse-supervisors—knowing how crucial good supervision was to such a program. But it felt pinched for funding, did not want to appear to be moving against the popular wave of sympathy for decentralization—which was seen as part and parcel of the transition from military to civilian government—and needed at least some tacit support from elected local officials in order for the program to function smoothly.[14]

While contributing to the program's good performance, the state's control over the hiring of the health agents also inadvertently turned the mayors into a potential source of opposition to the new program, because it reduced their power over patronage. The team from the Department of Health, that is, would first enter a município and explain to the mayor that he could join the program if he hired a nurse-supervisor and paid her salary. At the same time, however, he was to have no say over the hiring of a large number of new public employees in his município—ranging from roughly 30 to 150 persons, depending on the size of the município. To even join the program, moreover, the mayor had to finance his contribution to the program out of the newly mandated transfers from the federal government, which he was looking forward to using without such constraints on his power. No surprise, then, that some of the mayors were not enthusiastic about the program when it began. One actually hired his own health agents out of municipal funds to accompany the state-hired agents on their rounds to households, so that they (the mayor's agents) could distribute campaign leaflets on these visits. The new program strictly prohibited this practice, which is common among field-based public servants in many developing countries.

Reluctant Mayors

With this kind of discontent, why would the mayors have not used their new federal transfers as they liked, simply not joining the program at all? Was the state not running the risk—after noisily announcing a bold new

program of preventive health—of having only a small number of municípios join? There are three reasons why this did not happen.

The first relates to the fact that the program, in contrast to many such
programs, did not expand throughout the state according to a preordained
plan. Because a município's participation in the program was dependent
on the mayor's agreement to its conditions, the pace and pattern of spa-
tial expansion were dependent on the order in which mayors agreed to
join. As a result, the program spread gradually through the state over a
period of two or three years. This meant that a município that had joined
the program often bordered one that had not. News of the new program
therefore spread rapidly to nearby communities, which pressured their own
mayors to have a program like the one next door. By luring mayors into
the program one by one, then, the crazy-quilt pattern of expansion generated pressures for mayors to "voluntarily" join, whether they were skeptical or not.

A second source of pressure on the reluctant mayors relates to the state's
publicity about the program. The state government surrounded the health
program with an unusual and unending flurry of publicity—directly
through the media, particularly radio, and through the visits of the state
coordinating team to communities during the hiring process. The publicity had a major impact on worker morale, which is discussed in the following section. Suffice it to say here that these messages regaled citizens
with promises of dramatic improvements in the health of their babies. At
the same time, they instructed the public as to what they would have to
do in order to bring those improvements about: they were to urge their
mayors to hire a competent nurse, pay her salary, and run the program
cleanly. "Simply don't vote for your mayor," some of the program's managers advised or implied on their trips to the interior, "if he doesn't provide you access to our health program."

The third and final reason for the mayors being lured into supporting
the program relates to the health workers and nurses themselves. Once a
program was fully operating, its "army" of from 30 to 150 health agents
usually constituted the largest and most visible public-sector presence in
the município. Visiting several households a day, the agents worked mainly
outside rather than, in contrast to most public servants, inside the office.
They could be easily spotted in their uniforms of white T-shirts embla-
zoned with the name of the program, blue jeans, and blue backpacks with
their supplies.[15] They moved about the town from house to house or, in
their visits to more distant areas, traveled by bicycle, donkey, or canoe.

And, because they were doing work that endeared them to the community of which they themselves were a part, they represented a rather formidable local force, not easily ignored by any mayor. At least as important, the agents also saw it as their task to "educate" the mayors about public health initiatives they should support, like purchasing chlorine for campaigns against cholera, or about the need to provide means of transportation to the more remote and dispersed households. In this way, the agents elicited further and sustained financial support from the municípios.

Ultimately, the mayors found that if the program operated well, they could take substantial credit for it. In creating an informed and demanding community, in other words, the state had initiated a dynamic in which the mayors were rewarded politically for supporting the program. In so doing, the state had contributed toward replacing the old patronage dynamic with a more service-oriented one. In keeping such strict control from outside the município over the hiring of a workforce with strong social ties in the community, the state's actions represented a felicitous combination of centralized control and local "embeddedness."

Conclusion

In the name of a program that formally decentralized some responsibility and control to municipal government, the state government nevertheless kept control over certain crucial aspects of the program that caused mayors to initially lose a substantial opportunity to exercise patronage power in their domains. In addition, the state required an upfront contribution from the município before it could enter the program, rather than expanding according to a plan. And its style of operating "squeezed" the mayor in with pressures to commit additional resources once things got started. The state overcame the specter of possible mayoral intransigence, then, in a way that elicited eventual participation and capacity building.

With respect to the division of labor between state and municipal governments, the state's role did indeed correspond partly to that of the prevailing views of decentralization—the central arm of government, in this case, providing financing, supervision, medicines, and vaccines and other supplies.[16] Nevertheless, key to the program's success was the state's vigorous actions in an area of its supposed comparative *dis*advantage—namely, crucial aspects of the program's outreach, such as keeping the hiring and inspiring of the health agents to itself, and extensive publicity in the communities. This represents a more complex picture of the comparative advantages of central versus decentralized units of government, and of the proper division of labor between them.

These conclusions will become fully apparent only in the following section, which shows how the state actually carried out these particular functions and the important impact they had on worker commitment.

The Unskilled Meritocracy and Its Supervisors

"This town was nothing before the health program started," reminisced one of the health agents three years after being hired. "I was ready to leave and look for a job in São Paulo, but now I love my job and I would never leave—I would never abandon my community."

What accounted for the intense commitment and satisfaction expressed by many of the agents and their supervising nurses, and the high performance associated with it? How could the agents' jobs—with low pay, no job security, and no seeming potential for upward mobility—be associated with high worker commitment and performance? After all, the development literature singles out the "excessive" number of these kinds of employees as one of the causes of *poor* performance in developing-country public sectors.[17] Similarly, several studies of U.S. economic performance have pointed to these kinds of jobs as one of the causes of poor productivity in the United States today.[18] And an innovative U.S. program of preventive health for inner cities in the 1960s, with "barefoot doctors" hired from the community à la Ceará, led to "hostility" by these workers to the program they worked for because of the lack of opportunities to rise up in their work.[19] Why, in contrast, the high commitment, gratitude, and performance of Ceará's agents?

The Hiring Process

The origins of the strong commitment of the health program's workers can be traced back to something that happened before the health agents were hired—namely, a remarkable process of merit hiring. It goes without saying that such a process would help the state select the best applicants and therefore explain part of the good performance. In addition, the merit-hiring process was notable because good public managers in developing countries often face numerous obstacles when they attempt to use merit only as a criterion for hiring.[20] Several managers of successful infrastructure agencies operating in Northeast Brazil, for example, singled out merit-hiring victories as their greatest achievements, rather than getting roads built or wells dug (Tendler 1993a).

The hiring process itself had a major impact on the way the workers and the users subsequently viewed the program. The state-level coordinating team hired each health agent in three stages. It first required written applications from all applicants (family members and friends helped the less literate applicants fill out their forms), from which it culled out a list of people to be interviewed. Two members of the team (usually a nurse and a social worker) then traveled to each town for an interview with each applicant on the list, followed by a meeting with all applicants as a group. The group meeting was often followed by a subsequent round of individual interviews with those likely to be selected.

In the setting of Ceará's interior, the hiring of so many workers became an event of significance in the lives of the job seekers and the dozens of towns where they were to work. The number of jobs offered at any particular hiring was frequently the largest one-time public-sector hiring in the town—perhaps 20, 30, or 40 jobs at a time. This was the first time that most of the applicants had ever applied for a job or, at least, been interviewed for one. Many were sweating during their interview, and trembling with fear. Although the jobs paid only the minimum wage and carried no fringe benefits, this was considered a quite desirable income. Even those applicants who had worked as primary school teachers for the município had typically earned less than the minimum wage—quite common in rural Brazil, where teachers frequently have no more than an elementary school education. The minimum wage, moreover, was more than the wage paid to male agricultural labor, which was the principal occupation of the poor population of these areas.[21] Most significant, the health-agent jobs offered full-time work year-round, in an agricultural economy where employment was highly seasonal and those who had work frequently lost it during the dry season or the periodic droughts afflicting the region.

To be chosen for the job of health agent, in sum, was like being awarded an important prize in public. This meant that the newly hired workers started out their jobs strongly influenced by the prestige accorded them by the selection process and the jobs they were entering.

Rejects as Monitors

The coming of the state team to the interior towns evoked widespread curiosity and comment. That "important" professionals from the state capital would visit their town to run a job competition, sometimes even staying overnight, seemed to herald a new public service and a better future for the community. Townspeople avidly eavesdropped on the interview meetings from outside the open windows and doors, listening to the repeated messages of the state committee to the assembled applicants: "this program is yours, and it is you who will determine its success, whether you get the job or not"; "your community does not have to lose so many of its babies, it is not right to have such high infant mortality, you can do much better"; and, last but not least, "you have a right to demand from your mayors that they do what is necessary to start the program and support it." The applicants were also told that it would be an immense "honor" to be hired, and that the very act of applying for the job and getting interviewed was an "honor" in itself, which "had proven their commitment to the community" and their stature as "community leaders."

The traveling committee had a special message at these meetings for the applicants who would *not* be chosen. "Those of you who are not selected," they said, "must make sure that those who are chosen abide by the rules." The rules, spelled out in meeting after meeting, were the following: health agents had to live in the area where they worked, work eight hours a day, visit each household at least once a month, attend all training and review sessions, and not canvass for a political candidate or wear or distribute political propaganda. Although these requirements would seem routine, they are often not observed in Brazil, as well as in many other countries. "If these rules are breached," the committee warned the assembled applicants and eavesdroppers, "we want to hear about it." The warning was clinched with the admonition that "we are keeping all the applications, just in case any of those we hire do not perform well."

Needless to say, these promises turned dozens of rejected applicants into informed public monitors of a new program in which the potential for abuse was high. Community members did, indeed, frequently report to the nurse-supervisors when agents were violating the rules and not, for example, living in the community where they worked. (These agents were fired.) Less drastically, a family that had not seen its health agent in more than a month might mention this to the nurse-supervisor.

The image of disgruntled job seekers watching the job winners for one false step would certainly not seem to augur increased worker commitment and productivity, and even smacks of the scab-labor tactics reviled by labor unions. But the dynamic created by these instructions and admonitions was more complex, with strong positive elements. Because the selection committee's instructions to job applicants who were not chosen made them feel involved with the program, they also reported to the nurse-supervisors when they were satisfied with what a particular agent was doing. In addition, the hiring process and its warnings—far from intimidating the new workers—made the most dedicated ones feel *supported* by the state government versus local politicians and other powerful personages who commonly diverted programs to their own ends. These workers now had an excuse to say no, and knew they would be supported for their stand. The availability of this kind of "protection" to public servants—or lack of it—plays an important role in determining their accomplishments. Nonetheless, it has not received the same attention in explaining poor (or good) performance as has self-interested and rent-seeking behavior.[22] The admonitions to the rejected applicants, then, did not merely create opportunities and incentives for citizens to tell on public servants behind their backs. Rather, the hiring process's socialization of *all* the job applicants and the community at large to the program's mission led to the creation of a shared sense of collective responsibility for the program among all members of the community.

Because the health agents were not hired all at once, the salutary effect of the hiring process on the workers and the community extended long after the program's startup. First, the hiring for any particular município took place in batches over one, two, or three years, because the state did not think it prudent to hire so many new workers in one place at one time. In a município slated for 100 health agents, for example, the first competition might call for only 25 or 30; three or four subsequent competitions would hire the rest over as much as a three-year period, each time in the same way. Second, because the program expanded throughout the state slowly and unevenly, each one of these oft-repeated hiring events extended the process of "image creation" around the program well into the implementation period.

The Department of Health had initially resorted to publicity with the purpose of getting people to adopt preventive health measures. Early on, and with the governor's support, it succeeded in convincing some large private firms to contribute funding for radio and television campaigns advertising the program and its preventive health messages.[23] Later, and with

the same broad publicity, the state awarded prizes to the municípios achieving the best immunization coverage. By 1992, 43 of the state's 178 municípios had received prizes for the best DPT-III (diphtheria, pertussis, and
tetanus) coverage. The prizes were set up partly with the goal of getting
program personnel to take seriously the collection of health data—always
a problem in rural health programs. At the same time, the fanfare surrounding the granting of the prizes, as well as the program's broader publicity and its language of mission, bestowed substantial recognition on
the agents and their supervising nurses as well as enhancing their prestige
in the communities where they worked and lived.

As the program started to have important effects in reducing infant mortality, the publicity also reflected the state's capitalizing politically on its
successes. The two governors who ran the state during this period clearly
had national political ambitions, and the publicity obviously served these
ends. By the early 1990s, the first governor had become president of his
party, and the second was highly conspicuous politically on the national
scene—both because of their successes in administering the state.[24] Skeptics said that the publicity exaggerated the two governors' accomplishments. Some described the publicity as a modern version of "populist"
manipulation of the electorate, involving sophisticated "marketing" of a
government's image.[25] Whether this was true—and whether the accomplishments were exaggerated—the publicity nevertheless had the effect of
placing the health agents and their supervisors in an unusual spotlight of
public appreciation for their work. These effects were not necessarily intended, and their importance in worker commitment and the program's
performance did not seem to be fully understood.[26]

With this understanding of how the publicity complemented the effects
of the selection process, I now contrast the meritocracy created in this
program to more typical ones. In so doing, I return to the concerns about
productivity with which this section started.

Tenure as Problem and Solution

The literature of industrial performance has pointed to the lack of job
security and of prospects for upward mobility among many workers as
reasons for stagnant productivity growth in the United States. The development literature, in contrast, has identified "too much" job security
as a cause of poor performance in the public sector. The preventive health
case suggests one possible way of resolving this paradox.

That a meritocratic job selection process could bestow prestige on the job winners is not new. Professionals who work in public agencies known for serious merit-hiring procedures often cite that fact, like an item on their curriculum vitae, even when the competition took place many years ago. They proudly and often disdainfully set themselves off from others in the public sector who were not hired in this way. In Brazil, Bank of Brazil managers and professionals in the National Development Bank talk this way.[27] Outside Brazil, the Indian Administrative Service is an excellent example of civil servants who feel themselves an elite simply for having won their jobs. In all these cases, the prestige is linked to the particular service into which one is recruited, in addition to the larger elite group of trained professionals to which one belongs.[28]

The health program's hiring process differed in certain ways from these typical cases of meritocratic public agencies. First, it linked the prestige not just to the particular individuals who passed a rigorous competition, but also to the program's "noble" mission of bringing the community "into the twentieth century" by reducing infant mortality and disease. This was reinforced by the staging of the hiring process as a public event in the very areas where the job applicants were to work. Also in contrast to most elite public service corps, the prestige accorded by the hiring process was not grounded in the particular agency that did the hiring—namely, the state government's Department of Health. Neither the agents nor their supervisors "belonged" to the agency that conferred so much prestige on them because, although the Department of Health hired the health agents and funded their salaries, the agents worked under the direction of nurses hired and paid by the município.

Also distinct from the more typical case of meritocratic public service, the status enjoyed by the health agents was not the result of their being an educated elite. Rather, education was something that the job would eventually confer on these workers as a reward for their having been "chosen." It took the form of three months of full-time training (unusually long, particularly for unskilled, minimum-wage workers), subsequent in-service trainings, and substantial feedback from supervisors. For most people living in Ceará's interior, access to this kind of training was unimaginable.

In addition, and also in contrast to typical civil service hiring procedures, the reward for having passed the job competition did not come in the form of job tenure. As had become the practice of other fiscally strapped state governments in the 1980s, Ceará had gone out of its way to contract these new workers rather than hire them, so as to make it clear that they were not winning a permanent home in the state's public sector. Indeed, the governor and architects of the program liked to stress this as one of the keys to its success. The governor even publicly boasted of how he had resisted pressures to turn the agents "into state employees," claiming that to do so would cause the program to "die" (UNICEF 1993). Does this not amount to the "low-road" approach to getting performance out of workers—an approach said to lead to poor productivity?

At the time of this writing, the health agents' lack of job security had started to become more of a problem, as the program's architects had predicted, and not just the felicitous solution that it had seemed at the beginning. The agents were organizing to demand, among other things, greater job security and fringe benefits accorded to other public workers. The story of how the state reacted to this turn of events—together with other features of these jobs—reveals some significant differences from the way many other governments use low-paid or contract labor. The state, in brief, did not turn a deaf ear to the organizing and the demands of the health agents for greater security, and agreed to participate in discussing approaches to the problem.

The health program's architects had admitted that they had been leery about bringing on such a large contingent of new workers in a way that would doubtless imply legal responsibility to give them tenure in the future. But they had felt, at the program's beginning, that they would have a short "honeymoon" period of two or three years before such demands would arise. By then, they assumed, these workers would start to bring claims of "de facto tenure" before the labor courts, which had customarily decided such cases in favor of the worker. The program's founders did not worry too much about this eventuality because they felt that if the program were successful by the time the "honeymoon" ended, the state would want to upgrade the status and training of the agents anyway. When the health agents started to organize and issue demands, then, the state was willing to entertain the idea of "qualifying" a certain number of the agents through a process of selection and further training. The state government also supported initiatives among the health agents of some municípios to form associations or cooperatives. The state planned to then contract these associations, which would provide the fringe benefits (jointly financed by the state) the agents did not have. Although these new measures had not fully evolved at the time of this writing, the state's interest in increasing the status of at least some of the existing workers would, if carried out, represent a granting of job security as a reward for performance and as part of a larger process of upskilling.

There were other factors that made these jobs different from typical no-security, no-upward-mobility jobs. The three full months of training provided by the state to these contract laborers, as well as substantial in-service training, were more than many governments provided to their tenured workers. Given that health was an expanding sector, moreover, the training and the job experience were clearly "transportable" to other jobs in the public or private sector, if these workers were to lose their jobs. The high status conferred by these jobs on the workers also helped compensate for their lack of security. In addition, the jobs were "low-paid" only in relation to other jobs in the public sector or in public health, but not in terms of the perceptions and alternative opportunities of these particular workers. Finally, the jobs were more satisfying in terms of their greater variety of tasks, their greater discretion, and their satisfying relationship with citizen-clients. Recent research on large firms in the United States also suggests that job insecurity may be less problematic when counterbalanced by other features of the work environment valued by employees and associated with high performance (Osterman 1994).

In conclusion, then, the state's approach to its temporary and unskilled health agents seemed to avoid, whether intentionally or not, some of the problematic aspects of both job insecurity and job tenure. On the one hand, the state provided invaluable training to these workers and conferred unimagined status on them. On the other hand, it ultimately offered some job security—or seemed to be moving in that direction—but only after some time and only as a reward for work performed well.

The Good Nurse

Evaluations of preventive health programs, even of some good ones, routinely point to problems of poor supervision.[29] One explanation for poor supervision is that supervisors, usually nurses, are not included in the planning of the programs they are to administer and are allowed little discretion in their work (Walt et al. 1990). The past decade's literature of business schools on management concerns itself with a more generic version of this problem, pointing to the importance of the neglected middle managers in the literature on innovation and the need to "empower" them.[30] Any study of the achievements of Ceará's program, then, must ask why supervision was better than in most such programs, and whether the nurse-supervisors had greater discretion and were included more in designing their programs. The answer to these questions also helps explain why the program was not plagued with the all-too-common resistance of physicians and nurses to the introduction of paraprofessional workers.[31]

In the urban clinics and hospitals where many of the nurse-supervisors had worked previously, they had been inferior in status to the doctors they assisted, who treated them as subordinates rather than co-professionals. Now, each nurse was supervising and training an average of 30 paraprofessional agents, who referred to their supervisor as "doctor" and hung on her every word. Local people also addressed her as "doctor" when they passed her on the street, and she suddenly felt like an important local personage in the community.[32]

In addition, the nurse-supervisors felt that they had not really been able to "practice nursing" in their previous jobs. Hospitals had given them more and more administrative work while, at the same time, meeting nursing needs increasingly by hiring less-trained and lower-paid paraprofessional workers to carry out "nursing" tasks such as assisting physicians in surgery. On the one hand, then, the nurses had been angered in their previous jobs by the lack of "professionalism" in the way management ran nursing in their hospitals and, on the other hand, by the increasing administrative chores they had to take on without being given increased managerial discretion or status. This had led to various protest meetings at hospitals and professional nursing associations, which were of little avail and left the nurses feeling powerless, alienated from their work, and ignored as professionals.

In the preventive health program, the situation was quite different. The state Department of Health had deliberately left the nurse-supervisors with substantial control over the way they ran the program in their município, not pressing standardization too strictly. As a result, there was a good deal of variation in programs from one município to the next. Some supervisors instructed their agents on how to give shots and remove sutures, for example, while others were adamantly against teaching these "curative" tasks; some included family-planning messages in the advice giving of the agents, while others were against it. (Indeed, one nurse-supervisor initiated family planning in her município when she learned that many of her own agents had sexually transmittable diseases and did not know how to prevent, identify, or treat them.)

All this was a far cry from the nurse's subordinate relation to the physicians of her previous job, her exclusion from decisions that were central to her identity as a professional, and her administrative burdens that came without the discretion usually accorded to a manager. As the supervisor of a preventive health program, of course, she also was not "practicing nursing" any more than in her old job. But she felt more "like a professional" in her new job because she was making decisions about how to run a public health program, and she saw the direct health impacts of her work. That the nurse-supervisors' salaries in the preventive health program were higher than in their previous urban jobs, of course, must have been important in attracting some of the better nursing professionals and ensuring their dedication.

The resistance of health professionals to the introduction of paraprofessionals into health programs like Ceará's often contributes to the difficulty of getting the public sector to pay adequate attention and funding to preventive health, as compared to curative health programs. Part of the resistance is due to a genuine concern about compromising professional standards and jeopardizing the health and safety of patients. Another part, of course, bespeaks worries about losing power, professional distinction, remuneration, and access to jobs. It is remarkable, then, that the very nurses who had criticized the use of paraprofessionals in their previous hospital jobs became the ardent advocates in their new jobs of a program that relied heavily on just such workers. The new nurse-supervisors also adamantly defended the use of paraprofessionals in the preventive health program against the predictable criticisms that came, eventually, from their urban colleagues in nursing. Clearly, the new power of the program's nurse-supervisors to decide what their paraprofessional workers could or could not do was key to their change of heart.[33]

The Self-Enlarging Job

Many of the workers in the municípios where the health program performed best did things that did not fall strictly within the definition of their jobs. The extra tasks fell into three categories: (1) the carrying out of some simple curative, as opposed to preventive, practices; (2) the initiation of community-wide campaigns to reduce public health hazards; and (3) assistance to mothers with mundane tasks not directly related to health. In all these areas, the agents took on this larger variety of tasks voluntarily, and they liked their jobs better for having done so.

Extra activities of this nature often creep into preventive health and other public services involving considerable contact between workers and clients—as also occurred in the cases of best performance in the subsequent chapters on agricultural extension, drought relief, and business extension. Even as different a setting as that of the well-known success story in preschool education in the United States, the Head Start program, documents the same phenomenon (Schorr 1988). In health, experts sometimes view these extra activities as undermining the proper functioning of the service, for reasons explained below; similarly, agricultural extension experts see the myriad activities as taking agents away from their "real" work and hence contributing to poor results. In the eyes of the experts, then, the "nonessential" activities are associated with bad performance. But the workers of these cases see the extra activities as increasing their effectiveness and enhancing their commitment to their jobs. This section tries to understand the reasons for these opposing views by looking, in the following three subsections, at the three different forms taken by such extra activities in the case of preventive health.

Creeping Curativism

The health agents found it quite difficult to gain access to people's homes when they started working. Mothers would not answer their knocks on the door, or would hide their children when the agent crossed the threshold. Health programs, of course, frequently encounter this problem when working in areas like rural Ceará, where people rely on traditional medicine and local faith healers.[34] But, as in many other countries, this reaction was also grounded in the legacy of mistrust of anything that came from "government." Brazil's 18-year period of military government ending in presidential elections in 1984—with its repression of peasant organizing in the interior of the Northeast—had made that mistrust even more profound. It is against this background that the agents viewed the simple curative tasks as an "entryway" into preventive care.

The curative procedures performed by the agents were quite simple ones— removing sutures, treating wounds, giving shots, providing advice on treating colds and flus, taking a sick child to the hospital. The agents contrasted the immediate results of their curative procedures with the "tedious and frustrating process" of getting people to change their health and hygiene practices—teaching mothers how to take care of themselves during pregnancy, instructing mothers in caring for newborns, convincing people to take their medicines regularly, and cajoling people into washing their hands before preparing food, filtering their water, and adding nutritious foods to their diet. It took considerable patience and perseverance to convince new mothers, who usually preferred bottle-feeding, that breast milk was not "sour" and distasteful to their babies, or that they should take time out of their day to attend prenatal appointments.

The perseverance paid off. "I first earned the respect and trust of families by treating wounds or giving a shot . . . ," one agent reported, "so that now families listen to me when I talk to them about breastfeeding, or better hygiene, or nutrition—things that don't show immediate results." In the same vein, the agents liked administering oral rehydration solutions because "they are like cures," to agents as well as desperate mothers. A severely dehydrated baby, seemingly near death, would be happily playing only hours after taking the rehydration solution recommended by the health agent.

Using curative tasks to get one's foot in the door for the less dramatic, longer haul of changing people's health thinking and practices would seem to represent a quite sensible admixture to a preventive health program— especially if that helped the program to be more effective on the preventive side. Curative care, however, tends to crowd out preventive care in practice and in funding—just as road construction crowds out road maintenance. This is due not only to the greater lure of curative care to paraprofessionals and users. More significantly, physicians, who are powerful actors in health planning, find the less capital-intensive and less high-tech work of preventive care programs to be less challenging and low status— just as road maintenance is less prestigious and challenging to civil engineers than road construction.[35] Many public health reformers, therefore, believe that even a little curative care in a preventive health program is "dangerous."[36]

Partly for these reasons, the "creeping" curative care in Ceará's program did not go unnoticed. Nursing professionals in the state's capital complained that unskilled workers should not dispense curative care, no matter how minimal, without at least receiving training as nurse-assistants. Responding to this criticism, the coordinating team agreed to provide some formal nurse-assistant training to at least some of its health agents. This solution, of course, runs the risk of enabling the health agents to go too far in the curative direction—exactly what preventive health planners worry about. Preventive health agents cannot simply be allowed to do as much curative care as they want, just to keep them and their clients happy.

From Household to Community

In addition to their task of visiting households, many health agents took on, of their own accord, community-wide activities meant to reduce public health hazards. In one case, for example, agents obtained free air time on the radio in order to name families leaving garbage in front of their homes; in another, agents pressured workers and management in a bakery to wear hair nets and wash their hands; in yet another, agents worked with their supervisor to introduce meetings on family planning and female sexuality, which were not part of the program. In part, this taking on of larger causes was the result of the program's initial socialization of these workers into public service with images of "doing good" and the dedicated public servant.

Health agents also liked their work when they were pulled away from their routine preventive tasks to participate in community-wide campaigns against disease epidemics, the most recent example being the state's campaign against cholera. When participating in these campaigns, the agents felt swept up in a serious and dramatic public mission, in which the topmost officials of the state were intimately involved. This was more appealing to them than "giving mothers the same message over and over again" about breastfeeding or prenatal care. The lure of these kinds of tasks is not peculiar to health. Observers of agricultural extension workers have pointed to a similar dynamic in explaining the sudden bursts of good performance by agricultural extension services during epidemics of disease or pests that threaten to decimate the crops of an entire region.[37]

Many public health reformers, reflecting a strong current of thinking in the fields of social medicine and medical anthropology, encourage preventive health workers to see themselves as "agents of change" and of "empowerment" of citizens in the communities where they work.[38] Others worry about the tension that such challenges to community power structures create between the program and local elites; or they dislike the "distraction" of such activities from the more "basic" tasks of preventive health. These differences of opinion, and the concern of experts about disrupting "basic" work, have their parallel in the field of agricultural extension, as will become clear in the following two chapters.[39]

Good arguments may well exist, then, for defining a hard core of basic tasks from which workers in such services should not deviate—as in the case of preventive versus curative care. Workers may be doing more than basic tasks, moreover, for bad reasons as well as good. They may be subject to outside pressure unrelated to their mission—other agencies or individual politicians, for example, taking advantage of the field presence of a particular group of workers to pursue their own ends. In this sense, narrowly defined job definitions can also contribute to "protecting" workers so that they can do their "real" work. It is important to understand, nevertheless, that something else is also causing the variety of tasks to grow. The best workers are themselves pushing the boundaries of their job definitions—or simply letting it happen—because they view these broader realms of operation as profoundly fulfilling and, at the same time, consistent with their mission as public servants.

Trust and the Mundane

The third area in which health workers went beyond their mandate voluntarily related to matters of trust between workers and their client-citizens. When agents talked about why they liked their jobs, the subject of respect from clients and from "my community" often dominated their conversation—much more, interestingly, than the subject of respect from supervisors or other superiors.

The trust that was central to the workings of the health program was inspired by quite mundane activities. Because agents visited homes during the day when mothers were there alone with young children, they sometimes assisted with cooking, cleaning, or child care—giving a baby a bath, cutting its fingernails, or trimming its hair. The mothers, often lonely and overburdened, found considerable solace in this support and in sharing their problems with agents. "She is a true friend," a mother said of the health agent working in her community. "She's done more for us than she'll ever realize." The field-workers of the above-noted Head Start program of preschool education in the United States reported remarkably similar activities and perspectives on them—down to the cutting of the baby's fingernails and the washing of its hair (Schorr 1988).

The additional attention paid by field-workers to the mothers they visited might seem to burden an already heavy work agenda, which required several household visits per day, often to places of difficult access. Both the health agents and the Head Start workers reported, however, that the extra help they offered was crucial to their gaining these mothers' trust, as well as that of the community in general. This, they said, was the most difficult task of their work—at least in the beginning. Just as important to understanding these workers' worlds, the agents saw their clients not only as subjects whose behavior they wanted to change, but as people from whom they actually wanted and needed respect. It is these kinds of relations of mutual trust between workers and their clients—and, more broadly, between governments and the social networks in the larger society outside them—that are now receiving attention in the recent attempts of scholars to explain successful developmental states, public programs, and large private firms.[40] But the mainstream development literature's presumption of self-interest makes it difficult to recognize these relations when they appear, and to take them as a point of departure in thinking about how to improve government.

Conclusion

In an era of contempt for government, Ceará's state government and its Department of Health succeeded in creating an aura of mission around the preventive health program and remarkable respect for its workers in the communities where they worked. This was accomplished through a merit-hiring process for the 7,300 health agents—unusual for such a large force of low-wage and nontenured public employees—and incessant advertising about the program and its achievements. Partly informational, and later also representing sheer boasting by the state about its accomplishments, the advertising also placed the program's workers in a public limelight that brought them widespread recognition. Repeated prizes for municípios that reduced their infant death rate and other indicators of disease, and the accompanying publicity, had the same effect.

Workers often took on tasks, voluntarily, that fell outside their job descriptions. The health agents provided some curative care in addition to their preventive work, took on environmental health offenders in the community, or helped mothers with household chores. This broader set of tasks, sometimes viewed by experts as distractions from "real" work, cohered together as a more customized way of providing service to clients. This, in turn, formed the basis for relations of trust between workers and citizens. The greater discretion embodied in the broader job definitions was repeated in the greater formal autonomy and stature granted by the state to the program's nurse-supervisors, who had typically come from more subordinate roles in their previous jobs in hospitals and clinics.

In an environment already rife with rent-seeking opportunities, the greater ambiguity of these job boundaries would seem to make supervision of workers even more difficult. But the more amorphous boundaries were counterbalanced by new outside pressures to perform from the community. Through the same advertising that created the public recognition of the workers—and the "socialization" of job candidates, including the majority who would be rejected—the state raised the community's hopes about what to expect from its government, and then educated them precisely about what workers, supervisors, and mayors should be doing. This turned the community, and particularly the dozens of rejected applicants, into informed public monitors of a new program in which the potential for abuse was high. This aspect of the state's action was consistent with the user-driven accountability now in vogue in today's mainstream development advice. But it also involved something quite the opposite, a point I explain momentarily.

Together, these interlinked features of the state's actions added up to an approach to the treatment of public-sector workers that differed in key ways from the standard practices of many governments, let alone firms. On the one hand, the state lavished invaluable and "transportable" training on this large and unskilled temporary labor force, and conferred unimagined status on them. On the other hand, it ultimately ceded them some job security—or seemed to be moving in that direction—but only after some time and only as a reward for good performance. In this sense, and not necessarily intentionally, the state seemed to be avoiding some of the worst aspects of job insecurity *and* "excessive" job security.

Two other explanations of the health program's achievements should by now be at least partly clear from the above. Although this case might be seen as a success in decentralization of public service from state to municipal government, the success had more to do with something done by *central*, rather than local, government. The state kept an iron hand on the hiring, training, and socialization of an essentially municipal labor force. It swamped the public with inspirational and educational messages about the program. And it chose not to extend the service to municípios according to a preordained plan or pace but, rather, to let the expansion be determined by which mayors first showed good faith in hiring a nurse-supervisor and coming up with funds to pay her salary.

In addition, the health program did not suffer from the kind of opposition that frequently aborts or dilutes these kinds of attempts to extend public service broadly. One source of potentially crippling opposition was the mayors, who resented the state government's "usurpation" of their patronage power over the hiring of a large number of workers on their own turfs. Through its constant messages to citizens, the state government indirectly "incited" them to demand that mayors commit resources to the program, and run it cleanly, in return for their vote. In addition, because the health agents became the largest and most visible public-sector presence in the towns where they worked, they themselves represented a similar source of pressure on mayors and, most important, helped "educate" them about public health problems and concrete ways to support the program. In this sense, they were more like an "independent" civic presence than municipal workers subject to a mayor's clientelistic whims. The state's actions, in other words, made it more politically rewarding to provide good service and more politically costly to hire the party faithful. This amounted to changing the dynamics of patronage politics as it related to public service at the local level.

The second source of potential opposition was the physicians and nurses. Like professionals in other sectors, they frequently resist reforms that "lower" standards in order to extend service to much larger numbers of citizens—in this case, by using low-wage, unskilled paraprofessionals. By markedly enhancing the status of nurses as professionals, and by working in the rural areas where most physicians did not tread, the program turned a large number of potential resisters into ardent advocates (the nurse-supervisors), or at least kept them at a safe and uninterested distance (the physicians).

I may have conveyed more intentionality about what the state did, and implied more of an understanding of cause and effect, than was actually the case. The state considered second-best, after all, what I described as an ingenious way of dividing the labor between state and municipal governments. The state reluctantly ceded the hiring of the nurse-supervisors to the municípios, although keeping to itself the hiring of the agents. The effect of the state's boasting about the program's successes in the media is another example of lack of intentionality—the impact of this publicity on worker morale having not been foreseen or, retrospectively, perceived.

In closing, I return to the question of how to explain the kind of public-serving behavior that emerges in cases like these. Part of the explanation in the health case had to do with the hemming in of government workers with outside pressures from the community to perform. In this sense, my findings are not inconsistent with the prevailing mainstream conception of civil servants as inherently self-interested and, therefore, with the corresponding importance attributed to outside pressures as keeping them from misbehaving. But this was only half the story. The other half had to do with the state's nurturing of an inclination toward public-serving behavior among its workers, and its enabling of already public-minded government workers to do what they wanted to do. To identify what happened as the hemming-in of public workers with outside pressures to perform, then, may actually constitute a misreading of that part of the story—or, at least, an incomplete reading. As must by now have become clear, the story of the community as outside "monitors" of the health workers is irretrievably entangled with the story of the workers as embedded in that community through close relationships of respect and trust—a combination already discovered by others outside the mainstream development community.[41] What happened, in other words, was just as much a coming together of the workers and their clients as it was a sense of workers being watched by those who would report any wrongdoing.

The findings of this chapter might seem, at first blush, to be relevant only to the health sector, and to preventive health programs in particular. They might also seem to be a function of the particulars of the Ceará case—namely, the hiring of 7,300 never-before-salaried rural women. Clearly, this kind of workforce would be extremely grateful for its "scarce" public-sector employment. Also, these workers partook of that special excitement of participating in a bold new public venture. And in places where infant mortality is so high, like rural Ceará, it is less difficult to obtain a rapid initial drop in that rate than to achieve other more complex and less conspicuous goals pursued by preventive health programs. Most public programs, in contrast, do not operate in this kind of "honeymoon" environment, including those described in the subsequent chapters.

It was surprising, then, that loosely similar findings emerged in the other sectors studied—employment-creating drought relief, agricultural extension, and business extension linked to public procurement from small firms. And in these programs, in contrast to health, no new workers were hired. Indeed, the period under review was one of layoffs, budget cuts, and other privations. With certain sectoral variations, however, the workers in these other programs also showed higher dedication to their jobs and higher performance. As in the health case, client appreciation of their work was central to this outcome. Similarly, relations of trust had developed between agents and their clients. And workers were doing things that development advisors would, if they had their preferences, not normally have them do. I start with the emergency employment-creating program because it is closest to the health case.

· *3* ·

The Emergency Employment Program
and Its Unlikely Heroes

IN 1987, A 12-MONTH drought decimated the agricultural economy of rural Ceará and left a large part of the rural population without work, food, and drinking water. The state government responded, as it had to previous droughts, with emergency food and water supplies and a public works construction program that employed, at its peak, 235,000 persons— 30 percent of the economically active male and rural population.[1] Though Northeast state governments had rapidly mobilized for such emergency programs in past droughts for almost a century,[2] the response of Ceará in 1987 represented a radical departure from the past and from that of other states. Mainly, the state government succeeded in overcoming a deeply entrenched tradition of clientelism in the allocation of works projects, jobs, and relief supplies. On the one hand, it took power away from local elites, asserting strong central control over drought relief administration. On the other hand, it initiated a highly decentralized and orderly system of decision making around the allocation of jobs, construction projects, and relief supplies. The new approach built "from the bottom up" on decisions taken by community assemblies and sent to new municipal councils convened especially for that purpose. The process was guided by the agronomist-heads of the regional offices of the state's Agricultural Extension Service, according to strict criteria dictated by the state government.

The new approach to the drought emergency, though couched in the language of decentralization and grassroots decision making, clearly placed greater burdens on state administration. It is remarkable, then, that the 1987 effort performed better than those of previous administrations and other Northeast states, as revealed by two key indicators. First, relief and works projects arrived in the stricken communities more quickly—within 10 to 20 days rather than the four weeks typical of previous droughts. Second, the share of expenditures devoted to employing labor in works construction was significantly higher than in previous droughts and in other Northeast states, as well as higher than in many such programs around the world—80 percent versus the more typical 50 to 65 percent.[3]

How was all this possible, given the history of clientelism in Ceará, the incentives for state officials to collaborate with it, and the greater demands for honesty and fairness that the new approach placed on the public sector? Exploring this question uncovered another nest of puzzling questions. In the field, responsibility for the program's administration fell to the state's army of resident agricultural extension agents, whom villagers praised again and again as their "saviors," as the "heroes" of the 1987 program. This was somewhat surprising. Although agricultural extension agents frequently became important figures in the towns where they worked and resided, they were not necessarily able or willing to stand up to the powerful local elites that dominated previous programs. In addition, many from the Agricultural Extension Service saw drought relief as drudgery, taking them away from their "real" work. Like such services elsewhere in Northeast Brazil and around the world, moreover, Ceará's Extension Service did not have a reputation for outstanding results, among either farmers or experts.[4] Agricultural extension agents, finally and obviously, did not have the expertise required of a program concentrated so heavily on construction. How could such an unlikely cast of characters have been so central, in other words, to the greatly improved administration of an emergency employment-creating program?

Similarly challenging questions were posed by the fact that the 1987 program shifted its focus to smaller, community-based construction projects—schools, cisterns, wells, grain storage facilities, community meeting halls, small dams, and minor road repairs and structures. This compared to the much larger dams, reservoirs, and roads built under past drought programs. To be sure, the larger number of smaller projects in the 1987 program—and the numerous new local bodies formed to decide upon and monitor them—reflected more "democratic" decision making.

At the same time, the more numerous and dispersed small projects would also seem to have increased the opportunities for graft and clientelism that had plagued previous programs. In face of these continuing opportunities for rent seeking, how was program administration actually de-clientelized? With respect to the state's capacity to administer the program, moreover, why did the new insistence on smaller projects not run up against resistance from the building agencies and their engineers, who typically prefer larger and more sophisticated projects and techniques relying more heavily on equipment? These agencies, along with large contractor firms and landowners, had been key players in executing drought relief programs in the past, and in the political support for them.

Finally, and related to the above considerations about the building agencies, the 1987 program's new structure seemed to be highly dependent on interagency coordination, bringing together 12 state or federal agencies and parastatals with seemingly little self-interest in collaborating with each other—the state Departments of Planning, Social Action, Agriculture, Roads, Waterworks, and Health; state parastatals in agricultural extension, housing, mining, and technology; and the federal Department of Public Health Campaigns and the railway parastatal.[5] Also seeming to complicate the already difficult problems of interagency coordination, the program placed the more powerful building agencies under the coordinating authority of the weaker Department of Social Action in the state's capital and, in the field, of the weaker Extension Service. When stronger agencies are supposed to be coordinated by weaker ones, this is usually a recipe for failure, not success.

My search for explanations for the accomplishments of the 1987 drought relief program led me to some of the same factors that characterized the previous case of preventive health. This in itself was surprising, not only because the sectors were so different, but because of the eminently temporary nature of the drought program in contrast to the health program's successful efforts to institutionalize itself.

The De-clientelization of Drought Relief

Ever since the nineteenth century, drought in Northeast Brazil's semiarid interior has been a recurrent event, leaving thousands of rural families out of work and without food. The droughts, which used to occur roughly every seven years but have now become more frequent, routinely trigger

relief in the form of employment-creating public works projects and supplies of food and drinking water. Mounted by the region's state governments and funded largely by the central government, these rapidly mobilized initiatives represent significant expenditures of public funds and
employ large numbers of people. In the more severe drought of 1983, for
example, $352 million was spent on relief supplies and works projects and
3.2 million persons were employed, almost half the economically active
population of the rural Northeast (not all of which is drought-prone); in
the less severe 1987 drought, expenditures were $196 million and one mil-
lion persons were employed (15% of the economically active rural population).[6] Among the Northeast states, Ceará stands out as the state most
severely affected by the droughts. Almost all of its territory lies in the
drought-prone area—94 percent, including 171 of its 178 municípios.
With less than 20 percent of the region's population, then, Ceará accounted for 33 percent of emergency drought spending in the Northeast
in the 1987 drought—$62 million, of which $48.3 million was from the
federal government and $13.4 million from the state.

For many years, observers of the Northeast have claimed that the drought
relief programs benefited the region's large landowners, private contractors, and suppliers of relief more than those needing jobs, food, and water.
These "drought industrialists"—a name made famous in a book with that
title written by Brazilian journalist Antônio Callado (1960)—have dominated the works programs and are portrayed as villains in the lore of the
Northeast droughts. Decisions about projects, jobs, and relief supplies in
any particular município typically emerged from conversations between
mayors, who consulted with the large landowners in their domain, and
state government offices based in the state capital, which passed on to them
the funds and the relief supplies. In giving out jobs and supplies, these
local figures frequently gave preference to the politically loyal or simply
to the workers of the most influential landowners. Many of the projects—
roads, dams, small watering points, and other civil works—were located
inside the property of large landowners, and hence were not accessible to
the public. Press reports typically told stories of cattle having preference
over people in getting access to drinking water in the reservoirs constructed
under the program—cattle being the principal economic activity of the
large farmers of the semiarid interior.

The 1987 drought relief effort stood out from the others in Ceará and
other Northeast states because it attempted to change all this and, thereby,
to challenge the power of the "drought industrialists." In droughts pre-

ceding that of 1987, the state Department of Social Action had loosely co-ordinated the emergency programs in conjunction with the state Departments of Agriculture, Roads, and Waterworks. In 1987, the state took greater control over the program and, at the same time, made it more decentralized—a combination also characteristic of the health program. On the one hand, the new governor called and presided over weekly meetings of his cabinet on the progress of the emergency program, and named a strong and capable manager to be director of the state Department of Social Action; the new director had the power to coordinate the actions of the other state departments, and announced clear criteria (described below) regarding the kinds of works projects that would qualify for financing and which applicants for jobs would receive them. On the other hand, the state took control of the decisions about projects and hiring away from mayors and local landowners and gave them to a newly formed and "representative" municipal council presided over not by the mayor, but by the head of the local agricultural extension office. Although the more than 1,000 professionals of the state's Extension Service had helped out in previous droughts, they did not play the key role they were to play in 1987.[7]

In the new local councils—named Community Action Groups (GACs/ Grupos de Ação Comunitária)—the mayor or his designate was now only one among 12 representatives. The municipal council (câmara de vereadores) and Departments of Health and Education each had one representative; assemblies from the various villages named three representatives; and "civil society" had three representatives, named from groups like the Catholic or Protestant Church, the rural labor union, the landowners' association, and service clubs like the chamber of commerce, Lions' Club, and Rotary Club. In a process that was quite unusual for rural Brazil, the GACs would deliberate in weekly meetings over a set of two lists submitted by each village or community in the município, the villages ranging in size from five to 200 families. One list ranked a set of projects desired by that particular community; the other ranked those families hardest hit by the drought and most in need of employment and relief supplies. In order to generate these lists of proposed projects and job applicants, from which the GAC made its choices, the extension officer/GAC head traveled throughout his territory to organize village assemblies and guide them through the process of ranking job candidates and potential works projects. Often scheduling meetings on Sundays so as not to disrupt work schedules, he would explain the state's criteria for acceptable projects and employable persons, and for supplying emergency food and water.

The new criteria for the works projects revealed the strong hand of the state government in limiting the available choices and, at the same time, represented a distinct break from past practices: (1) only one person per household could be employed (usually the male head of household);[8] (2) those receiving jobs had to be from the "neediest" families, as designated by the community; (3) projects had to be of value to the community and not just to particular individuals; (4) projects had to be completed within months and, hence, before the end of the drought; and (5) projects had to be located in or near the community so that workers could eat and sleep in their homes. These requirements ruled out, in effect, some of the most common and notorious projects of past drought relief programs—those inside a landowner's property and large and longer-maturing construction projects like dams and major roads. Such projects typically employed large concentrations of workers in earth-moving operations, assembled from throughout the state. Local landowners, on whose properties the projects were often constructed, provided food and housing to the laborers and deducted payments for these services from their wages.[9]

The state's new criteria for smaller, more dispersed works projects clearly contributed to reducing the share of funds expended for items other than labor. Many employment-creating works programs end up spending a significant share of their funds on nonlabor expenditures like equipment, materials, and administration. Whereas in other Northeast states expenditures for such nonlabor components accounted for as much as 35 percent to 50 percent during the 1987 drought, the Ceará program succeeded in limiting nonlabor costs to 20 percent, an impressively low figure for almost any such program. Even programs that do succeed in spending a large share of their funds on labor often drift away from their initial labor intensity, because the engineers working in public agencies and their contractors prefer equipment-using techniques of construction[10]—preferences that are reinforced by the pressures of equipment producers and dealers.

Together, these new projects and procedures signified the state's attempt to introduce a new process of decentralized and "democratic" decision making at the same time that it wrested control of the program from other local actors. No wonder, then, that some mayors complained that the new program reduced the "autonomy" of municipal government, and that it would result in the "excessive centralization" of drought relief by the state government, making it "impossible to respond quickly" to the emergency.[11] As it turned out, however, the opposite occurred. Whereas jobs and relief supplies had taken at least four weeks to materialize in past droughts, the

new program started works projects and delivered relief supplies within
10 to 20 days.

Although the past drought relief efforts had been rightly criticized for
the inequity of their ways of selecting projects and providing jobs, they
nevertheless placed less of a burden on state capacity than the more de-
mocratized 1987 program. In 1987, the decision to exclude projects employing large numbers of people at one site, and to employ people only
where they lived, translated into myriad small projects dispersed widely
throughout a countryside with a low population density (17 persons per
square kilometer). Having each community draw up ranked lists of projects and persons most in need of work, moreover, required protracted visits by the extension agent to many small communities, often of difficult
access. Reaching decisions at these meetings was slow and agonizing; the
agent would run down the names of unemployed workers one by one with
the community to determine which family needed work most, and led long
discussions about possible projects and the order in which the community would like to rank them.

With these new consultative processes and new criteria for choosing
projects and workers, then, the state had taken on three difficult challenges:
(1) coordinating demands from communities, (2) confronting the clientelism of rural areas as manifested in the "drought industry," and (3) publicly promising to deliver more timely drought relief. The political risk of
not coming through on the latter promise was significant. In past (and
subsequent) Northeast droughts, hungry peasants had sacked food warehouses and markets when relief did not appear; or they threatened to do
so in protest marches on the state or municipal capitals—all such events
being widely publicized in the press.

The final and key piece of the 1987 drought story was the agricultural
extension workers who, in the eyes of the villagers of Ceará's dry interior,
were the heroes of that event. Over the 12-month period, they voluntarily worked long hours and were remarkably effective at coordinating action throughout the state. They succeeded in steering a difficult course between the "democratically generated" claims from the new local councils
and the surprised objections from local politicians and landowners, still
powerful and accustomed to the old ways of handling drought relief and
works programs. The agents themselves had heady memories of this time,
reporting a profound sense of accomplishment and satisfaction with their
work—more so, some said, than with their regular work. This despite the
fact that the relief effort accounted for more than half their workload over

the long 12 months of the emergency, and had little to do with their strictly agricultural expertise.

Public disasters like floods, earthquakes, epidemics, and droughts almost always elicit high dedication and outstanding work from civil servants. They like being part of a venture that is more dramatic and "noble" than their everyday work, and that endows them with new, albeit temporary, power and dignity. In addition, the clarity of goals and the measurability of results are much greater in emergency work of this nature. During normal times, much of the work of public agencies, including agricultural extension, is embedded in more ambiguous goals and measures of performance and is subject to less marked deadlines. Part of the high performance during times of emergency, then, emerges from something more akin to a burst of adrenaline than to sustained capacity for good work.

For all these reasons, the high performance of the Extension Service during the drought might not seem particularly relevant to what happens when the drama ends and work returns to normal. By the end of this and the next chapters, however, it will become clear that looking at the worklife of the extension agents during the drought actually does throw considerable light on how to improve worker performance during normal times. Even if we admit that almost any corps of workers would probably rise to the demands of an emergency like Ceará's droughts, then, there are still serious reasons for surprise. They are the subject of the following section.

Some of the territory gained in improving the quality of drought administration in 1987 was lost in the subsequent and more extended drought of 1991–93. Local people and agricultural extension staff compared the administration of the later program unfavorably to that of 1987. Most significant, the state allowed the chairmanship of the new local council to pass from the extension agent to the mayor. This happened, in part, because the state's leadership could not continue to incur the political costs of disregarding the objections by the mayors to the state's attempt to reduce their power. The mayors' discontent translated into serious opposition in the state legislature to other reform initiatives of the two governors—or threatened to do so. The unfavorable comparison of the 1991–93 program to that of 1987 serves to make the significance of the 1987 achievements even clearer. It also shows that it is not politically easy to sustain such efforts to de-clientelize programs, even after such a heady first round of success. The slippage from the achievements of the 1987 program, then, raises some questions about the sustainability of the achievements described below. These concerns are better treated against the background of an understanding of how the program worked, and hence I return to the subject at the end of the chapter.

Unlike the health program, finally, the gains in the administration of drought relief were also more difficult to institutionalize simply because of the intermittent nature of the drought itself. The massive state apparatus mobilized to cope with Ceará's droughts almost disappears from sight in the intervening years, when the Department of Social Action carries out a mélange of less dramatic tasks. Our difficulty in finding people in the state capital who remembered how things worked in 1987 is testimony to this remarkable disappearance, between droughts, of such a large institutional presence. For the people in the towns and villages of the drought-prone interior, however, the drought and the drought programs were major events in their personal histories. Luckily for us, they remembered the 1987 program in considerable detail.

Destined for Poor Performance?

To any experienced evaluator of public programs, two key features of the 1987 drought relief program would seem to have spelled trouble. First, the program involved 12 different agencies, auguring a severe problem of interagency coordination. To make matters worse, the lead coordinating agencies—the state Department of Social Action and, in the field, the Extension Service—were weak vis-à-vis the powerful "building" agencies that traditionally carried out public works construction—the state Departments of Roads and of Waterworks. Second, professionals in the agricultural services usually dislike relief work and see it as undermining the "real" work of an extension service. More generally, agriculture planning experts and small farmers alike frequently hold extension services in low repute, a view from which Ceará's service was not exempt. This section starts by showing why coordination could have been expected to be a problem, given the particulars of this case together with the experience with such programs elsewhere, and follows with the reasons for the low repute of agricultural extension services in Ceará and elsewhere.

The Perils of Coordination

Engineering professionals and the building agencies where they work typically play a central role in emergency construction programs like that mounted during Northeast droughts. In Ceará's past droughts, the building agencies had also been subject to the coordination of the weaker Department of Social Action, but that coordination was much looser. In 1987, the Department of Social Action—together with the Extension Service— gained significantly greater control over the works program. In addition, the governor of the state "lent" the Extension Service to the director of Social Action for the 12-month duration of the drought. This temporary control of the staff of the principal field agency by another agency's director would also seem to create conditions under which the best performance might not be expected. Lending the Extension Service to another agency also helped fan the flames of a longstanding resentment by the Department of Agriculture, in which the Extension Service was located, over the taking away of some its power over agricultural planning.[12]

Just as potentially problematic, the 1987 drought relief program gave direct responsibility in the field to the Extension Service, rather than to the building agencies, for supervising a large share of the construction (44%). Most of this represented small works—small wells, reservoirs, and dams; maintenance, repair, and minor construction of roads; and buildings like schools, community centers, and storage depots for inputs and grains. Although the next largest share of construction projects (32%) did fall under the responsibility of a building agency—the Department of Roads—these projects were still to be coordinated in the field by the same extension officer who chaired the new municipal council.[13] In addition, the drought relief programs of the past had always included large numbers of water projects, which had fallen under the responsibility of the Department of Waterworks. In the 1987 program, however, that department was responsible for only 2 percent of the employment, and the Extension Service now had responsibility for the rest. Directly or indirectly, then, the Extension Service supervised a large program of construction projects seemingly beyond its expertise—projects that typically fall in the domain of the building agencies.

Traditionally, building agencies hold considerably more power in the world of public bureaucracies than do service agencies like Ceará's Extension Service or Department of Social Action, and because of the capital intensity of their tasks, control substantially greater funds than do such other agencies. The engineers who head and staff these agencies constitute a professional elite held in high esteem in both the public and private sectors. Their professional affinity with other engineers in private firms engaged in design, construction, and equipment manufacturing forms the basis for a strong coalition in support of the building agencies and their construction agendas. The appeal of public construction projects to politicians works to strengthen this support, as do the myriad opportunities for graft that lurk in large construction contracts. In programs dependent on interagency coordination, then, building agencies often dismiss with amused contempt the requests of the typically weaker agencies that coordinate such programs, and are able to protect their bureaucratic turfs almost effortlessly.

Images of Agricultural Extension

Many agricultural professionals, quite simply, do not like relief work. They resent being pulled off their regular work to do relief, which they consider "inferior" and a distraction from their normal work pursuits. It is not obvious, then, why they reminisced so favorably about their work during the 1987 drought. The international community of agricultural planners and advisors echo the agronomists' dislike of relief work in that they view it and other such extracurricular activities as one of the worst things that can happen to an extension service. Monitoring and evaluation reports on agricultural development projects, including those in Ceará, routinely bemoan the fact that agents are pulled away to do things unrelated to their "real" work. The major offenders, in addition to emergency relief programs, are the processing of bank credit applications for farmers, survey work for censuses undertaken by various government agencies, and public health campaigns.

The much touted Training-and-Visit model of agricultural extension (T&V) goes one step further than these critiques, as discussed in the next chapter. It even insists on trimming away some of the activities directly related to agriculture, like helping farmers get access to production inputs, and directs agents to focus more narrowly on their messages about planting and use of inputs. Together, these visions and preferences regarding what good extension agents should not be doing raise questions as to why the finest hour of the Ceará Extension Service came when it was doing precisely what it was *not* supposed to do.

In addition, although Ceará's extension agents turned into the "heroes" of the 1987 drought, they certainly were not seen that way in ordinary times. In the eyes of many planners and peasant farmers alike, the Extension Service was often the butt of disparaging remarks—for not having a workable "technical package," for employing young men fresh out of vocational school or the university with little farming experience, for staying in the office rather than visiting the farm (sometimes, but not always, due to the lack of funds for fuel and vehicle maintenance), for looking more after the interests of large farmers and other local elites than of peasant farmers, and for exploiting their position of power in rural communities in order to run for public office. This litany of complaints about extension agents is not peculiar to the Northeast or Brazil, as the discussion of the next chapter attests.

Even with respect to the drought relief programs, the halo surrounding the better extension agents in the interior was nowhere to be found in the state capital. In fact, the Extension Service was in some ways the last place one would have turned for a rescuing of the interior towns from clientelism. Residing in the towns where they worked, socializing with local elites, and working within the constraints of that particular power structure would all seem to make extension agents, of all public servants, least able to break out of it. This problem is not peculiar to agricultural extension, but arises in all public services in which frontline workers have one-to-one contacts with their clients, far from headquarters or out of sight of their supervisors—like the police, welfare workers, teachers, and the field or traveling staff of international donor agencies.[14]

Another aspect of this problem affected those agents who identified most with the reformist goals of programs like that of the 1987 drought or the programs targeted toward small farmers—exactly the kind of "good" civil servant said to be so lacking in the government of developing countries. In order for extension agents to work effectively in the município to which they were assigned during normal times, they had to have the tacit support of local notables. Although this should not necessarily have been a problem, many state governments in Northeast Brazil were trying to redirect their agricultural support services and subsidies in the 1980s away from these same notables—namely, large landholders—and toward poorer farmers. This happened in a context of widespread mobilization in Brazil around demands for democratization, and even a brief period of agrarian reform (1985–87), during which the power of large landowners over their tenants and the land in general was being widely questioned and challenged.[15] In addition, a 15-year $1.1 billion program of rural development targeted toward small farmers in the Northeast, and funded by the federal government and the World Bank, had the express purpose of directing the extension services of the nine Northeast states to work with small farmers.[16]

A large share of the small farmers newly assisted by the Extension Service worked as tenants or day laborers for large local landholders and merchants. Extension agents helped the small farmers gain direct access to bank credit, organized them into associations for buying inputs or for marketing, and even sometimes helped them obtain land of their own. When these initiatives were successful, they reduced the dependence of tenants and other small farmers on large landowners for access to land, jobs, credit, inputs, and marketing of crops. The political and economic power of many Northeast landowners, however, was grounded in this very dependence of their tenants and laborers—a common phenomenon in many developing regions of the world, especially those with high inequalities of landholding, wealth, and income.[17] Some landowners were not particularly happy, then, to see local extension agents helping their tenants and laborers. They, the landowners, had the political power to get agents transferred or, at least, to make their work life unpleasant. Many agents, understanding that they had to "know their place" in the community, felt hemmed in by this narrow political space. Not uncommonly, the most effective ones sometimes found themselves suddenly transferred elsewhere.[18] Though Brazil became particularly fertile ground for these kinds of problems in the 1980s and after, they are commonly found in the histories of government attempts to reduce poverty and increase agricultural incomes by assisting small farmers.[19]

Given this difficult political context for the agricultural extension workers who headed the municipal councils, how could the 1987 drought emergency have produced one of the state's finest achievements in public administration? The following two sections explain why these factors did not cause the trouble one would have expected and how, indeed, they actually *contributed* in certain ways to the program's achievements.

The Extension Agent as "Refrigerator"

Why did the Extension Service do so well during the 1987 drought if it was ill-suited to emergency works programs, if drought relief was resented as a disruption of the service's legitimate work, if field agents were themselves bound up in the web of clientelism that they were supposed to break, and if the structure of the program made it highly dependent on coordination among many agencies that were not likely to cooperate?

The answer to these questions lies in two parts. The first, treated in this section, relates to how the demands and rewards brought by the 1987 drought to the work of the extension agents differed from their work in normal times—and in a way that elicited more commitment from them. The second, treated in the following section, relates to a combination of actions taken by the state government vis-à-vis municipal government.

Given the negative views of emergency work expressed by many agricultural professionals, it was surprising to hear several extension agents describe their work during the drought as "not that different" from what they normally did. Some even considered drought relief as part of their "unwritten job description," and said they were the people "best suited" for it. The most telling way to explain this seeming paradox is through a story that the agents themselves jokingly told about a nickname people gave them in the communities where they worked—"Counsel." Counsel is a brand of household refrigerator advertised widely on television in Brazil.

The Counsel advertisement shows a mother overwhelmed with requests from her children or her husband for all kinds of things—not only those one might normally find in a refrigerator, but also those that one definitely would not, like a toy or a screwdriver. No matter what the child or husband asks for, the mother always responds by saying "Counsel," with a nod toward the refrigerator. Like the mother and the refrigerator, in other words, people saw the local extension service as the place to look for help with a wide variety of problems, whether the solution to these problems "belonged" in an extension service or not.

The extension agents liked being called "Counsel," considering it a term of endearment and appreciation. But to agricultural planning experts, the Counsel story—with its incongruous mix of items that should and should not go in a refrigerator—would illustrate exactly what was wrong with many extension services in developing countries. How could it be that the extension workers pointed to the Counsel "job description" as a sign of their good performance and a source of immense satisfaction, when many were identifying this same syndrome as a weakness?

Emergency drought relief and works construction require a public service that can respond rapidly, the mobilization of local groups, and prior awareness of possibilities for quick, bottleneck-removing works projects. In the eyes of the extension agents, their routine work had situated them perfectly for this. They had to travel extensively around their município, organizing farmers to buy, sell, or even produce in groups. They brokered for their client-farmers with the mayor, the branch bank manager, and other local notables; and they helped solve marketing problems, which made them acutely aware of transport bottlenecks.

In the same way that the drought relief program required extension agents to meet with stricken communities to set priorities and make requests for works projects, the agents had worked closely with small-farmer groups, helping them decide priorities and formulate plans for small projects such as seed banks, input-supply stores, small community-owned grain mills, and so on. Just as their drought work required them to oversee food distribution through community assemblies, their regular work had them routinely calling meetings with farmers to decide on procedures for allocation of and payment for improved seeds or credit advances.

Even in the realm of expertise, the agents felt that their responsibility for supervising small construction projects was not so far beyond the domain of their usual work. When small farmers sunk wells, for example, they often called on the agents to give a "second opinion" on a site that had been previously recommended by a "diviner" or "water witch"; these sites sometimes turned out to be unsuitable because of conditions, for example, making dynamiting difficult. Similarly, as told in the next chapter, extension agents might help farmers repair their irrigation equipment or broker their initial contacts with repair services. Although these activities might fall outside the agents' normal "job description" and expertise, their assistance in these matters often had significant effects on the productivity and incomes of farmers by linking them to important input and sales markets.

Small construction projects were also not so far beyond the realm of the extensionists' work in normal times. Many of the farmer groups they had helped organize routinely asked for their opinions and assistance in relation to small construction and repair projects undertaken by the groups themselves or by government agencies to which they had much less access than they did to the extension agent. Although these projects were not their specialty or their training, the agents' ability to link up their clients to the outside world of more knowledgeable sources of information and assistance—combined with their own knowledge of how things worked locally—positioned them to be of considerable help. And although these small works projects were not directly agricultural, they often had major bottleneck-breaking impacts on agriculture—for example, the repair of a stretch of road making transport of local produce out of the area difficult during the harvest season or the incoming supply of inputs difficult during the planting season.[20]

One of the standard ways of distinguishing good from mediocre extension workers is that the good ones like working in the field and the less effective ones tend to prefer staying in the office. Time spent in the field talking to farmers, needless to say, is central to good extension work, and the best agents reported these times to be the most satisfying aspect of their work. It was these better agents, not the mediocre ones, who saw drought relief as actually helping them to be more effective at extension work.

Drought relief actually facilitated the agents' work outside the office. First, and most obviously, much agricultural activity grinds to a halt during a drought, meaning that demand for the services of extension agents also falls as farmers struggle with their immediate need to feed their families. In these times of slack demand, drought relief work kept agents busy at something as challenging and satisfying—if not more so—than their routine work. Second, the emergency funding provided for the drought relief program brought with it greater funding for allowances for travel expenses, and for gasoline and repair and maintenance of the agents' vehicles. Extension services in developing countries typically suffer a chronic scarcity of such funding in normal times.[21] During the 1987 drought in Ceará, one agent recounted, he could go to the field to visit farmers three times a week, as opposed to once a month during "normal" times.

Third, and finally, drought relief work helped extension workers build enduring relationships with the communities where they worked. When the drought ended and the rains finally came, things were permanently different as the regular work of extension recommenced. The drought relief program had made the best agents better known to the communities they served in a way that left a legacy of trust; small farmers said they preferred working with these agents, whom they now knew and respected. Building this kind of trust was not particularly easy. Mistrust of persons working for government ran high in the rural areas of the Northeast. In the same way that the acts of curative care by health agents helped open the door for preventive care, the drought relief program had made better extension work possible.

The best agricultural extension agents enjoyed being called "Counsel," then, because they considered themselves as places where, like the refrigerator, you could find "everything." For them, as opposed to the experts on agricultural extension, the line between agriculture and "other things" was not such a clear one. This amounted to their describing their expertise in a way that was different from the usual. In their eyes, their "specialist" knowledge lay not just in expertise about how to increase crop yields or reduce infestations of pests; it also lay in their ability to make things happen, which was grounded in their past experience as brokers between communities and the larger world of government offices and private firms—first, on matters relating to agriculture, then, for "everything."

Given that no other agency in the state had this particular combination of expertise and experience in rural areas, perhaps this broader definition of "specialist" expertise was not so far-fetched. Although it might leave too much hanging for the experts on agricultural extension, such a definition is nevertheless consistent with the recent research findings on large organizations noted earlier, which show better performance to be associated with greater worker discretion and a greater variety of tasks.

Against this understanding of the broader experience and informal job descriptions of the extension agents, the questions raised at the beginning of this section are now easier to explain—(1) the seeming "unsuitability" of the Extension Service to administer what amounted to a construction program and (2) the potential for interagency trouble that seemed to underlie the coordination demands of the relief effort.

The broader "self-defined" job definitions of the best extension agents also reflected the fact that they were more sympathetic than the building agencies to that very aspect of the program that complicated its administration—its employment-creating goals and its elaborate attempt to create a process of decentralized, representative, and "rational" decision making. In the past, evaluators have often pointed to worker and managerial disinterest in these kinds of goals or processes, let alone sheer resistance to them, in trying to explain the disappointing results of attempts to improve performance.

In addition, such a large and newly decentralized relief program like that of the 1987 drought required rapid contact with myriad communities, widespread sharing of information across field offices, and substantial coordination of their actions. Because past drought relief programs had made decisions and allocated supplies in less deliberative and consultative ways, they did not rely so heavily on a strong local field presence of government combined with a statewide networking capacity. This combination is exactly what the Extension Service had developed in doing its normal work. Most agents knew each other from their period of training; and local extension offices routinely shared information with other municípios about climatic conditions, prices, shortages and excesses of production, inputs, and new research findings. No other agency of the state had this combination of a strong field presence with the capacity for instant and far-flung networking.

The final piece of this explanation relates to the 1987 program's injunction against the traditionally large works projects—mainly, construction of major roads and reservoirs—and the preference, instead, for smaller, community-based, and less equipment-based projects. The latter kinds of projects were technically easier for nonengineers to supervise, although in other ways they were more demanding in that they involved a larger number of projects in widely dispersed places. In contrast to the Extension Service, the building agencies found the more dispersed and rustic smaller projects less professionally "serious" and, hence, less appealing. This is why these agencies so surprisingly ceded control to the less powerful Extension Service and Department of Social Action. With the building agencies less interested and less in control of project design, it was simply easier for the state government to dedicate a large share of program expenditures (80%) to the hiring of unemployed workers.

Although the 1987 drought relief program kept the building agencies at a healthy distance and benefited from having field-workers who were profoundly committed to what they were doing, these explanations still leave some important questions unanswered. When towns started making decisions about how projects and jobs would be allocated, why would the "drought industrialists" of past emergencies have so easily yielded their power? How could field agents now hold power over the same local landholders and politicians who previously could bring about their transfer? How did the drought relief program take power from these local elites without eliciting overwhelming opposition from them? Given that all relief programs provide myriad opportunities for graft, how did this particular program succeed in eliciting such public-minded behavior from its army of field agents? What kept the mediocre agents from abusing their greatly increased discretion or, at least, from simply not rising to the occasion? I turn to these questions now.

State versus Municipal Government

The answer to the questions posed above lies in a combination of actions taken by the state government vis-à-vis the world of the municipality, and the dynamic unleashed by those actions. First, and quite simply, the new director of the Department of Social Action—a cabinet-level post—made his presence felt quite directly at the local level, an unusual management style for public managers. Among other things, this caused the program's field-workers to feel appreciated for their expertise and protected from local politics. Second, the state government's directions and strictures regarding how the program should operate locally created the conditions for a greater heterogeneity of opinion to emerge among local elites, and a forum for a more public-minded voice to be developed by some elite actors. Third, the state government surrounded rural communities and towns with public messages about the program that, as in the preventive health initiative, created some constraints on rent-seeking behavior by elites and government workers alike. These findings are laid out, respectively, in the following three subsections.

All three elements of this story involved the state government's increasing its control over local government and other local actors. Most stories about improved local administration, in contrast, emphasize the ceding of control by a more centralized arm of government to local government. Similarly, the story reveals that public-serving behavior by civil servants emerged as a result of the state government's protecting its field agents from the abuse of power by mayors and other influential local actors. Most current discussions of how to improve public service, however, focus on *increasing* the power of local actors over service providers—as consumers of these services. These concerns about increasing consumer sovereignty and "voice" as a way of improving public services are well placed and, indeed, represent major advances in the thinking about public-sector reform. At the same time, this has also resulted in a neglect of the darker side of "consumer sovereignty"—the side that wields influence in a way that undermines public-minded goals of equity and efficiency. The focus on local actors, in short, has kept the development field from understanding the strong and innovative moves that central government must make if decentralized programs are to be successful.

Management by Wandering

How could the new director of the Department of Social Action have successfully coordinated the field staff of another agency, the Extension Service—only temporarily and almost overnight—and elicited such dedicated performance? The answer involves a greater presence by top management of the central level of government in local affairs—just the opposite of what is envisioned by the current thinking on decentralization.

For the duration of the drought, this particular director spent large amounts of time traveling in the drought-stricken areas, checking up on the distribution of food and water and on the works projects, receiving requests and complaints, resolving difficult disputes, and, in the process, participating in the various community and town meetings presided over by the extension agents. He even took a group of managers from the state agencies working in the drought relief program on a bus trip throughout the drought-stricken area in order that they could "experience it directly"—a first for some of these urban bureaucrats. Five years after the 1987 drought, people in the drought-stricken communities still recalled the visits of the director, referring to him by name and telling of how surprised they were to see an agency manager in their midst, let alone a cabinet secretary.

The opportunities provided by the director's travels for face-to-face contact with the extension agents changed their work environment markedly. They were now able to have one-to-one and informal contacts on their own, often remote, turf with the chief executive officer of their agency. In addition, the state government's actions served to provide more protection to field-workers from attempted diversions of the program by disgruntled landowners and others. Suddenly, extension professionals said, management and the state's leadership in general were treating them like "authority figures," acknowledging them as "competent professionals," and backing them strongly. The visibility of their contacts with such a "high dignitary," as witnessed by people in the interior communities, enhanced the agents' prestige. They felt more respected by management and in the towns where they worked.

The itinerant agency director represents an unusual phenomenon in the public sector of Brazil. His management style, however, resembled that of the "wandering-around" manager celebrated by Peters and Waterman (1982:122) in their book of more than 10 years ago on best management practice among large corporations in the United States.[22] Partly as a critique of the penchant of that time for "strategic planning," and based on the best-practice corporations studied by the authors, Peters and Waterman—and later Behn (1988, 1991) for the public sector—presented a manager who gets away from his desk and spends time with his customers, suppliers, and employees. This manager finds out what they are thinking, what problems they confront, and what ideas they have, making them "feel wanted, respected, and valued" (Behn 1988:650).

The public-sector manager in Ceará—and, for that matter, in many other countries—is often just the opposite of the good manager of Peters, Waterman, and Behn. He "spends all his time at his desk, reading and dictating

memos, or in meetings with [his] immediate staff and direct subordinates"
(Behn, ibid.). Unfortunately, as Behn says, "management by wandering"
has not acquired the cachet in the field of public management that Peters
and Waterman gave to it in private management. Evaluation reports and
the press often portray travels by public managers pejoratively as "jun-
kets" and "goofing off" and, for this reason, frequently reduce travel funds
or cut them off as "nonessential" (651).

One of the reasons public-sector managers do not wander, as Wilson
(1989) points out, is that they are too busy to do so. Public emergencies
like droughts require more "wandering," of course, than the normal work
of a public agency. The lesson to be learned from the case, nevertheless,
is obvious. The state's extension workers responded positively and quickly
to a seemingly quite simple change in the way they were treated.

Diversifying Local Elites

As with decentralizing programs in other parts of Brazil and other countries, the discourse about the 1987 drought relief program emphasized its
newly "democratic" nature. Less noted was the fact that the program
brought changes to the social and political dynamic within the local elite
community. In explaining the program's achievements, these changes were
at least as significant as the increased representation of poor communities—those intended to be served by the program.

Supporters and critics alike of successful decentralizations tend to place
too much weight, in depicting and judging what happened, on the issue
of control by the local citizenry and intended program beneficiaries. As
with Ceará's drought relief program, and the preventive health program
as well, enthusiasts exaggerate the degree to which decision making is actually more inclusive, while skeptics triumphantly ferret out cases that prove
the contrary. The reality is usually more complex. To expect that local
decision processes could suddenly turn so democratic is unrealistic. To describe these processes as such, after the fact, is often inaccurate or, at
least, it does not quite capture the essence of the change. The current enthusiasm of the development literature and project designers for "consumer choice" tends to work in the same direction, predicting that major
improvements will result from increased "consumer sovereignty." The end
result of this particular set of enthusiasms, predictions, and explanations
is that it is often difficult to understand the nature of the changes that actually cause government to work better. This subsection illustrates, with

some material from the case, the elements of a more complete, and hence accurate, explanation.

As described earlier, the 1987 drought relief program named the extension agent in charge of the local field office to be chair of the new municipal council, the Community Action Group (GAC/Grupo de Ação Comunitária). In doing so, the state government bypassed the mayor as the most likely choice to preside over such a body; it "packed" the council with members of "civil society"; and it turned the head of the state's local extension office into the foremost "expert" on the drought relief program in his particular município—the "front man," as extensionists said, through which all information on the município's needs would now be channeled. Municipal leaders and other local elites, though represented on the council, were now at least formally subject to a process in which the extension agent presided over decisions about drought relief that were taken only after painstaking and public deliberation.

On closer observation, the composition of the new municipal councils would not necessarily seem to have guaranteed a wresting of control from local elites. At least six of the 12 committee members might be expected to be under the thumb of the mayor or vote with the large landowners—four from city hall and from the municipal Departments of Health and Education, plus at least two from business groups like the landowners' association or Rotary Club. These latter groups were considered to be part of the representation from "civil society," even though they did not represent the jobless and the hungry for whom the emergency program was intended. Even some of the council members seen as truly representing the interests of the program's intended beneficiaries—the local parish priest and the head of the local rural workers' union—could not necessarily be counted on to vote against the desires of local landowning groups, depending on the politics of the particular município.

Signs that local elite control did not simply crumble with the advent of the new council came from one of the municípios where the new drought relief program worked best, Crateús. There, the three GAC members who represented the communities complained that, when it came to voting, they were too small a minority on the 12-member committee and that the communities' wishes were therefore not adequately represented. They asked the Department of Social Action, which granted the request, to authorize an increase in the number of community representatives from three to seven, thereby increasing the size of the council from 12 to 16. Although community representation still fell two short of a majority, the parish priest and the president of the rural workers' union in that particular município could be counted on to vote with the community representatives which, along with the vote of the extension agent, guaranteed the communities a majority.

Regardless of whether poorer groups were able to gain sufficient voice in the new local council, the new decision-making procedure had an independent effect on the dynamics within elites of the towns and villages. The broad elite representations on the new GAC council, and the vigorous discussions at its weekly meetings, allowed for a division of opinions to develop among elites themselves. This led to broader and more public-serving elite involvement in the council's decisions. For example, merchants and others with businesses in the municipal seat—usually the largest town in the município—feared that if the drought relief program were mismanaged, those without work and food would migrate to their town, live on the streets, loiter outside their places of business, and generally disrupt the climate for business. With rural poverty and rural-urban migration having become more and more of a problem over the preceding several years, especially during and after the droughts, town governments and business elites were feeling increasingly threatened by such migration and its attendant impacts on the town.[23] Merchants from smaller towns and villages also wanted to reduce migration to larger towns and to outside the region, but for different reasons. In that the rural poor were their customers, they worried about the permanent loss of customers resulting from the "draining" *(esvaziamento)* of the population from the countryside. This caused them to be sympathetic to opportunities to improve the quality of administration of drought relief and other measures, like agrarian reform, that did not seem to be in their interests as a rural elite class. To the extent that these particular elite voices were represented on the new municipal councils, then, this introduced heterogeneity into elite influence on local government and sometimes helped generate fairer and more carefully crafted decisions about the allocation of projects, jobs, and relief supplies.

The state government, in sum, constituted a formal deliberative process at the municipal level, laid down strict criteria for decisions, and presided over council meetings. This was central to the better outcomes achieved for these intended beneficiaries, whether or not they were fairly represented on the new local councils. By broadening elite representation in the decision making about the drought, and formalizing it in a newly created deliberative body, the drought program created an environment in which more public-minded visions of fairness could emerge from among local elites themselves. The extent to which this actually occurred, of course, varied from one município to the next, depending on the political and economic dynamics of each one.

All this is not to conclude that the determinants of the better outcomes described above are more "complex" than typically portrayed. Rather, this case and my interpretation of it suggest something more precise than the naming of decentralization and consumer sovereignty as the most recommended path to improved government, and the criticism that the poor do not really participate. First, the strong hand of state government—in dictating the criteria for choosing projects and beneficiaries, as well as the form of the local decision-making council—was crucial to the emergence of better local decision making, in those cases where it actually happened. Second, although the nature of what emerged in the best cases involved less consumer sovereignty and voice than decentralization enthusiasts would like, the evolution of public-mindedness among local elites—not necessarily direct consumers of the services—was crucial to improved local administration. Third, whether local elites will be public-minded or mean-spirited depends on the political, social, and economic dynamics of each particular locale. Decentralization and increased consumer sovereignty, in other words, may sometimes lead to better and fairer government service provision, but not always.

Surveillance and Trust Entangled

The drought relief program's effect on the emergence of intra-elite differences was not enough, in itself, to change the clientelistic dynamic of previous drought relief programs. Just as important were the decisive actions of the state government in another area—public information and a certain kind of public discourse.

From the inception of the drought relief program, the state government repeatedly told a wide spectrum of community associations and municipal councils, directly and through the extension agents, that they now had a formal say in decisions about projects, jobs, and relief provisions. As in the health program, the state conveyed this information with the language of a "transformational" public purpose. A new state government was vowing to modernize a socially and economically "backward" state by ending clientelism in the administration of drought works and relief, replacing it with a more "rational" and "democratic" decision-making process through which communities could exercise power. These messages had a monitoring effect on the behavior of workers and local elites while, at the same time, conveying a sense of serious public mission to all those who served on the new local councils. As one GAC member reported, anyone sitting on the council now had to serve the interests of the large majority of drought victims, if only to "maintain his reputation."

One of the better-known forms of graft in emergency employment programs throughout the world takes place around the payment of workers. Supervisors, or local notables in charge of community payments to workers, overreport the number of workers on the rolls or the days worked; they keep the payments for these "ghost-worker" days for themselves, or give them to other persons who have not worked, including members of their own families.[24] To deal with this problem, legendary in the Northeast drought relief programs, the state government issued public warnings to the 235,000 people who received jobs under the program. In language quite similar to that used by the state in recruiting the 7,300 agents for the preventive health program, the state government said it did not have the funding to hire everyone who was unemployed. Those who did receive jobs should consider employment as "a privilege rather than a guarantee," and should "take pride" in their jobs. Those who were not hired, in turn, should become "monitors" of those who did get the scarce jobs. In several cases, as a result, communities reported workers who, although paid by the program, did not show up for work. This new awareness of the community reduced the level of infractions below that of previous drought relief programs.

Concerns other than monitoring, interestingly, also motivated the state's admonitions to workers and communities. In the 1987 drought, partly because of fiscal constraints, the state government was not able to employ as large a percentage of the unemployed as it had in the previous drought of 1983. Leading to the same result, the state had decided to pay each worker more over the employment period in real terms than in past droughts, meaning that fewer could be employed. This was accomplished by paying the full minimum wage (rather than one-quarter the minimum, as in the previous 1983 drought), by the timely indexing of the minimum-wage salary to keep up with Brazil's double-digit monthly inflation of that period (in previous programs, wages were not indexed), and by paying workers for six more weeks after the drought ended, so that they would not fail—for lack of income—to prepare their fields for planting.[25] Since these new guidelines meant employment for a smaller share of unemployed workers than in the past, state officials felt they needed to have a public justification for employing some workers and not others. This is where the public admonitions about "privileged" jobs came in.

Recent studies of employment-creating works programs like Ceará's, but in other parts of the world, have criticized their choice to pay each worker a "decent" income rather than hire more workers and pay each one less. This, these researchers suggest, causes the "scarce" jobs to be rationed among the better-off of those seeking jobs and therefore undermines the very attempt of the program to target those most in need.[26] It was not possible to determine whether the wage paid in Ceará's program was indeed higher than market-clearing in this case, and whether this particular problem of mistargeting occurred. Nevertheless, the government's admonitions to the community about monitoring, and its approach to drawing up lists of the eligible, might be seen as another way of dealing with the problem of mistargeting, which has been of such concern to these particular analysts. The approach to mistargeting in this case, that is, relied on the working of community norms and pressures to allocate jobs in socially desirable ways, rather than on prices.

The state government was not the only bearer of tidings about the drought relief program to the public. In the municípios where the program was most successful, the new local councils used public information as a way of capturing the public's attention, instructing them, and creating a new environment for the taking of decisions. Many of the GACs blanketed their communities with information about the program—through the radio and, in some cases, with monthly information bulletins several pages long. In Tauá, one of the best-performing municípios in the drought relief program, the GAC circulated its bulletins to 40 public agencies, civic groups, political parties, and the media. It even allowed radio reporters to attend its meetings and broadcast the meetings or summarized reports of them over the radio, sometimes to the discomfort of committee members.[27]

All this public awareness, and the numerous meetings at which claims could be made and discussed, added to the creation of an environment in which new voices emerged in the interior towns and villages. These new voices made for a more complex picture of local elite views, in contrast to the simpler elite agenda previously dominated by large landowners and mayors who were beholden to them. At the same time, those government field-workers who had previously given in to the constraints on their operation placed by powerful landowners or clientelistic mayors, now found it more difficult to do so. With more divergent elite interests swirling around the distribution of drought funds and supplies, moreover, the agents saw their role as having changed. With the state's backing, they now had the power and the "solomonic" responsibility to preside over the new variety of opinions and pressures in their work world.

The public messages about the drought relief program, in sum, served to check the possible abuse of power by both clientelistic local elites and government workers. Ironically, and as occurred in the health program, the same public information that was keeping workers in check was also having a remarkably supportive effect on their morale and commitment. At the same time that the drought relief program was giving field-workers the power and the protection to serve the public interest better, that is, it was also forcing them to do so.

Lessons for Normal Times

At first glance, those concerned about issues of institutional sustainability might question whether there is anything enduring to be learned from the achievements of the 1987 drought relief program. Like many such public responses to crisis, it was an episode and not an ongoing program, operating for the 12 months of the drought emergency and closing up shop soon after the rains came. In addition, the agricultural extension workers who showed such high commitment to their job during the drought were doing something not directly related to their regular work—indeed, something considered to be undermining of "real" extension work. Finally, the drought relief program mounted three years later by the same state apparatus lost some of the ground it had gained over clientelism in 1987. Not able to withstand the discontent of the mayors, the state government allowed them to replace the extension officer as head of the local council.

The story of the 1987 drought turns out to reveal more that is relevant to our understanding of public-sector performance than might at first appear. For one, some of the findings that emerged from this case are strikingly similar to those of the previous chapter's health program. This despite the fact that the health case lies on the opposite end of the spectrum with respect to its ongoing character and the institutionalization of its achievements. Both stories reveal that poor performance resulted not only from self-interested public servants surrounded by rent-seeking opportunities, but also from work arrangements that kept worker morale and productivity low. Both cases, moreover, involved a decentralization success that had at its core a strong and new role played by central government. Finally, although both programs were rife with opportunities for public servants to misbehave, the state government provided new attractions to not do so. By repeated "coaching" of its workers and the public, the state increased the attractiveness of public-minded behavior to civil servants and citizens alike while, at the same time, stirring up communities to demand better performance from their government. That an exploration of the reasons for improved government performance in two such different activities could lead to these same findings endows them with a significance above and beyond the peculiarities of each activity and case.

The lesson of the drought story, finally, is not that extension agents can perform well only when they work on "other" things, like drought emergencies, vaccination campaigns, or credit applications for their small-farmer clients. Various findings reported above bear directly on the *routine* work of extension workers: the agency director who spent so much time away from headquarters with his field-workers and his clients, the respect conveyed by the state to the public about its workers, the state's call on the public to monitor its workers and to contribute to the decisions taken by field offices, and the greater autonomy and responsibility of workers in setting their work agendas. All of these give substantial food for thought about how to increase the dedication and dignity of extension workers and, for that matter, of various others in public services that rely so much on frontline workers.

The following chapter makes this clearer by fashioning the lessons of the drought case in terms that can be applied to the work of agricultural extension itself. It tells a story of agricultural extension agents liking their jobs better and contributing to increased productivity in agriculture while they were doing what they were supposed to do—namely, agricultural extension itself. Together with the subsequent chapter on small business extension, the agricultural extension story also reveals the significance of another important theme that ran across these cases—that of customized versus standardized jobs.

· 4 ·

Frontline Workers and
Agricultural Productivity

Fᴏʀ ᴀ sᴛᴀᴛᴇ so traditionally agricultural, with 40 percent of its people dwelling and earning a living in rural areas, it was puzzling to find that none of the widely publicized achievements of this innovative state government fell in the agricultural sector. For more than a half century, the traditional agricultural economy of Ceará has revolved around the interplanting of perennial cotton with cassava and beans under a sharecropping system, together with the pasturing of large livestock. The productivity of these crops has been generally stagnant or declining over the past two decades, and the production of tree cotton has been decimated by an infestation of the cotton boll weevil, starting in the mid-1980s. The latter has dealt a permanent blow to the cotton economy in its traditional form, and the share of agriculture and livestock in the state's output has declined from roughly 33 percent in the early 1980s to between 7 percent and 15 percent in the 1990s.[1] Cotton, cassava, beans, and livestock products still rank, nevertheless, among the state's six most important agro-livestock activities in terms of value and acreage occupied, the other two being cashew nuts and rice. To the extent that there has been dynamism in the agro-livestock sector, it has occurred outside the traditional activities, particularly in cashew nuts, irrigated rice, and poultry.

Since the early 1980s, the agricultural planners of Ceará and the other

Northeast states have turned their attention increasingly to small farmers who, as in many countries, had been virtually ignored in the attempts to promote and subsidize the modernization of agriculture and livestock production. Despite the state's highly unequal distribution of land, small landowners and tenant farmers still account for a significant portion of the output of important crops.[2] Together with farm laborers, without land of their own, small farmers also account for 40 percent of the state's economically active population and for an equally serious share of its rural poverty.

Ceará's Extension Service has led the drive to extend state subsidies and production services to smaller farmers. As part of these initiatives, and like many extension services elsewhere, Ceará's service encouraged small farmers to organize into groups for purposes of obtaining access to subsidized inputs, credit, and agricultural research and extension assistance. The World Bank played an important role in promoting the turn toward small farmers in all of the Northeast states, including Ceará, through a 15-year $1.4 billion program of support for integrated rural development projects, jointly funded with the federal government. For more than 10 years, the Bank-funded Ceará projects—three in succession starting in 1977 for a total of $573 million—expended 25 percent of their funds on agricultural extension, covering approximately one-third of the salaries of the state's Extension Service.[3]

With this history, Ceará's agriculture sector stands out not only because of the absence of significant achievements during a period of otherwise remarkable improvement and innovation in state government. In addition, agriculture was the only sector to have received sustained funding throughout the 1980s and into the 1990s, as well as technical assistance, from foreign donors. Because of this history of attention to agriculture and small farmers in all the Northeast, including Ceará, observers have expressed considerable disappointment at the continually stagnant or even declining per-hectare yields of the Northeast's staple crops (cassava, beans, corn, and rice), grown largely by small farmers.[4] To the extent that these critics have blamed the institutions of state government in the agricultural sector, they have not spared the Northeast's agricultural extension services. Various studies had appeared in the 1980s, after all, showing that public investments in agricultural extension in other countries, and even in the more developed parts of Brazil, showed particularly high returns.[5] Why wasn't the Northeast's investment in agricultural extension, they asked, paying off? Although an answer to this question falls beyond the scope of this study, looking at a slice of this experience provides some interesting insights, as well as useful comparisons to the three other sectors studied.

Because of the concern about stagnant agricultural productivity among small farmers, together with the emphasis on their lack of access to agricultural production services, I chose to look at small-farmer associations that had received assistance from state government and succeeded in increasing their production or organizing their own viable services. A surprisingly large number of Ceará's agricultural technicians and other observers of the agricultural sector agreed that three farmer associations stood out in the state as having become quite successful. I wanted to know why these three had done better than the others, and what—if anything—was different about the kind of relationship they had with the state's agricultural institutions, particularly the Extension Service.

My findings link up to the preceding chapters not only because the agents of the Extension Service were the same frontline workers of the drought relief program analyzed in the previous chapter. In addition, extension workers were the most numerous and conspicuous force of public-sector frontline workers or "street-level bureaucrats" in rural areas after teachers, military and police, and health workers.[6] Issues of worker dedication to the job, and of relations between workers and client-citizens, were therefore also likely to be significant determinants of improved performance—namely, of whether small farmers actually achieved greater access to the state's production services and whether farm productivity actually increased.

I started by looking for themes running across the experience of the three farmer associations, which were all located in the cotton-growing, semiarid interior of the state. It turned out, however, that only one group showed a striking increase in output, incomes, and productivity—the 60-member Santana Agricultural Production Cooperative (Cooperativa de Produção do Assentamento Santana), located in the município of Monsenhor Tabosa. The two other, much larger, cooperatives—COSENA and COAPEC[7]—had 600 active members each and were located in two adjacent municípios in another part of the cotton-growing interior (Senador Pompeu and Piquet Carneiro, respectively). The histories of COSENA and COAPEC were impressive in terms of their having succeeded, after a long struggle, in throwing out of office their large-landowner leadership, who had also been the landlords of many of the rank and file. They then organized services for their small-farmer rank-and-file members—agricultural extension, tractor rental, improved seed distribution, credit. The farming of their members, nevertheless, did not demonstrate the impressive changes in production and productivity that Santana's did. Ironically, moreover, COSENA and COAPEC had received more lavish support and attention from the state's agencies, through the World Bank–funded programs, than had the more successful Santana. As a result of these findings, the focus of my interest shifted from the themes running across the three farmer groups to the question of why one group did so much better than the two others in terms of productivity. It was the lack of precisely this kind of productivity improvement, after all, that seemed to bedevil Northeast agriculture in the aggregate, and had fueled the repeated disappointments with public policy and programs in this sector. That COSENA and COAPEC did not generate a significant increase in the productivity or incomes of their members should not take away from their achievements in other areas, nor does this suggest that such improvements are not possible in the future.

Although Santana was different from the two other cooperatives in several ways,[8] one difference stood out. Briefly, Santana's farmers were served by the public extension service, whereas the two other successful cooperatives had their own private extension services—albeit with substantial initial assistance from the public sector. One would have expected the two cooperatives' own extension services to have done better than the public service, rather than vice versa. The Northeast's public extension services, as noted above, had certainly not proven their mettle in terms of the aggregate performance of the region's agriculture—although with some notable exceptions.[9] More generally, the mainstream development community has been arguing—consistent with its new thinking on public service delivery in general—that extension services provided by nongovernment entities often tend to be better.[10] Farmer cooperatives like COSENA and COAPEC, other nongovernment organizations, and private firms are considered to be more responsive to client needs and pressures, more locally knowledgeable, and more likely to engage in client-driven, consultative styles of problem solving—if only because they are forced to by being located so geographically close to their clients.

Contrary to these views on public-sector reform, the difference between the public extension service assisting Santana's farmers and the private services of the two other cooperatives seemed to have nothing to do with the public-private fault line, as this chapter shows. First, the public extension service to Santana emerged from a special relationship between the agent and the farmers, which was client-driven and customized—much like the case of business extension of the next chapter. In this sense, the Santana case and others like it came closer to the ideal of nongovernment provision cited above. Second, the two cooperatives with their own extension services organized the delivery of their services in a manner that was more akin to that of the "typical" public service—standardized and "top-down." These findings suggest that some of the problems of public extension may actually be resolvable within the public sector itself. They also suggest that switching to nongovernment provision of services may not necessarily cure the ills that are viewed to be inherent in public provision.

In developing this case of agricultural extension, I chose to look carefully at the history of one farmer association and to contrast it to the two other less successful associations and to the state's more typical ways of providing agricultural extension and of disseminating research results. I found this a useful way of illustrating the larger set of patterns I found in other sectors, as well as making clear the problems inherent in existing programs of agricultural extension and research in Ceará and elsewhere. In earlier research in the nine states of Northeast Brazil, I had already described a number of similar cases involving customized relationships between agricultural service providers and client-farmers (and also between such service providers and "intermediate" clients such as other government agencies).[11] In that material, however, I had dwelled exclusively on the "demand-driven" nature of the dynamic that ran across several cases of successful dissemination of productivity-increasing agricultural techniques. I was less attentive then to the particular nature of the customized relationship between the farmer and the extension agent or extension service, and the positive impact this had on the agent's dedication to the job, as well as on farmer productivity.

The first section of this chapter sets the stage with Santana's significant achievements in increasing productivity and member incomes. It shows how service delivery in this particular instance—as viewed by both farmers and the extension agent—was customized and client-driven, in contrast to the more standardized and top-down style followed by many public extension services.

The Story of Santana: Driven by Clients and Customized

In the late 1980s, during a two-year episode of statewide land distribution to small farmers, 60 landless and micro-landowning farmers in the district of Santana received 3,100 hectares of land, after a long struggle that had united them in a cohesive group. The group formed an association one year after receiving the land in 1987 and, two years after that, a cooperative. Previously, and like most small farmers of the cotton-growing areas of Northeast Brazil, Santana's farmers had worked individual parcels, cultivating annual subsistence crops (beans, corn, cassava) and perennial cotton, as sharecroppers or small landowning farmers. Their landlords had grazed cattle herds extensively, drawing for forage on the residues of cotton and subsistence crops, part of a low-productivity system of joint production of these products. Upon acquiring their land, and after an agonizing period of debate, the group decided to depart radically from their past farming patterns and go into intensive livestock production—dairy and beef cattle, goats, and sheep; some families already owned one to three head of cattle.

Santana decided to cultivate its pasture and graze its cattle collectively, using artificial pastures and introducing irrigation for their dairy pastures. At the same time, members retained individual plots of one to two hectares apiece for subsistence production of corn, cassava, and beans. They pooled their existing cattle, amounting to 100 head and, with credit from the state, bought additional improved stock. They busily subdivided their new land into large fenced paddocks, separating the bulls from the cows, giving frequent vaccinations and parasite baths to their improved stock, harvesting the pasture grass mechanically for feed and mixing it with wheat, melaze, and cottonseed meal to improve its quality, and caring religiously for their irrigation equipment. Five years after acquiring their land, Santana's 60 farmers were successfully grazing a herd of 418 dual-purpose cattle, 443 sheep, and 620 goats. They cultivated an additional 100 hectares in individual 1.5-hectare plots dedicated to food production.

Santana's new techniques of production, of course, were nothing new in terms of good livestock management. They contrasted markedly, however, with traditional livestock management in the Northeast. First, they involved a departure from prevailing low-productivity practices, involving extensive grazing on unimproved pastures. Second, and as in many countries, cattle raising had been the dream of many small farmers of Ceará's interior. But it had not been within their reach, let alone Santana's "higher-tech" approach to it, because of its large capital requirements and risks. These risks had left livestock production in the hands of large farmers, the only ones with the requisite capital, land, and access to state-sponsored investment credit. Small farmers had participated only indirectly in the livestock economy, as sharecroppers of cotton and subsistence crops on the lands of large livestock holders—a subject to which I return in the following section.

Unlike most small farmers of Ceará, including those belonging to COSENA and COAPEC, Santana's farmers succeeded in lifting themselves out of the traditional low-productivity cultivation of cotton and subsistence crops in conjunction with livestock. Within three or four years, the group almost doubled the number of animals grazed on the tract of land they had acquired—from 0.13 animal units per hectare by the previous large landowner to 0.22.[12] Though the latter figure was still low by international standards, productivity was particularly striking for the 110 head of dual-purpose dairy cattle grazed intensively on 157 hectares of the group's holdings: the number of dairy cattle grazed per hectare rose 12-fold, from the 0.13 head of the previous large landowner to the 1.6 of Santana. This figure was also eight times higher than the average of 0.2 for the município. Milk yields were even more impressive: at 458 liters per hectare per year, they were 33 times greater than the município's average of 13.7 liters per hectare.

Because of these striking results, Santana fast became the darling of the state's agricultural agencies and development banks. This was after the short-lived land distribution initiative had ended and, along with it, the state's enthusiasm for assisting the new settlers in producing collectively. Santana's achievements, then, also represented somewhat of a vindication of the rationale justifying the law under which the group's land was expropriated—namely, that land not being put to productive use would be expropriated and handed over to those who could use it productively. If only on these grounds alone, the case merits attention—especially since the state government subsequently lost interest in land redistribution as key to its policy toward increasing agricultural production and productivity. In addition, and as described in this section, the findings of this case echo and therefore reinforce the lessons emerging from the other chapters about high organizational performance and worker commitment to the job.

A Client-Driven Bargain

Over several months after receiving their land, Santana's farmers worked out a "special deal" with an extension agent of their choosing. The deal gave rise to a type of service that was remarkably similar to the proposals for client-driven and consultative service delivery so in vogue among public-sector reformers today.

The Santana arrangement was born of the group's dissatisfaction with a previous agent assigned to them, and the infrequency of his visits. The group had complained to the local extension office that the agent had not been helpful because he did not visit them enough and did not sympathize with their decision to produce livestock collectively. Remembering an agent who had worked with them quite supportively when they were struggling to acquire the land, they successfully lobbied the Extension Service to bring him back and replace the existing agent.

The infrequent visits of the previous agent were not only a sign of his lack of sympathy for the group. As in many developing countries, Ceará's Extension Service was chronically short of funds to buy gasoline for its jeeps, to maintain them, and to reimburse its agents for the expenses of their field visits.[13] Santana solved this problem by offering to pay its favorite agent for a tankful of gas. This is common practice in developing countries, though never officially acknowledged.[14] For each of these visits, the group would present the agent with a written list of matters it wanted help on—how to acquire and administer livestock vaccinations, how to increase the yield of its pasture grass, how to operate and repair its irrigation equipment. After spending a full day or two at Santana, the agent would agree with the group on a date for his return visit two or three weeks hence. In the interim, he promised to consult with colleagues and superiors, research agronomists, and best-practice farmers in the region. In addition, the group encouraged its agent to spend some time, at its expense, attending to the requests for visits from six other farmer groups in surrounding communities. As a successful farmer group in the município, Santana's farmers said, they saw this as a way of acting "responsibly," as well as of demonstrating to their neighbors the fruits of collective action.

Santana placed particularly high value on the agent's assistance in helping it learn to use and repair its irrigation equipment, which was new to it and which suffered periodic breakdowns. Located in an area where repair services and expertise about irrigation were difficult to attain and costly, Santana would find its milk yields dropping dramatically within two days after a breakdown of its equipment. The group decided, therefore, that it would have to learn how to repair the equipment itself. With these kinds of returns to extension assistance, it is no wonder that the group was willing to provide the agent with food, lodging, and fuel in return for teaching it to repair the equipment or for helping it get access to repair service—even though he had no special expertise in irrigation equipment or its repair.

Both the extension agent and the farmers reported preferring their special arrangement. The agent said he liked his job much better when he worked this way, because he could be more "productive." With two or three weeks after each visit to "thoroughly research" the problems and requests posed to him by the group, he said, he could now arrive at the farms "knowing exactly what I have to do." He also enjoyed the challenge of working with farmers who were "demanding and receptive to technical advice"—an "ideal situation" for an extension agent. This contrasted with his regular work, where he had to start "trying to figure out what to do" only upon arriving at a village or farm, and did not have sufficient time to respond adequately to farmer questions and requests. At the same time, he did not view the farmers' "control" over his work agenda as undermining or slighting his own expertise. He participated fully in the group's technical decisions, he said, and did not simply accept its list of problems without giving his opinion or without changing the order of priority, if he saw fit.

Of particular importance to his commitment to the job, the agent liked the recognition he received for being associated with a farmer group that was doing well. The Santana farmers publicly praised his work and expressed profound appreciation for his support in front of the many visitors from state agencies and other farmer settlements who asked him to take them there. These episodes of public recognition took on the same meaning for the agent as the similar moments of public praise reported by the health agents and nurse-supervisors in chapter 2.

Santana's farmers had their own reasons for preferring this unusual arrangement with their extension agent. Their prior preparation of a list of requests helped them make the most of the agent's limited time with them, they said, and also gave them a basis for judging the quality of his work. They also stressed the element of trust that had set the stage for this particular arrangement: rather than being assigned an agent whom they did not know, they had chosen their agent—indeed, lobbied hard to get him. They had come to know him previously, when he had worked with them during their struggle for the land. He was committed to something they believed in profoundly—"the agrarian reform process"—a sharing of values that meant very much to farmers who had struggled many years to obtain land. The group's satisfaction with its agent could be seen not only in its comments, but in the ultimate "market test": even after the Extension Service started to receive adequate funding again for its operating costs, Santana continued to cover its agent's expenses.

Informal Performance Contracting

The arrangement between Santana and its extension agent was unusual only in the sense that it rarely appears in evaluations of extension services. Such "deals" between particular extension agents and farmer groups are common in Northeast Brazil, as well as in many other countries where extension services suffer from chronic shortfalls in funds for operating costs.[15] One could say that, in looking the other way, extension services are tacitly accepting an illegal form of performance contracting of their agents by farmer groups. How can a public agency that provides service to farmers free of charge justify a practice by which certain groups of farmers simply contract a particular worker while he is on duty in exchange for reimbursement of his expenses and, probably, an additional payment in cash or kind? And why would a public agency agree to this, if only tacitly? The answer is twofold.

First, any local extension office without funds for gasoline and fieldwork would be foolish to prohibit arrangements that allowed its agents to do their work rather than stay grounded in their offices. In Santana's case in particular, the local extension office would certainly not want to disrupt an arrangement that was facilitating one of the few production successes of small-farmer cooperatives in the state. Precisely because of this success, moreover, terminating the arrangement with Santana would have created other problems because, by that time, Santana had strong and aggressive defenders in the state capital.

Second, because these deals between farmers and particular extension agents are not officially acceptable, extension services cannot acknowledge them and, hence, do not have to justify them. For this reason, little is known about these kinds of arrangements, and under what circumstances they work. Despite the current enthusiasm for client-driven service among the international advocates of public-sector reform, then, they have not looked to this informal experience with performance contracting when searching for ways to reinvent agricultural extension.

Santana's arrangements with its extension agent, in sum, seemed eminently practical and wise. Indeed, to dwell on their virtues might seem to belabor an obvious point. Most extension services, however, show no sign of moving in this direction, and continue to organize their work along standardized and nonconsultative lines. Typically, the head of the local extension office and not the farmers provide the agents with their work agenda, usually a standardized set of messages and improved inputs to promote. To illustrate, the next section shows how the same extension service that assisted Santana operated according to the opposite, standardized style in another of its programs covering the same region—a campaign to combat the boll weevil in the state's cotton-growing interior, including those municípios where the three cooperatives were located and even involving the private extension services of the two cooperatives. The story of the boll weevil campaign serves to make clearer the difference between the customized and standardized style in agricultural extension.

Fighting the Boll Weevil
and Hurting Small Farmers

The glowing results of the collaboration between Ceará's Extension Service and Santana contrast sharply with those of its campaign to fight a major infestation of the cotton boll weevil with a new technical package for the crop. For more than a half century, cotton had been the state's main agricultural export, and the campaign covered the entire cotton-producing interior of the state. In the municípios where COSENA and COAPEC were located, the state Extension Service passed on its recommendations and input subsidies for cotton through the private extension services of the two groups. (Santana's cooperative was not involved, since its farmers no longer produced cotton.)

The boll weevil infestation decimated Ceará's cotton economy and employment in an even more sustained and calamitous way than had the 1987 drought. Just as during the campaign to combat the drought, the Extension Service played a key role. Yet whereas extension agents had been the heroes of the 1987 drought among the peoples of the interior, they gained no such reputation for their role in the boll weevil campaign. The explanation for this reveals an important similarity between the emergency drought relief program and the Santana case, even though both involve very different activities. In each case—and different from its usual operations—the Extension Service could not carry out its work without substantial consultation with its client-farmers. In the case of the drought, that is, the service needed the communities to provide a ranking of those eligible for jobs and of projects desired by the community; in the case of Santana, the extension agent needed the group to come forward with a list of the principal problems affecting its crops and to rank them in order of priority. This need for client input was both the cause and the effect of a customized, client-driven organization of the service. The cotton campaign, in contrast, shows the Extension Service in its more typically standardized and less consultative mode of operation.

The story of the boll weevil campaign illustrates the significant practical differences and outcomes that result when extension is delivered in its typical and less consultative form. The story also reveals that the two private extension services, as in the previous section, were just as nonconsultative as the public service. In conveying the harsh realities of the cotton economy of the Northeast interior, finally, the cotton story makes the achievements of the Santana farmers stand out, in contrast, even more. Under the Santana arrangements, the disappointments detailed below could not have occurred.

The Better Cotton

In the mid-1980s, the boll weevil attacked Northeast Brazil's major export staple, cotton, with disastrous consequences for the regional economy.[16] Between 1975/80 and 1987/91, the weevil infestation, along with declining international prices, caused the area under cotton cultivation in Ceará to fall by 73 percent and production by 63 percent;[17] during the same period, COSENA's purchases of cotton from its members fell by 40 percent. Throughout the Northeast's semiarid interior, a drought-resistant long-fiber variety of perennial cotton *(algodão mocó)*—in which the hot and dry Northeast had a comparative advantage—had long been cultivated in joint production with livestock and subsistence crops. The cotton bushes and the other crops left forage residues for the livestock during the dry season, which became an even more important source of feed for the cattle during drought years. Sharecroppers, who made up two-thirds of the membership of COSENA and COAPEC, typically cared for the perennial cotton bushes. They interplanted them with subsistence crops, for which they received from 30 to 50 percent of the value of the output—landowners requiring them to market that production through them as part of the sharecropping arrangement.

This way of producing cotton resulted in low average yields of 120 kilograms per hectare and was frequently quite inequitable to sharecroppers. In years of low rainfall, when pastures dried up early, landowners frequently released their cattle into the cropped area and cotton plantings before the harvest, indicating how important cotton was to the livestock economy. This practice, which both destroyed the tenants' subsistence crops and damaged the emerging cotton crop, was common enough that it was prohibited in the national labor and land tenancy legislation of 1964; until recently, however, the legislation was not enforced. The low-yielding production of cotton, then, was deeply embedded in a larger system of joint production with livestock and subsistence crops in which livestock rather than cotton was the landowners' principal concern.

Throughout the Northeast, state governments reacted strongly to the boll weevil's destruction of such a traditionally important export staple. As in many of the other states, Ceará's state agricultural research agency adopted a weevil-resistant annual variety used successfully in Southern Brazil. With a directive from the state's agriculture and agricultural planning agencies, the Extension Service vigorously promoted replacement of the long-fiber perennial cotton of the Northeast with the short-fiber annual cotton of the wetter, less tropical South. The technical package was composed of the new seeds, fertilizer and pesticides, and, if possible, irrigation. Yields were expected to be several times higher than for the existing perennial plantings, even without irrigation—800 kg per hectare, and 1,800 kg with irrigation.

Many public officials interested in modernizing Northeast agriculture saw the boll weevil infestation as a blessing in disguise. Although the option of the higher-productivity annual cotton had been around for some time, it had been difficult to get farmers to abandon the low-productivity system they used, for reasons explained momentarily. The destruction wrought by the weevil, planners hoped, would force the hands of the cotton farmers and jolt them out of their low-productivity trap, as well as fire up the state's agricultural agencies to promote the new variety vigorously.

The Sorry Results

In much of the cotton-producing part of the state, including the municípios where the three cooperatives were located, the campaign to introduce annual cotton had disappointing results. The new variety was not compatible with the joint production of livestock, let alone subsistence crops. It did not provide the same amount and quality of forage for livestock (the annual variety is a smaller plant that leaves fewer residues, and rows between the plants must be kept clear of the grasses and weeds that had been important sources of forage for the cattle). When interplanted with subsistence crops, the new variety's yields were not significantly higher than those of perennial cotton. Irrigation, moreover, tripled production costs, putting it beyond the reach of sharecroppers and beyond the interests of landowners for whom joint production with livestock was a major reason for producing cotton. During drought years (every three to seven years) the yields of the more common nonirrigated production of the new variety fell to the same levels as the drought-resistant perennial, or lower; this meant that average net returns for the new variety could be even less than for the old variety. In the drought year 1993, for example, only 20 percent of the land planted with the new annual variety was harvested, whereas that figure was 82 percent for land planted with the older perennial variety.[18] Because fertilizer and pesticides were costly, moreover, farmers tended to use them sparingly—a familiar story—also lowering the yield advantage of the new variety.

Out of convergence of landowner and tenant interests, both the sharecropper members of COSENA and COAPEC and their large-landowner members turned against the new cotton variety. Some agents of the extension service—public as well as private—were also not convinced, and actually encouraged farmers to keep on with the old drought-resistant variety. Some agents bitterly characterized the annual cotton promoted by their service as "an invention of the companies selling inputs." They complained that even with the boll weevil, the old variety still gave higher yields than the new variety under rainfed conditions. Rainfed farming was the only option for most farmers of the region.

Many large landowners, in an unusual alliance with the smallest farmers and the extension agents who sided with them, also resisted the new variety. Because of their primary interest in cotton residues as forage for livestock, and because the new variety would not serve this purpose, large landowners simply prohibited their sharecroppers from adopting the annual variety. Other landowners abandoned their weevil-infested cotton bushes, turned their lands exclusively to pasture, and evicted their share-croppers. Between 1975/76 and 1987/91, therefore, acreage planted in both old and new varieties of cotton had fallen by 73 percent and production by 63 percent; of the cotton land that remained, 68 percent continued to be planted with the old perennial variety, and 32 percent with the new variety.[19] Although the annual variety's share represented a fivefold increase from 6 percent in the mid-1970s, this still reflected a decline in lands planted with it since 1988, albeit a less rapid decline than that of lands planted with the older perennial variety.[20] In addition to the decline in cotton production, the conversion of cotton-and-crop land to pasture, with the accompanying eviction of sharecroppers, unleashed a wave of unemployment and poverty in the already-poor rural areas of the region, exacerbating migration from the countryside to the towns of the interior and the coastal cities—a matter of ever-growing concern to the mayors of those towns and to state policy makers. For a variety of reasons, these disastrous consequences had not occurred in the southern region of Brazil from whence the new variety had come and where it was widely cultivated.[21]

The sorry results of the campaign against the boll weevil need not have occurred if the state had engaged in a more consultative approach to the problem with farmers, and with its own field-workers, the extension agents. Contrast, for example, the more positive outcome resulting from Santana's help from the Extension Service and its client-driven context: it abandoned cotton completely in favor of the intensive production of dairy cattle and other livestock on improved pastures. These activities, in contrast to the traditional cotton economy, were more profitable. They were at least as labor-absorbing as the previous mixed combination of cotton, cattle, and subsistence crops. And they were obviously much more absorbing of labor than the exclusive livestock grazing into which many large cotton growers retreated.

Although Santana's way out of cotton was not a viable alternative for many farmers, it was not the only alternative available. If the state's agricultural planners had followed a more consultative approach with farmers and carefully watched their feedback to the initial plantings through the eyes and ears of their field agents, they would have discovered a felicitous way of fine-tuning their cotton campaign to produce better results. A closer look at the experience of the COSENA and COAPEC cooperatives, that is, reveals a missed opportunity to move away from low-productivity cotton production.

A Niche for the New Variety

Annual cotton *did* represent a desirable crop choice to a certain stratum of small farmers. In contrast to the large landowners and sharecroppers who were adamantly against the new variety, many small (and medium) farm owners liked it. Because of their small holdings, livestock production was not an option for them, and perennial cotton's advantage in terms of joint production with livestock therefore had no meaning in their case. They also felt they could manage the new annual variety's extra costs as long as the cooperative gave them credit for the inputs they had not used with the perennial variety.

Some of these small landowners became happy users of the new variety, then, and advocates at the cooperative for credit to finance their conversion. But the extension campaign against the boll weevil did not single them out for attention. In what might otherwise have seemed to be a logical decision, the campaign appealed broadly to the more numerous combination of large landowners and their sharecroppers. The latter were three times as numerous as small owners in the cotton-growing areas, represented the poorest among the state's farmers, and constituted a large majority of the membership of COSENA and COAPEC. Small landowning farmers, in contrast, accounted for only 25 percent of the membership of the two cooperatives, and an even smaller share of the state's small farmers of cotton. Singling them out for special attention, particularly in this context, might not have seemed to make particular sense, and would have been politically difficult. At the same time, however, significant increases in productivity and output by a critical mass of small farms in any particular region has been shown to have dynamic secondary or "linkage" effects on growth and income distribution in that region.[22]

The Northeast cotton-and-livestock economy, in sum, seemed impregnable to productivity-increasing attacks. For many farmers, there was simply no other economically viable crop alternative to cotton, unless the conditions under which small farmers gained access to credit and agricultural extension and research were to change markedly. But even within these constraints, a cotton-support strategy targeted at small-farm owners would have generated significantly better social and economic results than the dilution of the state's efforts across all farmers.

When new varieties or other innovations are carried from the experimental plot into the field, it is sometimes difficult to avoid big mistakes like those of the cotton campaign. It is difficult to imagine, nevertheless, that the learning period would have been so long, and the social consequences so dire, if more formal practices of consultation between farmers and the Extension Service, and between field agents and top management, had been in place. After all, the cotton story revealed that many extension agents themselves soon learned that the new variety was wrong for small farmers, and that neither their management nor the state research agencies paid them any heed. It is difficult to imagine the state's agricultural agencies having made this kind of extended mistake if the system had been organized as it was during the drought. In that case, as described in the previous chapter, the extension agent chaired a municipal council that *depended* on client input—in that case, on communities preparing a ranking of proposed projects and of needy candidates for jobs.

Conclusion

As projected against the story of Santana, the lessons of the cotton story are fourfold.

First, the Santana extension arrangement could not have produced this result because the farmers, who were also "paying" for their extension agent, would have rejected it.

Second, the state's agricultural agencies seemed uninterested in eliciting, and unable to respond to, the feedback of their own field-workers. Yet this is what they proved themselves quite capable of doing during the drought relief program—albeit under the command of a director from another state agency.

Third, the private extension services of the two cooperatives performed no better than the public service in the cotton campaign. Without a process of local trial and error, they simply passed on to their membership the latest wisdom on cotton from the state's agricultural agencies. Hence the results were no different than if these two cooperatives had been served directly by the public extension service.

Fourth, and by way of setting the stage for the next section, the cotton campaign actually represented quite good performance by the Extension Service—if seen simply as an exercise in aggressively disseminating a standardized set of recommendations. Into every corner of the cotton-growing region, extension agents fanned out with their standard package of messages and inputs meant to reduce the boll weevil infestation and increase the output and productivity of cotton. The only flaw was that the technical package was not quite right, as much a fault of the research agency as of the Extension Service. Technical packages, however, are usually "not quite right" until they are tested more widely in farmers' fields, adapted to agronomic variations among the microregions, and filtered through the kinds of market and institutional considerations that kept this particular new variety from being adopted. It is in this sense that the agricultural leadership in state government was to blame for not giving more importance to consultation with farmers and with its own field agents, and for not insisting on subsequent reconsiderations and iterations. These kinds of consultations and successive iterations, however, are in many ways incompatible with the standardized approaches followed by many governments in promoting agricultural modernization. The following section shows why.

The New Standardization: The Training-and-Visit System

The ill-fated campaign against the boll weevil illustrates some seemingly obvious problems with taking a standardized approach to service delivery in agricultural extension, especially when contrasted to the felicitous outcomes of the customized and client-driven arrangement with the farmers of Santana. But the most popular model of agricultural extension at the World Bank for many years was even more standardized than our cotton story. The Training-and-Visit system (T&V)[23] prides itself on greater standardization and even narrower limits on an agent's tasks than now exist in most extension services in developing countries, let alone in the customized model of the Santana case. This section compares the standardized T&V model with the customized approach of Santana in order not to convey the mistaken impression that "standardized" and "top-down" approaches to extension delivery are solely the result of deficient public administration in developing countries, and as a way of bringing out the importance of the findings about extension in this chapter, as well as in the preceding and following ones.

Starting in the late 1960s with cotton cultivation in Turkey and continuing with high-yielding varieties of rice and wheat in South Asia, the World Bank has promoted the T&V approach in a large proportion of its agricultural projects.[24] This model of agricultural extension became associated with some of the striking Green Revolution successes of India and Pakistan in the 1980s in increasing agricultural productivity, particularly in wheat and rice. Subsequently, 40 countries introduced the system in projects or as part of nationwide systems, usually with World Bank assistance. Among these cases, the Bank promoted the use of T&V in agricultural development projects in 31 countries of sub-Saharan Africa.[25]

In contrast to the broader jumble of tasks found in our cases, let alone most extension services in developing countries, T&V prunes back the extension agent's responsibilities markedly. As in the mass production model, it defines these responsibilities quite explicitly: agents must restrict themselves to messages "transferring information and technology," and their discretion is reduced. They are now trained to deliver standardized messages to farmers in a regular and rigorously observed schedule of fortnightly meetings in the countryside, announced in villages and hamlets with two to three weeks' notice. This reduces the common problem of farmers never knowing when agents will show up, as many complain, or of agents not showing up for meetings they previously scheduled.

T&V places this emphasis on the spreading of standardized messages to farmers about improved technical packages because many countries, its advocates say, already have such packages "on the shelf" of their research institutes and experiment stations. The lack of further field adaptation and a vigorous extension service, it is said, keeps these productivity-enhancing packages from being disseminated. T&V also strives to liberate extension agents from the "extraneous" tasks with which they are often burdened—or take on themselves—so they can focus better on simply disseminating the improved technical packages. This, and the stress on the agents observing a publicly announced calendar of regular visits to communities, is also meant to help reduce "the monitoring problem" in agricultural extension. The latter arises from the difficulty of adequately supervising such a large force of street-level bureaucrats, who work outside the office in dispersed and remote places and have one-on-one contact with clients that is not amenable to monitoring. Under T&V, if the extension agent does not show up in a community on the preannounced date, supervisors will hear about it from farmers.

The T&V model has generated considerable debate and a host of critics, including from within the World Bank itself, as ardent as its advocates.[26] The results of applying the model in sub-Saharan Africa have been less satisfactory than those of the earlier Turkish and South Asian successes, adding fuel to the debate. Two recent impact studies on T&V programs in Kenya and Burkina Faso, however, reported quite favorable impacts—to the pleasure of T&V supporters, since one of the studies' authors was a well-known academic agricultural economist and skeptic about T&V.[27] A more recent study by the Bank of its agricultural support programs, nevertheless, gives T&V mixed reviews at best (1994). Contrasting the standardized (T&V) model with the customized findings of the Santana case also brings out the clear difference in their treatment of problems of supervision and monitoring. These are, obviously, key factors in determining the quality of extension services and, indeed, of all public services that rely on street-level bureaucrats. I therefore turn to these issues now, and then return to the substance of the T&V critiques later in the following section.

Standardization versus Customization in Agricultural Extension

The customized service provided in the Santana case and others like it does not constitute a "model" of service delivery, unlike the T&V model, with its manuals and its incarnation in real projects. In the cases where customized service exists, it is usually an "accident" or deviation—something field evaluators run into from time to time. Indeed, I might not have noticed this deviation if its opposite, in the form of the T&V model, had not been so firmly in my mind. These deviations, moreover, would not have added up to anything in this research project if it were not for their likeness to the findings that emerged in some of the other sectors reviewed, particularly in the case of business extension of the following chapter. Put together, these findings also add up to a picture that is consistent with the models of good performance that are emerging from the studies of industrial restructuring and transformed work environments in the first world. In that latter world, customized service delivery, multitask jobs, and trusting relationships between workers and clients or between supplier firms and customer firms have now become almost as canonized as was T&V and its standardization in the World Bank. The same goes for management's giving frontline workers more discretion and paying more attention to their opinions about how to organize work.

In our stories, the agents seem to get involved in a larger variety of tasks than, according to T&V, they should have. This is analogous to the contrast between the more limited worker tasks of the earlier mass production model and the greater variety of tasks and customization found in the more "flexible" production of the late twentieth century. In the Santana story, for example, one of the agent's most important contributions to increasing farmer productivity and income was to help the farmers make their irrigation system work properly. The agent sometimes even repaired the equipment himself, teaching the farmers how to do it, or put them in contact with those who did know. Much of the agent's guidance, similarly, involved the management of livestock and pasture, although livestock was not his specialty. At the same time, however, the Santana agent was not merely taking on any particular problem he stumbled upon. The problems he chose to tackle were narrowly focused on increasing the output and productivity of that particular group. In the drought story, to go even further afield from the extensionist's normal responsibilities, the Extension Service's finest hour came when it was organizing communities to prepare lists of employment-creating projects and of needy job candidates, and coordinating the allocation of relief supplies of food and water—that is, when working on something other than agricultural extension.

In all of these instances, the extension agents were more committed to their jobs and their performance was higher—in line, again, with the findings of the large-firm experiences noted above. Yet a good part of the job in these cases did not really involve the "expertise," or even the typically prescribed tasks, of an agronomist or extension agent. Indeed, T&V advocates would consider these "extra" tasks—such as helping fix irrigation equipment, processing credit applications, or supervising small works projects during the drought—to be "diversions" from real extension work and to be part of the problem, rather than the solution. This is why the T&V model insists on narrowing the range of activities and advices of extension agents, and curtailing the occasions on which they get drawn off into "other" work. In so doing, T&V implicitly ignores the importance of these activities—which might be described as "brokering," "firefighting," and all-purpose advising—in building relations of trust between agents and farmers and, hence, in increasing worker commitment to the job and farmer productivity.

In certain ways, a client-driven model of service is, by its very nature, incompatible with the deliverance of standardized messages. For example, only after the extension agents of the cotton campaign had observed the results of applying the new weevil-resistant technical package, or listened to the objections of farmers to it, could they understand in what sense the standardized message they carried was not right. The agents' learning from their clients was cut short in this case, however, because learning from farmers and extension agents was not of central importance to the management of the state's agricultural extension and research agencies. Sadly, then, the unmodified recommendation about cotton continued to issue from the state government at the same time that field-workers were advising against it in private conversations with clients, ignoring it, or swallowing their doubts and continuing to pass the message along.

The cotton story also reveals another problem with standardized messages in agriculture. As seen above, the proposed new variety of annual cotton was not necessarily the wrong solution for all farmers. It made economic sense for the large minority of small farmers who owned land, though not for the sharecroppers who were more numerous nor for the large landowners and livestock producers who occupied a major part of the land planted with cotton. In this situation, more customized treatment—singling out the most relevant group of farmers or devising different messages for the different types of farmers—would have been more appropriate. But figuring this out would have required substantial interaction with farmers, responsiveness to what they were saying, and ability to offer more than one solution—in short, a nonstandardized approach.

Whereas trust between worker and client is central to the literature of industrial restructuring and workplace transformation, T&V gives much less attention to trust. Trust between agent and farmer enters the scheme, if at all, only in terms of the publicly announced schedules of dates for visits by agents to farms or villages which, if they are not observed, farmers can complain about to supervisors. This is certainly a pale substitute for the trusting relations, and the arrangements that gave rise to them, which were found in this case and in the better-performing firms studied by the researchers of restructuring. How can these trusting relations, however, be reconciled with T&V's legitimate concern about the need for supervision of such a dispersed workforce, and the enhanced opportunities for greater rent seeking that inhere in the greater discretion of customized work?

Sloppy Jobs and Hard Supervision

Without benefit of the framework of thinking provided by the literature of industrial restructuring, the more varied and heterogeneous tasks of the extension agents of our cases would seem to add up to rather "sloppy" job definitions and work schedules. By leaving public servants more on their own and with more discretion as to their work agendas, the customized approach seems to make even more difficult the task of supervising a large force of workers who are out of the office most of the time—the constant dilemma facing the managers of street-level bureaucrats. The whole concept of expertise, in addition, would seem to be jeopardized by this approach, with the extension agent becoming a kind of jack-of-all-trades rather than confidently conveying new methods of agriculture judged by "the experts" to be better. That is surely one reason why this way of thinking about job definitions is less appealing than a model of more bounded job descriptions and standardized sets of tasks or messages.

As in the more flexibly organized work environments of large firms, however, the customized jobs of the extension agents are anything but sloppy. They are paced by implicit rewards and penalties that can be at least as powerful in eliciting good performance as the more traditional job definitions and supervisorial relations. To illustrate, I return to the comparison of T&V to the case of Santana. T&V's pre-set schedule of appearances throughout the countryside gives supervisors clear marching orders for their subordinates, assures that workers know exactly where they are supposed to be, and allows farmers to be confident that extension workers will actually show up as promised. The workers have less room to slack off, since they, their supervisor, and their clients all know in advance that they must be at a certain place on a certain day. In the Santana story, in contrast, the supervisor's monitoring of the agent is partly substituted by monitoring by the farmer group. The agent also meets a promise, of his own in this case, to show up "two or three weeks later." But the reason for his returning as promised is the result of a bargain struck with his clients rather than of a schedule set by his superior.

In both T&V and the Santana case, then, the system works because the agent is penalized for not showing up. In T&V, the penalty takes the form of reprimands from a supervisor, who may have found out about the absence from complaining clients; in the Santana case, the client-farmers may complain, too, but they can also withdraw their allegiance to and "funding" of the agent, and look around for another one—as happened with Santana's first agent, whose replacement was successfully requested. Even more relevant to the issue of motivation, the two cases are different in that the Santana agent keeps his promise not only because of the threatened complaint to his supervisor for not showing up when promised, but because he likes his job better when he works this way. And he has developed a trusting relationship over a longer term that he does not want to breach. With respect to the farmers, moreover, their likelihood of complaining if the agent does not show up is considerably greater in the client-driven arrangement of Santana than in T&V. In the former, the farmers would certainly have good reason to be upset and to complain if their agent did not show up as promised, because they were the ones who had set an agenda of issues that were important to them and who agreed with the agent on a date for their next meeting. In the T&V model, the farmers may not necessarily need the agent on the date set by the agent's supervisor, may not find that date convenient, or may not be particularly interested in the topic of the standardized message brought by the agent. If the agent does not appear, in other words, these farmers will not necessarily have cause to complain, which reduces the penalty effect of this client-monitoring feature of T&V's standardized approach.

These matters of trust between agents and farmers, and of worker morale, are not insignificant. A recent World Bank review (1994:vi) of T&V and other extension programs noted that "*despite* T&V's objectives of using farmer feedback" in formulating recommendations, the "hierarchical structure and 'message-centered' delivery in T&V has done little to change the 'top-down' characteristic in formulating recommendations [to farmers] which has been traditional in most extension bureaucracies."[28] Given what is now understood from IPWT research on the importance of more discretion and customization to the job performance of frontline workers, however, it would seem that the standardization and regimentation of T&V were perfectly *compatible* with the "top-down" nature of traditional extension organizations, unresponsiveness to clients, and low worker morale. This was remarkably well understood by some careful observers of T&V workers more than 10 years prior to the above-cited review.

In a study of India's extension service during the best years of the Green Revolution, Mick Moore found that T&V's monitoring mechanisms had a strikingly "counter-productive" impact on worker morale: "The major formal supervisory mechanism was the setting and checking of 'targets'—for inputs distributed, practices adopted etc. . . . [T]he extremely authoritarian and (verbally) harsh fashion in which targets were set and performance was evaluated was both counter-productive in its own terms—leading to falsification of reports, ritualism and concentration of efforts on activities for which targets were set and expected to be checked—and in the long run damaging to the organisation. Rather than developing a sense of loyalty and commitment to their agency and immediate supervision, field agents responded with passivity, evasiveness and cynicism about their work."[29]

Moore goes on to identify the source of these problems in exactly the standardized routines that T&V considers the hallmarks of its success. He argues that T&V designers opted for the "'easy' road" of increasing job performance by "intensifying" supervision, "giving field agents precise visit and work schedules which could easily be checked." He contrasts this to what he considered the more desirable, albeit "very difficult," path of changing the relations between supervisors and agents in a way that would contribute to building "an *esprit de corps*" among field agents.[30]

The counterproductive supervisory measures found by Moore in the T&V system of the Indian Extension Service might have been less necessary if they had been replaced by, or at least complemented with, the more customized kinds of arrangements found between agents and their clients in the Santana case. The customized arrangements, in certain ways, represent a less "difficult" alternative to the ideal change in supervision that Moore says is needed. The increase in worker morale and performance, that is, does not necessarily depend on the emergence of a new set of relations between a supervisor and agents but, rather, on a change in relations between the agent and clients. Indeed, the Santana arrangement and others like it occurred over a period when superior-subordinate relations within the service hardly changed at all.[31] This lack of marked change in superior-subordinate relations made these cases of high worker performance even more striking testimony of the importance of intricate relations of trust between worker and farmer.

Even one of the most serious and most favorable studies of the impact of T&V on agriculture to date—that on Kenya, noted above—suggests that the extension service in that case was puzzlingly inadequate, and certainly lacking in some of the hallmark design features to be expected in a T&V success story. With respect to certain problems, in fact, the Kenya service came strangely close to that described by Moore for India more than 10 years earlier, and echoed complaints frequently made about poorly performing extension services in other countries. Although supervisors in the Kenya system were supposed to visit their agents in the field twice a month, for example, 40 percent of the agents reported receiving fewer visits (Bindlish and Evenson 1993:8). In addition, about half the field agents and supervisors reported training sessions took place only once a month rather than the required twice a month. (A majority of agents and supervisors, it should be noted, felt that once a month was adequate.) Poor transport and delays in reimbursement of expense claims for field travel, moreover, were ranked by all staff as significant "constraints on performance"—exactly the conditions afflicting Ceará's and other extension services with only average performance. Finally, and also similar to these other cases, linkages between extension and research were "weak" in the Kenya story, and research scientists seldom attended the monthly workshops meant to be the main forum for bringing research and extension together (ibid.:8–10).

Put together with Moore's findings on India, these studies reveal a puzzling combination of reported success, in terms of increased agricultural output and productivity, and extension services that are hard to distinguish from those portrayed in evaluations of the mediocre ones. If the institutions providing extension and research look the same, whether agricultural productivity increases or remains the same, this raises the question of whether it is the standardized regimen of T&V that actually explains the agricultural growth. One's mind immediately wanders to other obvious explanations, like the presence of aggressive private-sector suppliers of the improved inputs, or shifts in relative prices, or changes in the access of farmers to local markets and inputs—all of which would affect the expected returns from the new technology.[32] One also wonders, given the findings of the Ceará stories, if more customized ways of working with farmers might have actually crept into the routines of the T&V extension workers. This presents another possible, and more positive, way of interpreting the seeming contradictions in the African findings reported above.

Client-driven approaches to agricultural extension and other services, in sum, are very much in vogue on paper and in meeting rooms. Enmeshing these approaches in a series of considerations about worker dedication and performance, however, is not. The questions raised and alternative explanations offered in this section are meant to show, together with the comparison to Santana that precedes them, that there are other ways of thinking about improving the performance of extension agencies that rely on trust in and monitoring of workers by client-farmers, and an accompanying client-driven customization, rather than standardization. Despite the popularity of client-driven approaches, finally, one does not read or hear much about certain practical implications of using them. I turn to these issues now.

Conclusion: Implications for Practice

This chapter has described a set of customized and client-driven arrangements that have sprung up informally in various countries, including Brazil, between extension agents and farmers, using as an example the farmer cooperative of Santana. The frequency with which this kind of arrangement occurs in developing countries, and the good results it produced in this case in terms of agricultural productivity, suggest that this approach is superior to the standardized service delivery of many extension agencies—whether the standardization takes the form of the campaign against the cotton boll weevil in Ceará or the Training-and-Visit system promoted by the World Bank.

Extension services did not deliberately choose the customized arrangements described in this chapter. If they acknowledge them at all, they consider them makeshift, and to be abandoned as soon as budget normality returns. But these practices are quite consistent with the latest thinking about how to organize service delivery in the public and private sectors, including more accountability to and consultation with clients, more client feedback in evaluating worker performance, performance contracting, and charging for services. Historically, moreover, the Santana-like arrangements have quite distinguished forebears in the now-industrialized world. During the first half of the twentieth century, long before performance contracting came into style, the Northern Branch of the U.S. Agricultural Extension Service worked in precisely this client-driven way.[33]

In the late nineteenth and early twentieth centuries, at the county level in the United States, farmers customarily contracted an agronomist of the local extension service—or even one of their own—to work on a list of problems they presented. The formal relations between the extension agents and their client-farmers, then, were not that different from the informal relations between Santana's agent and his client-farmers. Only later did the independent local arrangements of U.S. farmers with extension agents at the county level evolve into statewide agriculture extension services and, even later, a nationwide extension system. Even then, state governments could not impose on counties and individual extension offices the kind of crop campaigns mounted against the boll weevil in Ceará and the other Northeast states—again, with the exception of the U.S. Southern states.[34] States frequently offered these campaigns to the counties, free of charge, but they first consulted with extension officers and farmers before adopting them. Northeast Brazil's extension services, created in the 1950s and 1960s by state governments, had not been through this formative demand-driven period. If the extension services of Northeast Brazil and of many other developing countries were inspired by any model, moreover, it was the less decentralized model of a much later period of the United States (and other now-industrialized countries), rather than the more relevant and client-driven earlier incarnation.

According to these "oldest" practices and "newest" wisdoms, then, the lessons of the Santana story and others like it should by now appear rather mundane. Then why aren't extension services adopting them? Even though extension services may tacitly condone the unofficial Santana-like performance contracts described in this chapter, many resist adopting more client-driven approaches to service provision.[35] Part of the resistance, of course, has to do with sheer bureaucratic inertia in the face of seemingly major change. Another part, however, represents concrete problems that need suggested solutions. Service delivery that becomes more client-driven, no matter how desirable on other grounds, makes things more difficult for managers because it reduces their control and certainty over budgeting, planning, and deployment of personnel.

What if groups dislike the results of working with a particular agent, and do not want to renew the contract? What does a supervisor do with that particular agent? What if, as is likely, some extension agents are requested more than others? How does a manager plan the deployment of personnel in these circumstances? How does an agency determine its areas of expertise when some farmer groups want to work on some crops and some kinds of problems and other groups want to work on others—and when the agency will not know these preferences, which may change from year to year, beforehand? In many ways, moreover, agricultural planners and technicians are bound to see client-driven approaches as a challenge to the very concept of their expertise. That such expertise exists, after all, underlies the justification for agricultural extension as conveying a set of "superior" agronomic techniques to farmers who, as a group, do not use them.

Although these dilemmas are not irresolvable, they do show that client-driven models of service delivery raise serious practical questions that must be faced. Even if the lessons of the Santana story seem obvious and mundane, then, they will not be so easily adopted by extension and research institutions. That is why it is important to stand back and see the similarities the Santana case shares with the other cases in this book, and to recognize the marked effect these kinds of relations between extension agent and client have in bringing about both improvements in worker commitment to the job and increases in agricultural productivity.

The following story of public procurement and business extension adds more to our understanding of the circumstances under which a more customized approach works. It also reveals another variation on the practical problems to be faced in implementing such an approach. In illustrating another manifestation of the contrast between standardized and customized jobs, the procurement case extends our understanding of this contrast beyond the particulars of agricultural extension.

· 5 ·

Small Firms and Large Buyers:
Demand-Driven Public Procurement

T HE DEMAND-DRIVEN approaches to agricultural extension described
in the previous chapter were informal and sporadic. Ceará's program
to redirect one-third of its public procurement expenditures to small firms,
in contrast, was a deliberate and major attempt to institutionalize what
amounted to a demand-driven approach to small-firm assistance. The program organized its assistance to small firms around a contract for purchase of their goods, and led to sustained growth among the assisted firms,
sometimes with strong linkage effects throughout the area where they were
located. In contrast to some other attempts by governments to assist small
firms by buying from them, the program also lowered the costs and increased the quality of goods and services purchased by the state government. It also reduced the inherent riskiness to government of procuring
from small firms, partly through contractual arrangements that forced the
support agency to both help and monitor the supplier firms and that required the firms to monitor each other.

In analyzing the demand-driven form of organizing service delivery,
the previous chapter emphasized the significance of the different relationship between the small-farmer client and the extension service. In
this chapter's case of public procurement, performance of the business
extension service and commitment of its workers were also high, and for

similar reasons. Instead of tracing out the same dynamic again for business extension, however, I have instead developed this case in a somewhat different light. The case is striking, that is, in that most programs of assistance to small firms and microenterprises (SFs)—so in vogue today in both developing and developed countries—are supply-driven and not demand-driven. They specialize in providing one or more ongoing services, like credit, courses in business management, or technical assistance. They try to serve as many firms and as many sectors as possible. The striking stories of SF growth, however, have tended to be driven by demand. They started in a certain sector and radiated out from it. Typically, large customers of small-firm suppliers—corporations, traders, state enterprises, or government agencies like those in this case—provided the small firms with a market, technical help, and often finance. These customers all fashioned their assistance around their particular needs, and around problems that arose as their suppliers worked to fill an order. In analyzing the success of Ceará's similarly demand-driven procurement initiative, this chapter raises questions as to why SF assistance programs have paid so little attention to demand-driven approaches and why the prevailing supply-driven approaches have continued to be the instrument of choice despite the paltry evidence of their effectiveness and impact.

In its first year or so, Ceará's procurement initiative enjoyed a limelight that most small-firm programs never experience. Launched by the new reformist governor just taking over in 1987, it was started as a minor part of the emergency program to reduce the unemployment resulting from the drought of that year, which left 600,000 rural workers unemployed for almost a year. Because the disaster relief funds made available by the federal government were substantially less than for earlier droughts, the traditional public works construction program discussed in chapter 3 could not employ as large a share as in previous droughts of the unemployed. Faced with these constraints, the state government decided to experiment with a novel approach that would require no additional expenditures. First, it directed that materials and tools for building the works projects—bricks, tiles, gravel, hoes and backhoes, buckets, shovels, wheelbarrows—be purchased from small producers in the drought-stricken interior. This gave rise to the expansion or opening of dozens of small brick-making operations, wood workshops, stone quarries, and lime-burners. Second, the state redirected some of its customary purchases—school furniture, repair and reconstruction services for public buildings, small metal grain silos—from large firms outside the state or their distributors to small firms located in the drought-stricken area.

These initial efforts were successful enough that they became permanent after the drought ended. In the subsequent three-year period (1989–91), the state spent US$15 million on such contracts, accounting for 30 percent of its total purchases of goods and services. The most important items were school furniture like desks (400,000 pieces) and tables, chairs, and bookcases (20,000), accounting for 55 percent of total expenditures; 550 service contracts with 200 informal firms for the repair, maintenance, and reconstruction of public buildings, particularly schools (23% of total expenditures); service contracts with 100 firms for the repair of 5,000 pieces of equipment, particularly televisions and videos in schools; and other miscellaneous items like electricity poles (500) and small metal silos (20,000) for on-farm storage of grains during subsequent good harvests.

Two agencies, which had already worked closely together in SF-support programs, were responsible for the procurement program—the state Department of Industry and Commerce (SIC) and the Brazilian Small Enterprise Assistance Service (SEBRAE), a semipublic technical-assistance agency found in most Brazilian states.[1] Financed originally by federal and regional institutions whose contributions subsequently declined, SEBRAE had been receiving an increasing share of its income from the state government through SIC—income that covered 70 percent of SEBRAE's expenditures in 1992. SEBRAE earned the remaining 30 percent of its income from charges to final users and commissions on government contracts. The agency's headquarters in Fortaleza operated with approximately 35 professionals (engineers, economists, business administration specialists, accountants), and it had five branches throughout the state with one or two professionals in each.

The most significant impact of the new public procurement policy fell on the previously sleepy district of São João do Aruaru (SJA). With 9,000 inhabitants, and located 130 kilometers from the capital city in a zone of excellent hardwoods, SJA was the home of four small sawmills with three employees each—certainly not the makings of the highly publicized success story that it soon became. Indeed, because the district's carpentry skills were not even known outside that locality, they came to the attention of the technicians of SIC and SEBRAE only through their conversations with a local priest about drought relief. After visiting the sawmill operators, the head of the state's drought relief program placed an order with them for 300 wooden wheelbarrows. (In the past, the state government had procured iron wheelbarrows from outside the state.) Although the woodmakers of SJA had never fabricated wheelbarrows, they had regularly produced other rustic items like truck sidings, roof frames, and wooden pans and trays for cassava and sugarcane mills. With SEBRAE assistance, the four sawmills successfully completed the order. Their wooden wheelbarrows turned out to be more desirable than the iron ones purchased by the state from large suppliers, because the latter product had a tendency to rust and dent. The wood product, in addition, cost 30 percent less.

Two years after its first order, SJA had completed four more orders for a total of 2,000 wheelbarrows, as well as handles for hoes and backhoes and wooden barrels for distribution of water. Even more significant, the woodmakers had completed a large order from the state Department of Education for 3,000 school desks and 100 tables—the first time they had produced these particular items. In so doing, SJA replaced two large furniture manufacturers in Southern Brazil, which had supplied 80 percent of the school desks bought by state government for more than 10 years. As with the wheelbarrows, the school desks cost 30 percent less than previous purchases, partly because of the large reduction in transport costs on items procured from within the state. By 1992, SJA was supplying 40 percent of the state's needs for school furniture, amounting to 90,000 pieces annually.

The impact of the procurement program on SJA was striking. Five years after the first order for 300 wheelbarrows, the number of sawmills in the town had increased from four to 42, each mill now averaging nine permanent workers. An additional four to seven temporary workers per mill felled trees, cut them into lumber, and transported the lumber to the mills. All in all, this added up to a total of 1,000 persons employed directly or indirectly by the mills—more than 10 percent of the total population of the district. More than half of the mills increased their productivity by acquiring power equipment that they did not have before—electric planers, power lathes, routers, and presses.

Although the procurement-induced development of SJA would certainly not have occurred without the state's contracts and accompanying technical assistance, the town and its sawmills did not become dependent on the continuation of these contracts. They used their public contracts and their new skills and contacts gained through the state's technical assistance to break into new private markets (furniture for summer homes and for hotels), where they became permanently ensconced. Indeed, five years after the program's start, these private markets had come to account for 70 percent of their sales. In addition, the woodmakers were starting to receive orders from other state governments, the first being for 20,000 school desks from the neighboring state of Paraíba. Many of the new private and public customers learned about the quality of the town's furniture through the state's repeated advertising about the program's success. (Because the publicity around the program had several other positive effects, it is treated separately in the fourth section.)

In terms of sustained developmental effects, the SJA success represented the program's most conspicuous achievement. This was partly because only in this case did the program concentrate so much of its procurement and assistance in one small district—40 percent of the total purchases of school furniture under the program. Not seeming to be able to apply this lesson about concentrating program efforts in certain places, however, the state government dispersed the rest of its purchases for school furniture among 43 additional municípios; and it distributed its contracts for other products across 90 of the state's 178 municípios. The fourth section of this chapter explains the reasons for this strange failure to apply elsewhere the lesson of the SJA success about procurement as an instrument of developmental policy.

For anyone familiar with the innovative, demand-driven style of the procurement program, it would have been surprising to discover that SIC and SEBRAE continued to operate a set of older, uninspired supply-driven programs. This presented an unusual opportunity to compare supply-driven and demand-driven approaches within the same agency. Like many such programs elsewhere in Brazil and other countries, these two agencies had traditionally provided fairly standardized assistance and messages to firms across many sectors. They normally organized their work along functional lines, with three or four professionals assigned to separate divisions—credit, training, and marketing assistance. Consistent with this supply-driven approach, the technicians of SIC and SEBRAE tended to characterize the problems afflicting their clients—lack of access to credit, limited technical and managerial capacity, and difficulties in marketing—as endemic to small firms. Although SF programs in many countries typically define their clients' problems this way, a growing literature shows how the needs of firms differ markedly from one sector or subsector to another.[2] Likewise, the two agencies' evaluations of their programs and of staff rarely looked into the workings of particular sectors and instead charted generic indicators like the number of SF associations formed in a particular year, the number of firms participating in a program, and the number of courses given and of participants in them.

SEBRAE offered managerial training programs to firm owners from different sectors—the standard fare of so many such programs, providing instruction on how to write checks, use a bank, keep books, and so on. The state government, in addition, made special subsidized lines of credit available to SFs, to which SEBRAE helped firms gain access.[3] SEBRAE did provide some sector-specific services, including 200 different courses on assorted subjects ranging from repairing computers to bakery techniques. But the curriculum remained the same for every round of participants, rarely allowing instructors to meet requests from individual groups or to adapt to their particular circumstances. Taking place in a classroom rather than at the firm site, the courses demonstrated equipment in settings that were quite different from the conditions under which most firms operated, where the equipment was less sophisticated, the space more crowded, and the supply of public power frequently interrupted or nonexistent.

Appreciating the problems of their SF clients in finding customers, SIC built trading centers and "microenterprise palaces" in selected cities to provide small firms with a place to sell their wares locally. As frequently occurs with such initiatives, however, the results were disappointing. Although the agency blamed the low occupancy in one such center on the firms' "inability to run the shops," firm owners reported that they were not really that interested in a local trading center because opportunities for sales expansion were actually much greater outside the home market.[4] More successfully, and less ambitiously, SIC and SEBRAE encouraged and backed the participation of small firms in local and national fairs—the only other clearly demand-related initiative in these two agencies' programs.[5] The two agencies also encouraged small firms to form associations, partly to lobby for legislation and regulation favorable to small enterprises and partly to reap economies of scale in group purchasing and selling. All this, with the exception of the sponsoring of trade fairs, added up to a supply-driven program that had little impact on local economies or employment—in striking contrast to the two agencies' innovative demand-driven achievements.

At the outset, a few clarifications. Several of the important lessons of this case arose from the way relations were structured between four sets of actors, which therefore should be identified from the start: (1) the purchasing departments—the government agencies that purchased the goods and services; (2) the support agencies—the two agencies that provided technical, organizing, and other assistance to the small firms, and brokered the contract between them and the purchasing agencies; (3) the associations of firms or individual tradesmen with which all contracts were made; and (4) the individual firms themselves. In the case of school reconstruction, a fifth actor was also important, though not formally a part of the contract—the neighborhood or parent-teacher associations. In contrast to the Ceará program, many SF procurement programs do not separate the support and purchasing functions into different agencies, and many SF-support programs work with individual firms rather than associations.

Finally, although this case involves public procurement from small firms, it should also be seen as a variation on the more general theme of demand-driven approaches to organizing assistance to producers—whether in the context of public procurement or whether in the public or nongovernment sectors. I turn to that more general theme now, which will serve as a backdrop for the dynamics of the Ceará case and its lessons. As the following section will show, public procurement is not the only opportunity for structuring SF support in a demand-driven way, though it is clearly a significant one.

SF-Favoring Procurement: The Nonexistent Debate

Despite the fact that most SF assistance programs today are supply-driven, as noted above, many of the striking stories of SF growth have involved demand-driven assistance from these firms' customers. Two bodies of evidence bear on the theme of demand-assisted SF growth. First, in attempting to explain high performance in certain national, regional, or sectoral economies, students of industrial organization and development have pointed to the key role played by supportive and trusting relations between firms. Some of these researchers have focused on the relationships between SF suppliers and larger-firm customers; the most celebrated of such cases is the Japanese automobile industry.[6] Others have focused on small-firm clusters or "industrial districts," and their networks of interfirm cooperation and competition; the classic case is the north-central region of Italy, the so-called Third Italy.[7]

The second body of evidence on demand-driven assistance and SF growth is more fragmentary and less consciously argued. It comprises a number of case studies that reveal SF development to have been strongly influenced by government agencies or state enterprises through assistance tied to their procurement. In many of these cases, the government customer was both demanding and supportive with respect to quality. This contributed to sustained increases in the performance of the supplier firms. For developing countries, some of the products and sectors represented are school furniture, vehicle parts, milk, and specialized footwear and uniforms for public workers (such as police, hospital personnel, and electric-system repairmen).[8] For developed countries, one of the most famous cases of procurement-driven SF growth is Silicon Valley in the United States— the network of originally small semiconductor firms in the San Francisco Bay region of California, and their supplier-customer relation with the U.S. Defense Department.[9] There are other U.S. cases in which "sophisticated demand" from government played an important role in driving growth and international competitiveness—computers, chemicals, pharmaceuticals, and medical instruments—but they do not involve small firms exclusively or at all.[10]

The cumulative impression from reading these case studies is that the right kind of procurement-linked assistance could have significant impacts on SF productivity and employment. This is not a new idea. More than 20 years ago, the International Labor Organization argued forcefully about the employment-creating potential of directing public procurement toward small firms in the informal sector.[11] The impact of these arguments on most governments, however, was minimal.

More recently, and for somewhat different reasons, international donors have supported social investment funds (SIFs) in various countries with the purpose of counteracting the increased unemployment accompanying structural adjustment programs. Among other things, the SIFs have focused attention on the need to modify procurement regulations so as to make it easier for small firms to bid for public contracts to be executed by municipal governments, private firms, and nongovernment organizations.[12]

The SIFs are being watched more for the light they throw on matters of temporary unemployment reduction, decentralization, and community participation than on matters relating to sustained local growth. My perspective, in discussing the issue of small firms, is different from that of these initiatives. It draws attention to the large share of manufacturing and services output in most countries that is accounted for by government purchases at all levels—almost one-third of nonagricultural gross domestic product, for example, in India.[13] And it stresses the potential for local economic development that lies in the interaction between government customers and SF suppliers. As this case will show, together with those cited above, achieving this potential involves more than modifying procurement regulations so that small firms can bid.

The Case Against

If there were a debate on the subject of SF-favoring public procurement, opponents would be likely to express the following three reservations. First, public agencies do not like to buy from the kinds of small firms that normally do not qualify to bid for public contracts. As any conversation with a procurement officer will reveal, buying from small firms untutored in the ways of public tendering is viewed as a major headache, involving many contracts for small amounts, more paperwork, and the expectation that product costs will be higher, quality lower, and delivery unreliable.

Second, the unreliability of the public sector as a customer exacerbates the problems of small firms. Governments frequently pay erratically and late, and purchase only in large quantities that are difficult for many SFs to produce, at least within the stipulated time periods. Governments also cannot be relied on to come back soon for more orders. Because small suppliers typically overexpand to fill these contracts, they then languish or simply disappear in the long periods between contracts. They "gorge" themselves, in effect, on the government's large contracts and temporarily secure market, which render them unable to face the vicissitudes of the "real" market of private customers when their government purchaser disappears.[14]

Third, SF-favoring procurement programs are often too "soft" and overprotective with small firms. Among the programs criticized for this failing are those as different as India's policy of reserving certain markets for small firms and the U.S. government's favorable treatment of SF bidders, including minority-owned firms, with respect to certain products or services.[15] In these cases, the suppliers know they are entitled to a protected niche regardless of performance, and the public-sector customers know they must buy from these firms for "social" reasons. This does not bode well for either cost or quality. Advocates and providers of SF assistance themselves contribute unwittingly to these negative judgments about SF-favoring procurement and other assistance programs. They normally argue their case on the grounds of reducing poverty and portray the small firms they want to help as "the walking wounded."[16] Support to them, correspondingly, is presented as "only" a social strategy, unrelated to economic growth or the more efficient acquisition of goods and services by government.

These problems are, indeed, quite serious in many SF-favoring programs. But the Ceará case, along with some of the others noted above, shows that they are clearly not inevitable. Briefly, the procurement process did not take place in a protected environment devoid of concerns about cost and quality, and the SF suppliers produced a lower-cost and better-quality product than the established suppliers. The government contracts launched these small firms permanently into new private markets, with good-quality and competitively priced products. Their success, in some cases initiating a self-sustained process of local growth, did not require that subsequent public contracts or other assistance continue indefinitely. Much of this happened because the purchasing agency was not required to buy from the small firms. Two other agencies that assisted SFs helped the firms meet their contract specifications and deadlines vis-à-vis the purchasing agency. Most important, these two support agencies had to prove to the purchasing agency that the SF product or service was at least as good and competitive as that procured previously from larger firms.

Why did the Ceará case and the others noted above produce better results than the programs for which SF-favoring procurement has gained its bad reputation? I outline an answer to this question now, and suggest how the better results might be made to happen.

The Case For

The case to be made for a demand-driven approach (DDA) to SF assistance has four parts, which are set forth in the order in which production occurs.

First, DDA directly tackles one of the major problems facing most struggling small firms—that of finding a reliable customer and thereby having sufficient assurance about the future so as to be able to focus on improving productivity. The supply-driven approach (SDA), of course, does not simply ignore the problem of marketing, but the method of dealing with this problem is open-ended: a final sale or subsequent contracts are not guaranteed at the end of the assistance, and the service provider is not judged to be at fault if the firms it assists cannot produce something that sells.

Second, DDA structures the work of the support agency quite differently from SDA. Instead of providing standardized assistance on a variety of subjects to the largest number of firms possible, DDA must devote its assistance at any moment in time to one set of firms producing the same product. It focuses on problems that come up in the course of trying to meet a contract's specifications and deadlines, from the acquisition and storage of raw materials, through matters of production, to delivery of the final product. All this often requires that a support agency concentrate its efforts on one or a few geographical areas where SFs producing a particular type of product are clustered—as occurred in the Ceará case.

Another way of characterizing DDA is to say that the approach is more problem-driven, iterative, and results-oriented than is SDA.[17] It is also more "client-driven" in the sense that the "client" to which the support agency provides services is the small firm. My brief for this style of operating, in other words, is nothing new. It has been advocated for almost 10 years in the literature on best-practice corporations that have successfully faced the challenges of global competition and industrial restructuring.[18] More recently, the "reinventers" of government have urged governments to move in this same direction.[19] The supply-driven approach dominates, nevertheless, in most SF programs.

A third strength of DDA will be forthcoming only if it is structured properly. As the above critiques show, this is often not the case. DDA works best when it subjects both the firms and the support agency to a tough test of performance: if the final product of the assisted firms does not meet competitive standards of cost, quality, and timely delivery, the customer (the government purchasing agency) will simply not accept the goods or will not renew the order. This impels the support agency to strive together with the supplier firms to improve quality and reliability. The Ceará program, along with the other cases noted above, had to face this kind of test. Supply-driven programs do not.

Fourth, SF-favoring procurement has some clear advantages over other approaches even as an employment-creating strategy. The quality and durability of the jobs left in the wake of successful SF-favoring employment-creating programs like Ceará's are far superior to other such programs, including the above-mentioned social investment funds. These latter programs rely heavily on construction for their job-creating impact—entailing unskilled, temporary, and low-wage work.[20] This contrasts with the clear upskilling of labor and other sustained impacts that were central to the Ceará case.

It should be clear by now that DDA's advantages over SDA play themselves out in two distinct realms. One is the world of the small firms them-selves; the other is that of the support agencies. SF practitioners and re-searchers, however, have tended to pay more attention to the constraints facing small firms than to those affecting the performance of the support agencies. The argument for DDA, in contrast, identifies the structure of incentives faced by SF support agencies as constituting an equally serious determinant of performance. My argument, then, rests strongly on the pressures that DDA brings to bear on the support agencies themselves.

Real-World Procurement

When small firms are "entitled" to special consideration, as noted above, both the customer and the supplier tend to suspend judgment about cost and quality. A surprisingly similar set of lapses can occur, however, when government makes contracts with its traditional suppliers of goods and services. The resulting inefficiencies are at least as serious as those caused by giving small firms an edge in procurement, although their origin is quite different. I set them forth briefly here. They show that the assumed healthy workings of the market mechanism—the background of existing procure-ment against which SF-favoring procurement is considered inferior—may be more of an ideal than a reality.

As is well known, the costs of complying with government procure-ment regulations often keep small firms from bidding. Or, SFs simply do not have the connections in government that make for successful bidding. In addition, government usually pays contractors only upon delivery and inspection, and without advances. This also keeps many efficient small firms from bidding for public contracts because they do not have suffi-cient reserves or outside finance for working capital. Finally, governments in developing countries frequently pay their suppliers after considerable delay, which eliminates yet another tier of potential small-firm bidders. Some of the firms excluded by these various circumstances may well pro-duce a cheaper or better product. This means that the competition faced by the firms that are capable of bidding successfully for public contracts is more restricted than it is assumed to be. The price and quality of goods and services procured by government, therefore, fall considerably short of the competitive ideal.[21]

Other less obvious characteristics of the playing field on which firms compete for government contracts emerged from examining the traditional context of public procurement in Ceará. Established suppliers, for example, often sell their lower-quality output to government because they perceive government to be a less demanding customer than the private firms to which they also sell. An interesting example comes from the case of the contracts for school reconstruction discussed below. The supplier, in this instance, treats government as a kind of "captive" customer or "customer of last resort." This is facilitated by the fact that side payments made to government officials by bidding firms contribute to government's becoming a less demanding customer. Government's delays in paying its suppliers, moreover, cause the suppliers to search for additional contracts from private customers to compensate. The additional contracts make it difficult for these suppliers to execute their public contract efficiently—again illustrated below in the case of school reconstruction. All these factors add up, inadvertently, to a set of disincentives to efficiency and a process of "adverse selection" among the firms that typically bid for and win government contracts.

One of the main arguments against SF procurement is that centralized purchases in substantial volumes from single large suppliers bring economies of scale in purchasing. That is why governments and international donors prefer "packaging" many small contracts into a single large contract.[22] Centralized purchasing and bundling of contracts, however, also can involve distinct diseconomies in that they often impose greater transport and storage costs. This is particularly true in public services like education and rural health, which buy goods and materials for numerous dispersed locations. When the state of São Paulo's Department of Education decentralized to municipalities its purchases of furniture, school lunches, and curriculum materials, costs decreased by almost 30 percent as a result of savings on transport and storage.[23]

The problem of quality and cost in public procurement, then, is far from being peculiar to buying from small firms. But the nature of the problem involving larger established suppliers is quite different. Established suppliers may not start with the quality problem and the high transaction costs that small firms present to government. But various factors conspire to cause the government suppliers to sell their lower-quality or higher-cost goods and services to government. The end result is the same disincentive to quality that occurs, for different reasons, in the SF-favoring procurement that "entitles" small firms to a fixed share of the government market. Smaller firms, in turn, may not produce exactly what government needs and require more guidance, but they may also value government more as a customer because they lack the market alternatives that large firms have.

Aided by demand-driven support such as that provided in Ceará, the quality of their product can be improved. This is what happened in the stories of the wheelbarrows, silos, and school desks to be told in the following sections.

These observations contain two implications for policy. First, the playing field on which firms bid for government contracts is less level than is implicitly assumed in the arguments against SF-favoring procurement. This is not to say that one imbalance should be corrected by another. Rather, there is a serious efficiency—not equity—argument for subsidizing the transaction costs of contracting with small firms through programs such as that described below. The case for special treatment, however, should not involve mere SF entitlement to government contracts. As will be seen, the demands for performance inherent in properly structured SF-favoring procurement are quite substantial. Second, contracting out for goods and services previously produced "in-house" by government is now a popular item on the agenda of public-sector reform. But given the above-noted disincentives to quality and efficiency in the existing environment of public procurement in developing countries, contracting out public services to private providers will not necessarily produce better results.

Customers, Suppliers, and Their Brokers: The Case of School Furniture

The demand-driven style of Ceará's procurement program worked through two sets of contracts. This section traces these dynamics through the case of public procurement of school furniture from the woodworkers of São João do Aruaru (SJA), and the following section does the same with respect to contracts for the maintenance, repair, and reconstruction of public schools.

The Contracting Process and Its Effects

The contracting procedure of Ceará's procurement program differed in one crucial way from many similar programs: if the agencies purchasing the products did not like their price or quality, they simply would not buy. This meant that SIC and SEBRAE had to convince the state Departments of Education and Agriculture and other such purchasers that the SF products were worth buying. The procedures surrounding this arrangement, though seemingly cumbersome, were key to the program's successful dynamic.

The purchasing agencies first contracted with SIC for the goods or services. SIC then made a second contract with SEBRAE to provide technical assistance to the small firms, paying SEBRAE a 5 percent commission on the value of the contract. SEBRAE, in turn, made yet a third contract to purchase the goods or services from an association of small firms, artisans, or building tradesmen located near each other. Key to the good results of these arrangements, SEBRAE would not contract individually with small firms. It instead sought out existing small-firm associations or encouraged and helped groups of potential suppliers located in one place to organize an association. Just as significant, SEBRAE worked out a system of product warranties with the producers—one year for school desks and other furniture, for example, and three years for the grain silos and electricity poles. In the case of school furniture, each item had a metal plate with the producer's name and the number of the contract. If an item proved defective, it was returned to the producer for repair or replacement; if that producer had closed down in the interim, the association of producers to which that firm had belonged was contractually responsible. All these arrangements reinforced the pressures on both the firms and the agencies to deliver a good product.

The Ceará program involved none of the traditional subsidies on inputs or subsidized bank credit for which SF programs have been criticized.[24] Even the technical assistance—one of the few currently accepted ways of subsidizing SF growth—was only partially subsidized, at most, given that SEBRAE charged for it through the 5 percent commission on the contracts.[25] The 50 percent advance on the contract, of course, might be viewed as an implicit subsidy of interest-free credit for working capital, especially given Brazil's high rates of inflation in the 1980s and early 1990s. Paying even partially in advance for goods and services, moreover, would seem to be risky business for government, as well as imposing high monitoring costs. But the advance payment differed importantly from the typical case of subsidized small-firm credit.

First, the advance payment mimicked the way many large private customers finance those of their small-firm suppliers who cannot obtain bank finance for working-capital costs. Namely, the customer pays a significant portion of the final payment upfront—in the form of credit, cash, or raw materials—and the remaining payment is tied to the delivery of the product. The advance therefore reduced the major financial obstacle to small-firm competition for public-sector business—an outcome also found in several other countries.[26] The importance of SFs being able to compete for public contracts, then, lies not only in the benefit to them, but also in terms of making available to government a better selection of goods and services from which to choose.

Second, if a particular producer did not deliver to the association on time, or produced a faulty product, the other firms in the association were jointly responsible. They had to make up for any shortfall in the association's total order before being paid for their own deliveries. In these cases, obviously, the better-performing firms had good reason to pressure the laggards to comply. Because of the visibility of the association in the community, the dissatisfaction of the better-performing firms damaged the reputation of the laggard firms. This disciplining mechanism was key to the quality and productivity improvements of the procurement program, and to the reduction of transaction costs to government of buying from small firms.

The intrafirm disciplining dynamic of these arrangements seems similar to the peer pressure used to ensure repayment in the microcredit programs that have now become so popular. Representing a significant advance in small lending over the past decade, these programs bring individuals together in small borrower groups with joint responsibility for repayment. The effect of grouping in the Ceará case, however, was greater than in most programs of microcredit. Each firm belonging to the groups of the Ceará program, that is, produced the same product, and was already an established producer. Microcredit groups, in contrast, bring together individuals who are often not experienced producers or who are not all engaged in the same activity. The discipline of the Ceará case, in other words, involved more than peer pressure around repayment: in the course of pressuring the laggards, the better-performing firms also persuaded the weaker ones to improve the quality of their product, and helped them do so. This was a key contributing factor to the ongoing increases in product quality among the program's suppliers.

The arrangements described above, in sum, brought four important factors into play. First, they created a healthy distance between two sets of government actors—SIC/SEBRAE and the purchasing departments. Second, they made SEBRAE's income dependent on the performance of the producers to which it provided technical assistance, through the commission SEBRAE earned on the contract. Third, SEBRAE's insistence on working only with associations of SFs, not individual firms, helped overcome one of the major problems of procuring from small firms—the need to make many small contracts. Fourth, this combination of arrangements introduced both discipline and technical support regarding quality and other aspects of performance among the firms themselves. This combination of pressures and incentives is rarely found in programs of SF-favoring procurement, SF bank credit, or SF extension. The following two sections illustrate how it all worked.

Industrial Cluster and Growth Pole

Under the guidance of the procurement program, SJA turned into the classic case of a small-firm cluster or industrial district.[27] The Aruaru Association of Furniture-Makers (Associação dos Moveleiros de Aruaru), which was formed at the state's urging to produce the first orders, had started with only four firms and had grown, five years later, to 42. In addition to serving its members, the association had become a major civic institution in the town. Among other activities, it formed a permanent committee for group purchase of timber and other materials (with correspondingly increased bargaining power vis-à-vis suppliers); organized the sharing of equipment among members; shared information about opportunities to purchase secondhand equipment; and sought ways of preventing sawmill accidents, also pressuring the state to provide an expert on occupational safety. The association also constructed its own building, dubbed by the townspeople as their "church" because producers met there almost every night. The building also served as a store for raw materials, and job seekers frequented the place for leads on possible work.

When SEBRAE first started working with the SJA producers, the agency's frequent rejections of defective products or parts translated into a self-imposed pressure to improve the quality of the labor force. As a result, the sawmill association took upon itself the cause of upgrading skills in the town. To this end, the association successfully lobbied the mayor of the município to arrange night-school sessions for high-school-age sawmill workers who worked during the day in the sawmills. Teachers arrived every evening by bus from a town 45 minutes away. Such a thing was almost unheard of in the interior towns of the Northeast. Led by the association, moreover, SJA struggled to become independent of the município of Morada Nova and become its own município, as faster-growing districts throughout the state had tended to do.

In addition to the dynamic interfirm cooperation of this new small-firm cluster, backward and forward linkages to firms in other sectors emerged in almost textbook fashion and with remarkable spontaneity. The sawmills of SJA moved "backward" into repair, then assembly of sawmill equipment like bandsaws, and then equipment for sugarcane and cassava mills operating in the region, as well as for local manufacturers of cheese. Five storeowners bought trucks to transport the timber from the forest to the sawmills. A new supplier of Amazonian hardwood set up business in the town. A private bus company opened a new line between the town and the state's largest city and capital 130 kilometers away—a bus ride of almost three hours. The Bank of Brazil opened a new branch—quite unusual for a district of only 9,000 inhabitants, particularly given that the bank was streamlining its operations and closing existing branches in several larger districts. The flurry of new manufacturing activity and employment in SJA, in turn, led to a spurt of housing construction. A new brickmaking operation opened up and hired 20 workers. Townspeople who had lived in mud huts before, and then built adobe houses, proudly showed visitors the old mud structures, which they had left standing so all could see how their lives had improved since the 1987 drought.

The unforeseen development of linkages in SJA was striking, especially in contrast to the many programs that have tried unsuccessfully to create such linkages through a series of "integrated" and significantly more costly public investments in industrial development. The managers of SIC and SEBRAE, after all, were not even thinking about possible linkage effects when they chose to purchase wheelbarrows and school furniture from SJA. This was not for lack of interest in linkage dynamics or of appreciation for the virtues of interfirm cooperation. Indeed, these agencies were at the same time implementing a full-blown scheme to create interfirm cooperation and linkage dynamics among small footwear producers in the state's third largest city, Sobral. They even used the language of linkage in their name for the project, "the footwear growth pole of Sobral."[28]

Sobral, with 100,000 inhabitants and numerous small leather footwear firms, certainly seemed to provide more scope for fashioning an industrial district than did tiny São João do Aruaru. At the time of this research, however, the prospects for the forging of this kind of SF growth pole in Sobral seemed dim even though the two agencies, ironically, had tried much harder there than they had in SJA. They imposed a grand developmental scheme that set out to change the basic structure of production in the footwear sector, generously providing finance, training, leather inputs, and fully equipped workshops. In that the Sobral and SJA programs were the products of the same agencies and persons, their contrast drives home the importance of the organization of service delivery in determining whether SF programs work well or poorly—as distinct from the expertise of a particular agency's staff, the quality of its leadership, or the particulars of the historical moment.

The state's role in unleashing the growth of SJA's small-firm cluster, with its attendant linkage effects, poses an important challenge to the literature of small-firm industrial districts. These studies report that small-firm clustering has always preceded public support and cannot be created by "some government agency."[29] Yet in the case of São João do Aruaru, the state created a small-firm cluster or district almost "from scratch," and out of the raw material of only four small sawmills of three employees each. If for this reason alone, the state's approach in this case merits scrutiny.

Forced by Procurement

Unlike many SF programs, the Ceará program did three important things. First, it linked small firms to a customer that was already accustomed to purchasing large quantities of school furniture, uniforms, and wheelbarrows, whether from small firms or not. Second, by bringing the support agency together with the firms through a contract for procurement, the program forced the agency, in effect, to provide "training" at the firm site rather than in the classroom, and as problems were discovered. Third, this process helped the support agency discover the critical bottlenecks and learn how to break them.

During a visit to one of the sawmills, for example, a SEBRAE engineer discovered that timber for school desks was being stored without appropriate protection from rain or humidity. This prevented proper drying and caused the wood to crack later. Prior to this, SEBRAE's standard technical advice had covered design of the furniture and wood selection, but not drying or storage. In the case of the small metal grain silos purchased by the Department of Agriculture for on-farm storage, some firms had had difficulty producing an adequate seal through their soldering process. Correcting this was imperative, given that an imperfect seal created the danger of pest infestation. SEBRAE's engineers suggested a different approach to the soldering process, and worked side by side with the producers until they achieved a perfect seal. In a final example from the school repair case, presented below, SEBRAE technicians discovered—upon observing the building tradesmen working—that they were not waterproofing ceilings or protecting the cement of the school courtyards from cracking in Ceará's intense equatorial sunlight. The technicians showed the contractors how to use a ceiling product made of oil for waterproofing and how to add a plastic-based material to the concrete to prevent cracking.

Firm owners working under the procurement program took the impending visits of the agency technicians quite seriously. The woodworking firms of SJA, for example, told how they would meet together before a visit by the SEBRAE technician in order to draw up a list of common problems they were facing in the course of fulfilling their order. The technicians, in turn, reported that they liked working this way much better. It made their task "easier," they said, because they could concentrate on the problems brought to them by their clients. On those occasions when they were unable to come up with immediate solutions, they could research the problems and bring suggestions on their next visit.

The technicians' advice and their understanding of the sector, in sum, emerged from working together with the producers at the firm site. This contrasts with the pre-set agendas and packages so common in other business extension services, with much of these two agencies' other programs, and with the agricultural extension services of the previous chapter.

Quality, Price, and the Reluctant Buyer

The school principals who received the new school desks made in SJA reported that they were actually better than the desks they had received previously. They complained that the latter, produced by two large manufacturers located in the more developed southern state of Paraná, had not lasted more than three years. Whereas the Paraná desks were made of laminated wood, which swelled and warped when exposed to dampness, the SJA desks were made of the solid hardwood available locally. This section attempts to explain how rustic firms that had not even produced school desks before, let alone in such large quantity, could have produced a product of higher quality and lower cost than a larger, more sophisticated manufacturer.

In most SF-assisting procurement programs, the buying agency uses the product or service itself or resells it, usually at a subsidized price, to final consumers. Either the buying agency is an advocate of SFs, or a higher authority has mandated that it buy from SFs. This case was different: the support and the purchasing functions were housed in different agencies (the support agencies neither used the products nor resold them), and the purchasing departments were not required to buy from SFs. This meant that the support agencies had to prove to another entity—the purchasing department—that buying from small firms was no more costly or burdensome than these departments' standard procedures.

Reinforcing these pressures on the support agencies, the state's purchasing units were distinctly unenthusiastic about switching some of their purchases from a few large manufacturers or distributors to numerous unknown small producers. The Department of Education predicted that school desks made by rustic small producers of the interior would "fall apart within a year," that the producers would never be able to deliver on time, that the heavier solid-wood desks would be more difficult to move around (they were), and that unit costs could not be as low as those of the large manufacturers in southern Brazil, from which the desks were normally purchased. The Department of Agriculture worried, in turn, that the seal on the 2,000 small grain silos provided to farmers for on-farm storage would be faulty. They also did not like the idea of buying wooden wheelbarrows rather than the sturdier iron ones they normally purchased. In the course of complaining about anticipated problems, the skeptical purchasers conveyed useful information about the kinds of products, materials, and parts that tended to break down or wear poorly. This information clearly helped the technicians of the support agencies and the new supplier firms learn how to produce a better product.

Even when the purchasing departments had had positive experiences with their new SF suppliers, they wanted to show their "neutrality" with respect to small firms. As a procurement officer from the state Department of Education said, "I only purchase from small firms if they charge lower prices and offer good quality, but at the moment they stop doing that, I quit." Likewise, the Department of Agriculture warned that it decided to purchase grain silos from small firms "not just" because SIC was promoting SF procurement, but because "it was a better deal—better prices, good quality, guaranteed delivery in a short time." The initial skepticism of the purchasing departments, finally, was reinforced by disgruntled local dealers, who had handled the previous purchases from outside the state, earning a 15 percent commission. Now they were being displaced by an intermediary, SEBRAE, that was earning "only 5 percent." In their eyes, this was a case of "unfair competition."

While the constructive pressures to perform caused by all this skepticism were impressive, SIC and SEBRAE had a much less charitable interpretation. In a litany of complaints that would be familiar to many program evaluators, the two agencies dwelled on how much time they had had to spend overcoming the resistances of the purchasing departments and outsmarting their subterfuges. They peppered their complaints with tales of alleged collusion between these agencies' procurement departments and the displaced suppliers and distributors, and of untoward pressures by them on the state's governor. Regardless of the truth of these complaints, it was clear that the "lack of cooperation" by the purchasing agencies pressured the support agencies to focus their assistance on improving the quality of the SF product.

The procurement program's conspicuous origins in the 1987 drought created similar pressures to perform. The state government had broadly advertised the procurement program to its citizenry as a bold new approach to reducing the unemployment resulting from the drought emergency. Although SF-assisting programs often couch their goals in the language of employment creation, they are rarely faced with the urgency posed by an intense drought and its specter of famine, sickness and death, and widespread looting of food stores and warehouses—let alone the possible loss of votes by a newly elected governor who had promised reform.

Under the pressure of the limelight and the reluctant purchasing departments, any failing in goods and services provided by the program's clients would have been more conspicuous than usual. If the wooden wheelbarrows were to break down, this would have clearly discredited the new experiment. If the solder on the grain silos were to prove defective, this would have endangered the supplies of the many small farmers who had stored their grain in the 2,000 silos distributed after the drought. Paying careful attention to problems like these enabled the two agencies to avoid embarrassing failures. The urgency and the high stakes, then, gave these otherwise minor agencies a chance to prove their mettle in the face of a major crisis.

SEBRAE technicians had to maintain their vigilance around quality even after a producer association had completed its order, because of the contractual requirements for payment and the system of warranties. When an order was completed, the technicians inspected it at the site of production, rejected those items that did not meet quality standards, and required that the firm replace any defective article promptly. When the program first started, the rejection rate was 15 percent. Some desks were built with a poor-quality wood, for example, and some had a desk arm of the wrong length. Because SEBRAE would not authorize payment to the association until the defects were corrected, this caused the good-quality producers to pressure the laggards, threatening to exclude them from subsequent contracts and sometimes actually doing so.

Making the groups responsible for any misbehaving members elicited self-monitoring mechanisms among the firms. These were crucial to the improvement of quality and to the state government's ability to pay its suppliers 50 percent in advance without, at the same time, creating a new set of monitoring troubles. The self-monitoring also reduced the monitoring burden of the support agencies. Because the firms valued the public contracts so highly, together with the technical assistance that accompanied them and the 50 percent payment advanced by the state, they had strong incentives to comply. In addition, the small producers took pride in their new role as suppliers to government. They would often honor the warranty beyond the legal period, or help with problems that were not their responsibility. In one case, for example, the Department of Education of the state's capital city had stored 2,000 school desks, chairs, and bookcases it had purchased from the program for more than a year without adequate protection from humidity and heat. Even though the producers were not responsible for the ensuing damage and the warranty period had expired, the association of woodworking firms sent some of its members to repair the furniture, asking only for reimbursement for their bus tickets to the city.

The final piece of reinforcement for these market-like tests was the 5 percent commission earned by SEBRAE on every procurement contract. Five years after the program started, these commissions added up to 15 percent of the agency's revenues, having become an important new source of income in an era of declining support from other sources. SEBRAE definitely had something to lose, then, if the producers they were coaching did not perform well under their contracts.

When Small Firms Deliver Better:
School Maintenance, Repair, and Reconstruction

The early part of this chapter laid out the reasons why government agencies look askance at purchasing from small firms, and why governments and experts have shown little interest in the matter. Some of their reasons have to do with the seemingly reasonable assumption that purchasing from larger, more established firms or distributors is less costly and less time-consuming, and that small firms cannot promptly deliver a product of equal quality and price. I challenged this view, explaining how established suppliers divide their work between their public and private customers in a way that can lead to lower quality and higher cost in the services purchased by government. The gap in quality and cost between the larger and smaller firms, then, is not always as great as is commonly assumed. This section provides an example from the experience of the Ceará program with the maintenance, repair, and reconstruction of schools and other public buildings.

The contracting of small firms to provide maintenance and repair services for public schools started with 109 schools under the municipal jurisdiction of the state's capital city, Fortaleza. The mayor who introduced the innovation in Fortaleza expanded it subsequently, when he became governor, to an additional 225 state schools in that city and in some of the other larger towns in the interior. In reminiscing about the initiative, the ex-mayor liked to describe the remarkable state of disrepair in which he had found the city's school buildings when he took over in 1989. Inspired by what he had heard about the early successes of the state's procurement program in other sectors, he ordered the city's Department of Education to let out small contracts for school maintenance, repair, and reconstruction to informal tradesmen and small firms. The department contracted 26 informal contractors—small associations of electricians, plumbers, bricklayers, and painters, as well as small contractor firms—to repair all its school buildings, for a sum total of US$190,000. This first project took only 45 days to complete—very important for a new mayor wanting to start his term of office impressively.

As a result of reforms taking place in the education sector at the same time, the state and city Departments of Education were also experimenting with the decentralization of school repair decisions to school principals. The principals distinctly preferred the new approach, which led to greater accountability, better-quality work from contractors, and significant savings. This section explains why. For purposes of brevity, I refer to this program as "school repair," which also includes the repair of school equipment such as videos and projectors.

From Equity to Efficiency

Prior to the new procurement program in education, decisions about school repair had been taken by the headquarters of the respective Departments of Education. For major repairs and reconstruction, another department dedicated exclusively to building construction would carry out these tasks itself or contract them out to private firms. When a school or its equipment needed repair, the school principal would requisition education headquarters or the other state or municipal department responsible for such works. The response often took many weeks or even months, and sometimes never came at all.

Compared to contracts for school construction and reconstruction, contracts for school and equipment repair are typically small, averaging US$5,000. The work involves discrete tasks such as building outside walls, laying sidewalks, fixing roofs, or installing water connections, electricity, and gates. Given the distances between schools, the work is dispersed. Medium and large building contractors lose valuable time and capital moving their costly fleets of heavy equipment from one small work site to the next. They therefore find the repair and reconstruction contracts less attractive than construction-only contracts, and the school construction contracts less attractive than larger single-site construction jobs. They nevertheless bid on these less desirable jobs when times are bad, or as "fill" in between large contracts—a common practice in other places.[30] Because contractors view this work as "second-best," they are frequently hurried and do shoddy work; poor supervision by fiscally strapped city and state administrations does not help. In addition, larger contractors frequently leave these jobs before they are completed—promising to return later— as soon as a larger, more desirable contract appears.

In the case of school repair in Ceará, issues of decentralization were intertwined with those related to procuring from small firms. The inefficiencies of existing procurement practices, as described above, had two related causes. One lay in the previously centralized approach to the procurement of school services, and the other in diseconomies involved in using larger contractors, including a procurement environment that allowed contractors to do shoddy work. The next subsection explains how these inefficiencies were reduced through a combination of SF procurement and decentralization to school principals of decision making about repair.

Decentralization, Community Associations, and Monitoring

In the beginning of the school repair program, and as in the case of SJA, SEBRAE encouraged individual building tradesmen to form associations, and then brokered the contracting process between these associations and state or municipal Departments of Education. Soon after, SEBRAE gradually resorted to another mechanism that was considerably less time-consuming than seeking out and evaluating the work of each individual tradesman or small contractor. It turned to another party—neighborhood and parent-teacher associations in the vicinity of each school. These groups already existed, having formed to pressure city government about the supply of water, sewerage, and other services, including the quality of their children's schooling and school buildings. Some of the tradesmen belonged to these associations themselves.

In a further lessening of the burden on SEBRAE, the school principals took over the task of consulting with the neighborhood association about the choice of a contractor and the supervision of the work. In some cases, the members of the neighborhood associations themselves took turns supervising the work. SEBRAE staff had previously explained to the neighborhood associations what they should watch for if they wanted to "monitor" the contractors' work. When work on a school commenced, members of the better-organized associations passed by the school site regularly to see how work was progressing, and whether the contractors were using acceptable materials and carrying out other required practices. It was not unusual that association members would report back to the principal on the quality of work, good as well as bad.

The involvement of the neighborhood associations in the selection of the contractor, and their subsequent monitoring presence while work was being done, clearly contributed to better results—an outcome reported in similar programs elsewhere.[31] The local contractors understood that they could not afford to get a reputation in the neighborhood for doing shoddy work, and they felt grateful for work they never before had. As a result, the better organized the neighborhood association in the area of a particular school, the better the repair and reconstruction work tended to be. Also, the stealing of materials stored at the site, a major problem at construction sites and with significant cost implications, was much less frequent because of informal monitoring by parent associations.

By providing each school principal with a budget for maintenance and repair and leaving the expenditure of those funds up to her or him, the Department of Education had freed itself of the burden of dealing with many small contracts for repair and maintenance. The principals, in turn, liked having control over maintenance and repair—in brief, over the physical quality of life in their schools. They also liked getting help from the neighborhood association in identifying local contractors and in supervision, since that reduced the new burdens placed on them by decentralization. In contrast to the previous situation, then, contracting for and monitoring of school repair were now in the hands of two new and more watchful "stakeholders"—the school principals and the neighborhood associations—with considerable self-interest in making sure good-quality work was done. Contracting centrally with one large firm did not bring such self-interested monitors to the numerous work sites. It is remarkable, actually, that governments do not take more advantage of these opportunities for cost-free monitoring in order to ensure better-quality work and less pilfering, particularly in contract work involving many widely dispersed work sites.

As in the case of the SJA woodworkers, finally, the public contracts helped launch these small producers into new, private markets. Some gained work as subcontractors to two large construction firms building dams under contract to the state; for jobs like this, which required the contracting of so much labor, these firms found it less costly and time-consuming to contract a group of workers and their "master craftsman," all of whom already had proven experience working together. Other small contractors subsequently bid successfully, for the first time, for contracts to repair or reconstruct other public buildings throughout the interior of the state. The contracting agencies had come to know of the small contractors' work through the praise of the school principals, as well as through the intense publicity surrounding the program, to which I turn now.

Publicity, Opposition, and the Unreplicated Success

From the description of the procurement program so far, one would have no inkling of the political maelstrom stirred up by the effort to buy from small firms, nor of the incessant publicity surrounding it. The state government played an important role in contributing to the maelstrom, and then contended with it quite cleverly.[32] I end the story here because it brings out three issues of significance for public procurement as an instrument of SF development, and for SF programs in general. First is the opposition to SF procurement from supplier firms and distributors that are displaced or fear they will be. Second is the high commitment to the job found among the technicians who work in more customized programs like this one. Third is the fact that the most successful case of local development resulting from this program emerged out of the concentration of assistance on a cluster of four firms producing the same product in one district. Though these three lessons do not seem related, they were all intertwined in the story of intense publicity.

Starting with the procurement program's beginnings in the 1987 drought, the state government went out of its way to publicize its achievements on television and radio and in newspapers and posters. At first, the national as well as local news media picked up the stories because the Northeast's chronic sufferings from drought, together with clientelism and graft, always made for good copy. In contrast to the usual tale of inadequate public preparedness and malfeasance in the distribution of relief supplies and jobs, these reports gave wide coverage to the "speed" with which the state government had mobilized small firms to produce the wheelbarrows in 1987 and, later, the grain silos.

The publicity did not stop with the ending of the drought, and was still going strong four years after the program's start. It portrayed the procurement initiative in quite noble terms: the state had "turned public procurement democratic," had economized during hard times, and had shifted its purchases from outside the state to within—creating a program that was an outstanding example of "austerity and morality." The state government organized a public seminar on the program, inviting other governors and high-level public managers from throughout the country. The occasion culminated in a visit to São João do Aruaru and its makers of school furniture. This was one of an endless number of occasions on which SIC or SEBRAE took visiting dignitaries by bus on the almost three-hour trip to SJA.

There were obvious political reasons for the state's exuberant proclamations about the procurement program. The two reformist governors who presided over its founding and growth had serious national political ambitions. They busily touted their achievements outside the state, including that of the procurement program. The publicity helped protect the program from demise by way of the fierce opposition it provoked from the manufacturers or dealers that it displaced. Although the state did not attack the protesting suppliers directly in publicizing the program—the out-of-state products having been sold by local distributors—it went out of its way to advertise that it was "coming to the rescue of local industry," reducing problems of unemployment, and mending its bad habits of purchasing from outside the state.

The state government also fended off large-supplier opposition to the program by appealing directly to the new and less powerful constituency of small firms and self-employed tradesmen who were, at the least, numerically larger. As reported above, SIC and SEBRAE encouraged these firms to organize into associations that could then bid for state contracts. But this was not the only intention: they also encouraged the associations to become a counter-lobby to the hitherto more powerful displaced firms, as well as to lobby in favor of tax exemptions for small firms. For every round of opposition from the previous suppliers, SIC and SEBRAE mobilized a wave of presidents of local small-firm associations to pressure the governor to preserve the program or to extend it to their towns. When the governor or SIC officials visited interior towns, they were regaled with pleas to give orders to firms. Mayors and other local leaders joined in the clamor, wanting to take credit for bringing the new "democratic procurement" to their town. With the backing of this newborn constituency, SIC and SEBRAE successfully lobbied the state's Industrial Council to formally include small-firm representation—for the first time in the state's history.

The public attention swirling around the procurement program had a second positive effect, similar to that among the workers of the preventive health program. Those staff members who worked in the program saw the constant "showing off" of the program, and their frequent escorting of visiting dignitaries to production sites, as amounting to an unusual recognition of their work—as if they had received prizes for outstanding achievement. One SEBRAE technician told of what it meant to him to accompany such important personages to visit "his" producers, and to hear them speak publicly about how they valued his assistance. It is not surprising, then, that SEBRAE technicians said they did not mind the increase in their workload resulting from the new program, because the results brought them "prestige"—not only locally, but throughout the country. The publicity had similar effects on the morale of the new small-firm suppliers themselves: all of São João do Aruaru, for example, felt immense pride at having provided the wheelbarrows for such a major emergency as the 1987 drought.

The publicity around the procurement program, in sum, had transparent political purposes as well as significant positive effects. It contributed to substantial popular support for the program, helped the state overcome serious opposition from the displaced suppliers, enabled other towns to learn about the program and enlist in it, and, by making those who worked in the program feel recognized, elicited high dedication from them. Not all the effects of the publicity, however, were felicitous. In the concentrated assistance provided to the woodworkers of SJA, that is, SIC and SEBRAE had clearly developed a quite successful demand-driven model of assistance to small firms. But the publicity-driven popularity of the program throughout the state created broadly dispersed demands for the procurement contracts. As a SIC official explained, "I had to help the largest number of firms and districts possible." It was politically difficult, in other words, for the state to heed the lesson of success in SJA. That would have required concentrating contracts and assistance in a few municípios at a time, where at least embryonic clusters of producers were already operating, while denying support to many other contenders. SIC and SEBRAE, then, dispersed the contracts subsequent to SJA across the state's municípios, seeming to fail to learn the lesson of this success.

Governments frequently fail to notice certain successes, especially when they take place in such remote corners of the territory like SJA. But the state government in this case clearly noticed what was happening in SJA and even capitalized on it, making the case into an ongoing public-relations event. This, ironically, contributed to spoiling the possibility for replication. In ceding to the pressures to expand to various municípios, then, the state had to violate the lesson underlying its first success. That it ceded in this particular case, however, does not violate the validity of the lesson.

Conclusion

Governments and NGOs have become more and more interested in small firms, and programs to assist them, because of their alleged potential to create employment and reduce poverty. But the resulting rapidly proliferating programs of support to SFs, whether government or NGO, are largely supply-driven despite the fact that demand-driven models are significantly more effective. This chapter has raised questions about the persistence of the prevailing supply-driven model, and has showed why the demand-driven approach is better.

DDA outperforms SDA on four fronts. First, it produces better results in terms of sustained SF-based growth and, hence, provides a stronger argument for assisting SFs than the current "social" arguments that portray small firms as pathetic. Second, it elicits better performance from support agencies, whether in the public or nongovernment sectors, and technicians show greater dedication to their work. These institutional actors tend to be neglected in the SF literature, which focuses largely on the weaknesses and needs of SFs. Third, it does more than SDA to reduce the problematic transaction and monitoring costs of purchasing from small firms, and at the same time helps them improve the quality of their product. Fourth, and with respect to SF-favoring public procurement in particular, it can lead to government's procuring goods and services of better quality and lower cost. This will happen if SF-favoring procurement is structured along the lines suggested below, and also because the existing market in which developing country governments procure goods and services is less efficient than it is normally assumed to be.

One part of my argument related to the strengths of DDA as a way of organizing SF assistance—whether in the government, NGO, or for-profit sector. The second part related to the particular form of DDA seen in the Ceará case—the procurement of goods and services by government. I focused on procurement because government customers have been significant actors in many stories of SF-based growth, although less studied than similar cases in the private sector. Also, government purchases, including all levels of government, account for a large share of total expenditures in developing countries. They represent a major untapped opportunity for promoting SF-based local growth, which dwarfs the resources devoted to date to supply-driven SF programs. SF-favoring procurement programs, nevertheless, have been plagued by certain problems. Through the Ceará case and others like it, it was possible to discover the conditions under which DDA around procurement could work well. This conclusion first sums up the case for DDA as opposed to SDA, and then the conditions under which procurement-focused DDA in particular can be effective.

Demand-driven support to SFs mimics history. Assistance to small firms from large purchasers, whether private or public, has tended to play an important role in the stories of significant SF-based growth. DDA works better because it forces support agencies to fashion customized assistance—to firms that produce the same product and are located near each other—around production for a particular contract. If the product is not up to standard, it is rejected or the contract is not renewed. Under SDA, neither the firm nor the support agency is subjected to this market test. SDA delivers standardized service—business advice, training, production assistance, or credit—to as large a number of firms, often quite diverse, as possible. This assumes, implicitly, that there are problems that are generic to all SFs, which can be reduced by offering standardized services—an assumption proven wrong by almost two decades of evaluation research on SFs and SF-support programs. In recent years, moreover, customized assistance has become increasingly recognized as a better model of service delivery in general in the public as well as the private sectors because it is more problem- and results-oriented.

In organizing its services to SFs around a particular contract for goods or services, DDA necessarily tends to work with groups of small firms rather than individual firms. This contributes to the development of certain growth-promoting externalities among the firms themselves—the possibility of sharing orders, specialization among firms, joint purchase of inputs, and joint action toward solving other problems. Students of SF clusters or industrial districts have shown that these externalities are key elements in the dynamic growth of successful clusters. Although SDA may also encourage firms to organize in some cases, the effect is not the same: the support agency does not link the organizing, and the service that goes with it, to a contract and the problems that arise in meeting it.

SF-favoring procurement in particular must observe the following four criteria if it is to work its magic. These criteria emerged from the study of the Ceará case and others like it.

First, and in contrast to many SF-favoring procurement programs, purchasing units should not be *required* to buy from small firms. Otherwise, these units will not be demanding with respect to price and quality. This criterion also suggests that the SF-support functions be kept separate from the purchasing function, so that the support agency, together with the firms, will have to prove to the purchasing unit that SF products can be delivered at the same price and quality as those of the government's existing suppliers. Although the support and purchase functions in the Ceará case were actually housed in different public agencies, this need not be the case. The support unit can be a nongovernment agency; or, as in some cases of SF-favoring private customers, it can be housed in a unit within the purchasing department itself.

Second, SF-favoring procurement should contract only with groups of firms, and pay each producer only upon delivery of a satisfactory product of the whole group. This is crucial to reducing the transaction and monitoring burdens of government purchase from SFs, as well as to reducing the risks of adverse selection. Working this way automatically shifts a significant part of the responsibility for monitoring from the support (or purchasing) agency to the firms themselves. This creates a dynamic of joint responsibility that resembles the peer pressure of today's popular micro-lending programs. The better firms sanction the laggards and, in the process, assist the laggards in improving the quality of their product.

Third, to work properly, SF-favoring procurement must make a substantial part of the payment to suppliers up front—in the Ceará case, 50 percent. This is how many successful SFs actually acquire working-capital finance, namely, from large private customers; this is already being done in some of the social investment funds, albeit at a typically smaller share of contract value than that of the Ceará program. The advance also solves one of the major problems bedeviling SF-favoring procurement—the failure of SFs to deliver because of insufficient working capital. Although advance payment would seem to increase monitoring costs and the risks of nondelivery, the contractual arrangements suggested above virtually eliminate these problems: they elicit self-monitoring and self-imposed sanctions among the firms themselves. Advance payment, finally, is a more effective method of providing working-capital finance to small firms than the special lines of subsidized credit that are typical of SF programs.

Fourth, the support agency must earn a small commission on the contract. This makes the agency at least partly dependent on the performance of the firms it serves for its income, which elicits more concern about improving the effectiveness of service. SDA, in contrast, not only frequently operates with full subsidy, but suffers from the absence of this built-in incentive to critically evaluate its work.

In closing, I emphasize that SF-favoring procurement requires little additional expenditure of resources and, as the Ceará story shows, may actually reduce the costs of running government. Most of its employment-creating and growth-inducing effects derive from government purchases that would have been made in any case, with or without the SF-favoring program. The need for subsidy is less than in existing supply-driven programs, since the contract presents an opportunity for the support agency to charge a commission, and no subsidized credit is offered to firms. The only additional expenditure is for technical support—minuscule in relation to the procurement itself. This support could be easily mobilized, in fact, by commandeering the organizational resources of the myriad SF programs now operating in the supply-driven mold.

· 6 ·

Civil Servants and Civil Society, Governments Central and Local

THIS BOOK HAS ARGUED that much of the current advice offered to developing countries, and the thinking that underlies it, is misguided. The advice ignores a substantial body of evidence about the conditions under which service organizations perform well. Those who formulate the advice have not been curious enough about the evidence embedded in instances of good government in the countries being advised, the case described in this book being a small example. This chapter reviews the contrasts between the advice and the reality as they emerged from these cases. It then uses the findings to suggest a way of interpreting the behavior of governments and of formulating advice that sticks more closely to the evidence.

Work Transformed

All the programs or parts of them reviewed in this book showed signs of high performance and significant impacts. In preventive health, infant mortality declined and vaccination coverage increased dramatically. In agricultural extension, the output and productivity of client-farmers increased significantly and measurably. The procurement program did the same for its small-firm suppliers, in addition to causing significant spillovers in the form of local economic development. The program of public works construction during the drought emergency created jobs more rapidly than usual, succeeded in dedicating an unusually high share of expenditures to labor as opposed to equipment and administration, and de-clientelized the distribution of jobs, projects, and relief supplies.

Four explanations for the better performance ran across these cases. Although the explanations are closely entwined, it is worth separating them out for purposes of discussion.

First, the workers in these programs showed high dedication to their jobs. Either they came to the jobs dedicated and their work environment rewarded and hence perpetuated that dedication, or the circumstances of their work elicited commitment from them. Although the importance of committed workers to improved performance would seem obvious, I start the chain of explanation here. This is because mainstream development advice pays little attention to the matter of worker commitment, except to argue that government workers are doomed by their self-interest to be uncommitted. And it does not worry about the array of practices now widely known to bring about dedication to the job. This despite the large body of IPWT evidence pointing to worker dedication as not only quite possible but as indispensable to improved performance in large service organizations. While this latter realm of inquiry tries to understand the conditions under which worker dedication increases, the development community occupies its mind with ways of protecting the public from the self-interest of workers.

Second, government itself fed the high dedication of these workers with repeated public demonstrations of admiration and respect for what they were doing. It built a sense of calling around these particular programs and their workers. It publicized the programs incessantly, even their minor successes. It gave prizes for good performance, with much pomp and ceremony. It lured journalists, politicians, and other dignitaries into visiting the communities where the programs were producing results. When it recruited and trained workers for some of these programs, it talked to them like a chosen people. Simply by virtue of working in these programs, they were told, they stood above the rest as leaders, and this placed a special burden on them to behave responsibly. All this contributed to a new respect for these workers by the public—remarkable in a time of widespread contempt for government. Workers reveled in the new respect and, in a kind of virtuous circle, they wanted to live up to it. Note the difference in this sequence of improved performance from that implicit in development advice, where the public servant is presumed guilty of self-interest unless proven otherwise.

The "chosenness" felt by Ceará's public servants in these particular instances, it should be added, was different from that of the typical case in which government is successful at creating the notion of a chosen elite in public service. Among these latter "mandarin" or "closed" systems of recruitment, the French and Japanese cases are the best known.[1] They tend to form an elite cadre within a larger body of public servants, partly through selection of candidates from prestigious, elite educational institutions that exist mainly to serve this purpose. But in the Ceará case, the sense of chosenness cut across all categories of workers, including the temporary and less educated ones. Although there is certainly no comparison between the performance of the French and Japanese civil services and that of Ceará, even in its best-performing programs, the sense of calling and chosenness of the Ceará cases did not involve the much-noted pitfalls of the mandarin systems: elitist attitudes among the elite cadre toward the public and toward noncadre co-workers, the inequity and perceived violation of egalitarian values inherent in recruitment through elite educational institutions with few opportunities for entry, and the absence of qualified subordinate cadres within the public service.

In publicizing its programs, Ceará's state government often had purposes in mind other than those of bestowing respect on its best workers. By granting prizes to the municípios with the best improvements in vaccination coverage and reduction of infant mortality, the state wanted to encourage the regular collection and analysis of health indicators at the local level. In explaining to the public exactly what kinds of services were supposed to be delivered by the health and drought relief programs, and what workers were supposed to be doing or not doing, the state wanted to get citizens to monitor both its workers and local governments.

The publicity also served the purpose of creating a new constituency that would help the governors and agency managers overcome political opposition. This came from large private suppliers in the case of public procurement from small firms, from nurses and physicians in the case of the paraprofessionalization of preventive health, and from mayors in the case of the drought relief program's attempts to de-clientelize the distribution of jobs, projects, and supplies. Finally, and most simply, the flurry of publicity served the purpose of projecting a highly favorable national image of two young reformist governors, for whom brilliant careers in national politics clearly lay ahead. To point out these other intentions is not to belittle them or to detract from the achievements, but to show how remarkably easy it can be, in certain instances, to induce public-sector workers into performing better.

Third, the recognition felt by these workers, and its contribution to their performance, was also related to the different way their work was organized. Workers carried out a larger and more varied set of tasks than normal, often voluntarily. Some of these additional tasks lay outside their expertise and prescribed functions, often requiring simply the brokering of connections between clients and the larger world of government agencies and private suppliers. Paraprofessional health agents, for example, provided a little curative care in addition to their preventive work. But curative care is normally reserved for and, indeed, jealously guarded by, physicians and nurses. Agricultural extension agents supervised numerous small construction projects in the drought relief program. But this is normally the task of engineers and associated supervisors.

In yet another example, the agricultural extension agent tackled an agenda of various and sundry problems prepared by the farmers themselves—in contrast to, as elsewhere in the state, delivering the typically standardized messages to all farmers about how to improve farming. Some of the problems for which these farmers asked his help were beyond his immediate expertise or responsibilities, like repairing irrigation equipment or getting access to an unsympathetic bank. Business extension specialists, similarly, went to the firm site rather than offer advice in their offices or the classroom. Normally specialized in certain functions like technical assistance, credit, or training, they provided a little of all these things and even others in the course of helping their clients solve unforeseen problems that came up while they were producing to fulfill a contract.

This seeming jumble of tasks, sometimes involving more brokering than expertise, cohered together in a client-centric, problem-solving approach to service delivery. It gave rise to trusting and respectful relationships between clients and public servants—both parties repeatedly using the language of trust and respect to describe these arrangements. The more customized the work, both sides reported, the better the results.

These findings would come as no surprise to the students of improved performance in large firms or, more recently, even to some of those studying how to improve the performance of the public sector in industrialized countries. Job enlargement, multitask work, customization, one-stop shopping for customers, and greater discretion of worker and client in driving the work agenda are by now standard features of the stories of best practice in large firms. But in the world of development advice, experts view the multitask jobs as distinctly *bad* practice: the extra tasks, they say, distract workers from their "real" work, undermine program objectives, and increase worker discretion more than is desirable in a public-sector world full of opportunities to misbehave.

Each sector has its own variation on this critique of "extra" tasks. Public health experts say, and with good reason, that preventive health goals are already compromised by the lure of curative care to health workers, professionals, and clients alike. Agricultural extension experts say that agents are already too burdened with processing credit applications for farmers and with doing special duty in the wake of natural disasters. One of the most explicit attempts by development experts to keep these distractions at a safe distance can be found in the Training-and-Visit (T&V) model of agricultural extension, promoted for many years by the World Bank. T&V prides itself on specifying tasks more narrowly, stripping away the "extra" tasks that plague extension agents, and tightening up the "sloppy" job definitions to a basic core of agricultural expertise. T&V's stripped-down job involves a carefully specified schedule of field visits to deliver standardized messages to all farmers about good farming practices. This circumscription of job boundaries is just the opposite of what occurred in the best-practice Ceará cases recounted here.

Fourth, it is important to note that the concerns of T&V experts and others who would circumscribe worker tasks need to be taken quite seriously. The greater variety of tasks can indeed burden workers and certainly does allow more space for shirking and rent seeking. In these cases, however, such problems were kept under control by two mechanisms: the state's messages to the public and the customization of work. As with the best-practice firms of the industrialized world moving toward a more customized organization of work, moreover, the extra tasks of the Ceará cases were not simply slapped onto existing jobs without rhyme or reason. They cohered together as a set of activities that were necessary to achieve the program's goals, whether it was improved health, greater agricultural productivity, or growth of small firms. The proof of the pudding was the greater output increases of client farms and firms that occurred when work was organized this way.

Because the multitask nature of these jobs arose partly out of a process of consultation between workers and clients, they also contained certain self-monitoring processes. Farmers would complain to supervisors, for example, when they felt that a particular agent was not helping them progress on their mutually agreed-upon agenda of work. Just as important to the issue of shirking, the state government's messages to the public about its programs drew in the public as outside monitors. Ironically, this was the flip side of the same messages that made these workers feel recognized and honored by citizens. The health and drought relief programs articulated the monitoring messages most explicitly: they informed citizens of what public servants should actually be doing and not doing, such as working eight hours a day, living in the communities where they worked, or not distributing political campaign information during visits to households.

In a variation on this theme, the school maintenance and repair program drew neighborhood associations into the process of selecting small contractors. And to enable these associations to informally monitor the repair and reconstruction work, agency technicians instructed them in some basic procedures that contractors should be following, like the proper preparation of wall surfaces for receiving tiles. In yet another variation, the public procurement, drought relief, and health programs repeatedly advised communities to pressure mayors, state legislators, and agency managers to provide them with services. This made the workers in these programs more visible to the public, and subjected them to the impatience of communities not yet receiving service. On the face of it, these messages and their virtual deputization of a band of community monitors might seem to create a rather unpleasant environment in which to work. But that was not the case because of the larger context of respect for public service in which the messages were delivered.

In order to make service delivery more customized along the lines suggested here, certain practical problems would need to be faced. For example, if the work agenda of the agricultural extension agency should be driven by problems defined by its client-farmers, this requires substantial modification of the planning and budgeting process. Many agricultural extension services function in a top-down way that channels to farmers a set of standardized messages about best practices, or carries out agricultural policies that provide special support to all farmers for particular crops. If farmer groups are to negotiate an agenda with their extension agents—meaning that one group will likely want help with one set of problems and another group with something else—the content of these mutually agreed-upon work agendas cannot be known much in advance, nor can it be standardized. This will significantly alter an extension service's approach to planning the year's activities, to budgeting, and to procedures for deploying and promoting staff. What does a manager do, for example, in the highly likely event that farmers request one extension agent much more than another?

Similarly, if small-business extension works better when it is demand-driven rather than supply-driven, as in our case, this has certain implications for the organization of small-firm support services. There would be no room in a customized approach, for example, for standardized courses on business management, provided in a classroom and away from the firm site. Yet standardized business extension courses are the stock-in-trade of many small-firm programs, in both the public and NGO sectors. How does a small-firm extension service move from standardized to customized delivery, however, without increasing unit costs markedly? The high costs of customizing business extension, after all, explain why this kind of service is usually standardized in the first place. This study revealed that public procurement, if done properly, can indeed become an attractive option for organizing service delivery in a customized way while, at the same time, covering costs and keeping them reasonable. Indeed, customization also turned out to resolve one of the major problems plaguing many small-firm-favoring public procurement programs in the past—the poor quality of products or services provided.

The procurement case revealed another dilemma posed by customization, which these particular agencies failed to resolve. The concentration of attention at any moment in time on certain groups of producers, often required by the customized approach, can create political problems in the form of allegations of inequity and favoritism by the unattended groups or regions. Because Ceará's leaders wanted to gain as many supporters as possible from the procurement initiative—an important feature of the political landscape of most such programs—the program's resources were ultimately spread too thinly across firms. This kept the most striking developmental success story of the program, involving the woodworkers of São João do Aruaru, from being repeated elsewhere. Whether or not the Ceará cases showed ways of meeting these practical challenges, they reveal the importance of identifying and facing them.

Finally, these cases revealed that government can be a remarkably strong moral presence in creating an imagery of calling around public service—in the eyes of the public and of public workers themselves. With this moral force, if it likes, government can get citizens to monitor its workers. With the same rhetoric and publicity, moreover, it can enlist the public to help protect its own workers from meddling by politicians and others with power in government itself. This particular problem is often neglected by the literature of reform because of the assumption that public servants are homogeneously self-interested, and that it is only the public that needs protection from their abuse or neglect. These cases showed, however, that it was just as important that dedicated and capable workers in government be protected from others in government—rent-seeking co-workers, superiors, and elected officials. The agronomists running the drought relief program showed great appreciation to state government for backing them against such meddlers, as did the health agents and nurse-supervisors of the health program. How does one build on the ability of governments to exert such moral force in reforming themselves? How does this work in a setting in which, like that of Ceará, the public-minded typically intermingle daily with the rent seekers? If government is viewed mainly as a stage for self-interested behavior, this makes it difficult to see the clear opportunity for putting government's strong moral presence to work toward improving its own performance.

Even though the development community is paying some obeisance to the new thinking about service delivery in large organizations, in sum, it is not grappling with many of the questions and challenges noted here. This is partly due to the lopsided attention paid to users as opposed to workers. It is also due to a set of beliefs widely held in the mainstream development community about the comparative disadvantages of central governments as opposed to local governments, and of governments as providers of services in comparison to nongovernment providers. According to these views, many of the issues and challenges posed above would take care of themselves if governments would only decentralize to some extent from central to local, and transfer some service provision from government to nongovernment providers. I turn to this set of beliefs now, and the evidence brought to bear on them by these cases and the literature.

Decentralization, Participation, and Other Things Local

Like the IPWT research, the better-performing Ceará programs operated in ways that elicited higher worker dedication, included a greater variety of tasks and more autonomy for workers, and were more client-sensitive and customized. The prevailing development wisdom says that these traits come more naturally to local rather than central governments, and to non-government rather than government providers. On these grounds, it is suggested that a good part of the responsibility for providing many public services be shifted from central to local governments, and from government to nongovernment providers. This set of arguments about inherent traits, or comparative advantages and disadvantages, lies behind the enthusiasm in the development field today for things local—decentralization to local government, the important role of civil society or associationalism in holding governments accountable, and service delivery by NGOs or private firms.

Local governments and nongovernment associations were, indeed, more active than usual in these state-sponsored programs. In preventive health, municipal governments had to hire and pay the salary of the nurse-supervisors (15% of total wage costs), and also voluntarily financed other expenses like the purchase of motorbikes and donkeys for the agents' household visits. In the drought relief program, village assemblies and new municipal-level councils decided who would get jobs and relief supplies, and which public works would be built and where. Although the cases of agricultural and business extension involved no formal decentralization to local government, the state government channeled support through associations of producers that became, in the process, important civic institutions in their municípios.

The experiences reviewed in this book did not confirm the picture of local governments and of nongovernment providers as being inherently better at tailoring services to client needs, or as having the comparative advantages assumed by the development literature. In this sense, the book's findings confirmed the ironic "paradox of decentralization" so aptly identified by Rudolf Hommes, an ex-minister of state from Colombia, one of the countries that has taken decentralization quite seriously. Decentralization, Hommes said, "demands more centralization and more sophisticated political skills at the national level."[2] This section offers my own interpretation of why this is the case, and draws on the Ceará cases to suggest a better way of understanding decentralization as well as customized service delivery.

The current thinking about public-sector reform and decentralization represents a blend of arguments from the field of economics, together with perspectives on civil society and participation from writings on political science, democracy, and NGOs.[3] Although these currents of thinking are in many ways quite distinct, they nevertheless converge in the policy world in a set of assertions and implicit assumptions that appear regularly in the myriad meetings, project papers, and donor tracts on how to improve government. For the sake of brevity, and at the risk of offending the parties to the blend, I refer to it as "decentralization and participation," and abbreviate it as "D&P." In drawing on the Ceará case for evidence, I sometimes use the terms *central government* and *state government* interchangeably, for reasons noted earlier.[4]

According to the D&P scenario, local government is better at the kinds of services discussed in this book partly because it is spatially closer than central government to its client-citizens. This greater proximity makes government more vulnerable to citizen pressures, and makes it easier for citizens to become more informed and hence more demanding of good service. The smaller area and number of citizens served by local government allow for a greater tailoring of service to the particular tastes and socioeconomic realities of each locality, in contrast to the "excessive" standardization and rigidity of faraway central governments.

After decentralization, in the D&P scenario, the central arm of government does considerably less than it did before. It has given up substantial power to collect taxes and spend them directly, and has retreated to a principally regulatory and standard-setting role. It continues to provide some supporting services, but only those in which it has a presumed comparative advantage—certain kinds of tax collection and expenditure, services requiring concentrations of skilled expertise like research and development, regulating and monitoring functions, and other activities with obvious externalities or economies of scale, like the manufacture of vaccines.

In the D&P scenario, then, central government moves in the direction of becoming a benevolent bystander of a mainly two-way dynamic between local government and a demanding civil society. D&P thinking, correspondingly, directs its attention almost exclusively to figuring out how to build local government, increasing its capacity to provide services, and getting it to impose and collect the charges and the taxes required for its new role. Similarly, D&P pays serious attention to making sure that local civil society does its part, building its strength to pressure and monitor government or, organized into NGOs or private firms, to become an alternative provider of public services.

There are three unstated assumptions in all this that, although obvious, set the stage for summarizing the Ceará findings. The first assumption is that the two-way dynamic between local government and civil society is, indeed, one of the best ways to improve the quality of government in general. The second assumption is that decentralization is the best way to embark on the long journey toward improved local government. The third assumption is that central governments will give up power or, at least, that advisors should invest considerable effort in persuading them to do so. The latter task, as any decentralization expert will report with exasperation, is anything but easy.

Two further assumptions—this time, about "civil society"—go into the D&P blend. The first is about causal arrows. It says that a robust civil society is a prerequisite to good government. The immense popularity in the development community of Robert Putnam's fine book on the determinants of good local government in Italy (1993) is testimony to how widely held this assumption is. Putnam marshalled an impressive array of evidence from the Italian case to argue that good regional governments were found where civil society was most developed. Those regions without this "social capital"—in his study, the regions of Southern Italy (with a few exceptions)—could not do much about it. They were path-dependently doomed to bad government. Or, at the least, they started with a distinct disadvantage.

The second assumption is that nongovernment organizations and other institutions of civil society are distinctly autonomous and independent of government. It is this outsider status that is said to make them particularly effective monitors of government, good advocates for citizens, and good protectors of those abused or neglected by government. The outsider status also makes for good service providers, preserving them from the afflictions of government, rigidity and rent seeking in particular, and freeing them up for more customized, client-friendly approaches. Put together with the assumption that local government is more vulnerable to civil society's wishes and watchfulness than central government, this adds up to a strong argument for decentralization on the grounds that it relocates government to a place where civil society can work its magic better. But this book revealed a picture of the relations among central government, local government, and civil society that differed in important ways from this scenario.

First, improvements in local government turned out to be less the result of decentralization than they were of a three-way dynamic among local government, civil society, and an active central government. Central government was in no way a pale vision of an overcentralized past. It was also doing different things than it had in the past—not less of the same, and not necessarily in line with its presumed comparative advantages.

Second, although civic and other nongovernment associations were often important actors in these cases, this was made possible in several instances by something government did first. In addition, the performance-inducing effects of civil society on government often worked their magic on central rather than local government. Some members of civic associations or nongovernment organizations, moreover, migrated to government, making alliances with like-minded colleagues already within government. Once in government, they spanned the public-private divide by continuing to relate to their outside networks. Although this process is quite familiar to any observer of the public sector, it is worth noting here because it means that the assumed clear boundary between government and nongovernment is actually quite blurred. Government was causing civil society to form, then, at the same time civil society was acting "independently" from outside government to challenge its wisdom and its actions, or to demand better service. To the extent that civil society contributed to good performance, then, it was not necessarily previously existing or totally independent of government. This finding of two-way causality between the formation of civil society and improvements in the quality of government makes for an explanation of how governments improve that is more complex than that of the D&P scenario. At the same time, the complexity opens up the possibility for more agency by planners in strengthening civil society than does the path-dependent view now so popular in the development community.

Third, these cases did not reveal an inherently greater flexibility and client-friendliness on the part of NGOs as opposed to government. This finding is backed up by a larger body of evidence from the literature, as explained in the fourth section.

The following two sections lay out the argument and summarize the evidence. It will be obvious from what follows that I am not suggesting that the dynamic described here is the only possible one, nor that the causal arrows assumed in the D&P scenario are in reality reversed. A careful reading will also show that I am not saying that central government should go back to its old centralized ways.

The Three-Way Dynamic: Local, Central, and Civic

To the extent that the Ceará cases involved decentralization, they revealed something quite different from the unidirectional transfer of power and funding from central to local that is at the heart of the stylized portrayal of decentralization. Most strikingly, the central government took power away from local government, even though its actions ultimately contributed to strengthening the capacity of local government.

The drought relief program took away the longstanding power of mayors to decide where the jobs and the construction projects would go. It replaced the mayor as head of the municipal decision-making council with the state government's own representative, the agronomist-head of the local extension office. It arbitrarily imposed standard criteria according to which local projects could be funded—criteria that virtually excluded the preferred projects of many a local notable, like large works projects or those located within private landholdings. And its director spent much more time "managing by wandering around" at the local level than central government agency directors normally do, personally meeting with community associations, municipal councils, and field staff.

The health program, similarly, kept local government from having any say over the hiring and firing of a municipally based force of health agents. These agents often became the largest public-sector presence in the town, the hiring of which is normally a function of municipal government. The state government also laid down rules of worker conduct that, in effect, also circumscribed the traditional power of local officials to wield their influence over a cadre of essentially municipal workers. For example, it prohibited health agents from the traditional practice of distributing political campaign leaflets in the course of their household visits, which advertised particular candidates, usually supported by the mayor.

Also in contrast to the D&P scenario, the state government did things it had not done before or did more of certain things it had done previously, at the same time that local government or other local actors were also doing more. It launched public information campaigns with a vengeance in the municípios where the programs operated. It went to dozens of towns in the interior to carry out time-consuming interviewing, hiring, and training of new municipally based workers. It required and supported the formation of civic associations with which it or local government then conducted public business.

D&P experts would be quick to point out, and rightly so, that the Ceará cases do not represent genuine decentralizations of power to local governments. At most, as in the cases of health and drought relief, they were only partial decentralizations. The cases of public procurement and agricultural extension, in turn, amounted "only" to deconcentration of service delivery within a central government agency. Whether or not these programs were the genuine thing, however, they were leading to some of the same outcomes that decentralization is supposed to achieve: stronger local institutions in the form of more capable local governments, and a more developed and demanding civil society. The preventive health program is a good example.

When the health program started, the state government kept iron control over the hiring, training, and payment of 7,300 municipally based health agents. The municipal government hired and paid the nurse-supervisor who managed the program, as well as other operating expenses like transport. After five or six years, however, the agents began to form associations among themselves at the municipal level and to demand fringe benefits, greater job security, and more training. The result, just emerging as of this writing, was that many municípios were starting to contract the health agent association as a new, local, and nongovernment provider of services. This is precisely the kind of outcome sought by decentralization. But it occurred in this case without decentralization. Indeed, this desirable development could not have occurred without the strong hold of central government on the health agents during the program's first years.

The health program provides another example of stronger local government resulting from something other than genuine decentralization. Starting in the mid-1980s, Brazil's central government carried out decentralizing fiscal reforms that would be the envy of most decentralization experts. (It has been criticized for doing much less, however, in terms of devolving actual responsibilities to local governments.)[5] The new constitution of 1988 and other measures had increased the revenues passed on by central government to municipal governments, and had given the municípios new responsibilities in health and education. But this often had little effect on the poor quality of health services in many municípios, where ambulances continued to be used by mayors and their families for personal travel, or mayors continued to dole out prescription medicines to ailing constituents from their homes.

The state government, now forced to share power with the municípios in health and at the same time having no authority or institutional capacity to enforce good behavior on them, could only resort to the carrot and stick. It provided its share of the financing (85% of wage costs) only to the municípios that would play according to its rules. Those that would not were left out, while at the same time being subjected to demands for inclusion from an electorate newly informed by the public information campaigns of its rights to good health services. For the same reason, those mayors who did enter the program were subjected to demands for account-able behavior from their constituents.

Driving the pace and pattern of municipal involvement, then, was not a balanced decentralization policy or a uniformly applied program. It was, rather, the idiosyncratic pattern of responses by mayors and their con-stituents to this particular set of inducements and penalties. The result was clearly messier and slower than D&P advocates would like. But it may have been at least as effective as genuine decentralization in strength-ening local government and civil society. And no realistic alternative may actually exist in many cases, given the unwillingness of central govern-ments to cede power and the initial incapacity of local governments to use it responsibly.

In trying to understand why these cases worked well, one cannot help but notice the magic that was worked by distrust between central and local governments. Distrust induced the state to monitor the municipal features of the programs aggressively, to socialize the municipal workers to stan-dards of excellence, to set criteria meant to prevent abuse and increase program effectiveness, and to educate citizens to keep watch. Distrust made the state keep for itself certain tasks that the D&P scenario normally al-locates to municipal government, like the hiring of municipally based health agents, engaging in outreach to local citizens, and presiding over the meetings of municipal councils and community assemblies making deci-sions about local projects.

Decentralization experts have little sympathy for central governments' mistrust of local government, and see it as a lame excuse for not giving up power. They portray partial decentralization to local government or decentralization of power to local offices of central agencies not as first steps toward the real thing or as alternative paths to improved local gov-ernment. They view these initiatives, rather, as smokescreens thrown up by central government to obscure the fact that nothing "real" is being done or, worse, in order to "further extend central control."[6] They point out, rightly, that central government itself is rife with the clientelism and incompetence that it fears in local government. But whether central gov-ernments use mistrust as an excuse has little relevance to the point being made here: it was precisely *because* central government was on the scene as a mistrustful outsider that the local "content" of these programs did better and expanded.

The D&P scenario, it should be noted, does include room for this constructive side of central government's mistrust of local government in that it almost always provides a monitoring role for central government. But D&P's monitoring is a pale version of what central government did in these cases, and does not really capture the significance of central government's key involvement in certain aspects of program execution. This gave it greater force, information, and presence which, ironically, increased its effectiveness in its role as outside monitor. Although experts on decentralization understand that there are as many opportunities for local government as for central government to engage in rent seeking and other undesirable behavior, the D&P scenario relies heavily on civil society, not central government, to keep this misbehavior in check. I take this matter up in the next section.

In the public procurement program, a similar healthy antagonism between different levels of government contributed to the better performance of the support agencies, as well as of the small firms that received technical assistance. In that case, it was different units within state government that distrusted each other, and in a way that experts often criticize as a lack of cooperation in carrying out a desirable policy. The purchasing departments in state government (Education, Agriculture, etc.) mistrusted the Industry and Commerce Department's procurement program, predicting that the new small-firm suppliers would produce inferior and costly products, delivered late. The skepticism took the form of being quite demanding with respect to quality and price. This forced the support agencies, which were sympathetic to the cause of small firms, to work hard to assist their client firms in improving their product. Needless to say, this constructive distrust had the same positive effects on the firms themselves, and is just the opposite of the laxness toward quality and price issues that characterizes many such programs. Whether it was distrust between agencies or between levels of government, then, the existence of a powerful and distrusting outsider on the scene contributed to making performance better.

What central government did in the name of distrust in these cases can also be seen as advocacy by it on the behalf of local citizens vis-à-vis local government. This is difficult to conceptualize in the D&P scenario. D&P leaves central government out of the mainly two-way dynamic between local government and civil society, in which the latter demands accountability from the former. Or, D&P portrays NGOs as independent entities outside, and often protecting citizens from, a monolithic entity called "government," whether central or local.[7] This takes us to the subject of the next section.

Civil Society and Good Government:
What Causes What?

In the D&P scenario, NGOs and civil society play two distinct roles in bringing about better government. The one is to advocate for citizens and to demand accountability from government. The other is to provide services contracted for by government. This distinction is not frequently mentioned in D&P rhetoric, although it has caused much soul searching within the NGO community about whether service provision "compromises" the autonomy of advocacy groups. I bring up the distinction here for another reason: each of the two roles has its own set of assumptions about the relationship between civil society and government. With respect to advocacy, civil society's special advantage in monitoring government is assumed to lie in its outsider status or independence from government. With respect to service provision, nongovernment organizations are assumed to have inherent traits that differ from those of public agencies, and which allow them to perform better than, or at least to create healthy competitive pressures on, government providers. This and the following sections raise some questions about the accuracy of these assumptions. This section discusses the advocacy role, and the next section the service-provider role.

The Ceará case did, in fact, reveal civic associations to be playing an important role in improving the performance of local government. The sequence of events and the causal arrows, however, differed from that assumed in the D&P scenario. In many instances, for example, the more central government—the state government—had itself induced the formation of these associations, sometimes in a prior period, or strengthened and educated those already in existence. The state's actions took three forms: (1) conducting public information campaigns and delivering similar messages locally in less formal ways; (2) insisting on providing services only through producer associations rather than to individuals or individual firms, and working with these groups through contract-like mechanisms; and (3) requiring the formal discussion of public investment decisions at the municipal level by decision-making bodies that included, at the state government's insistence, representatives from civil society and state government, as well as from municipal government. I take these up in turn.

The state's public information campaigns and exhortations to citizens to monitor and respect the public service were the most conspicuous examples of government's inducing of civic action. As described in the cases of health, drought relief, and public procurement, these messages increased the ability of citizens to pressure government for improved service. They put in people's minds a vision of better and more just government, implored citizens to stand up against the abuses of government, and explained how to recognize infractions and what to do about them. In certain ways, ironically, this "advocacy" by government on behalf of citizens was better than that of NGOs, in that it gave detailed instructions to the public on exactly what government workers or contractors should and should not be doing. There is no reason, of course, why NGOs could not do the same by first acquiring the necessary technical expertise.

The state government had more than advocacy for citizens in mind when it incited the public to expect more of government. It wanted the public to heed its advice about health or agricultural practices, to monitor a difficult-to-supervise workforce, and to discipline mayors who were out of its control. It wanted to make sure voters gave it, rather than municipal officials, credit for good programs and other improvements in service. And it was skillful in using the very discourse of empowerment invented by the advocacy NGOs themselves. Regardless of the varied intentions behind the state's messages, they nevertheless had awareness-raising impacts on the public that were similar to those of the more "purely" motivated messages of this nature from independent advocacy NGOs. The language of empowerment and instruction appropriated by government in these messages also raised citizen consciousness permanently. State government could not subsequently control what form the resulting demands would take or keep these demands from being turned on state government itself.

In agricultural and small-business extension, the state government also contributed to the conditions for an "independent" civil society to emerge. In these particular cases, the support agencies worked only through associations of small farms or firm owners, rather than individually. Where there were no such associations, it encouraged their creation and nurtured them. Many of these producer groups evolved into strong local civic institutions, serving the community beyond the immediate interests of the members. The Santana farmer cooperative, for example, paid for the extension agent to visit other farmer groups in the surrounding area. The woodworkers of São João do Aruaru financed daily trips by schoolteachers from elsewhere so their town could have a high school.

Servicing small producers through associations or cooperatives is nothing new. But the results have often been inconsequential in terms of the newly organized producers' productivity and ability to compete, let alone in terms of improved service delivery. These cases were different in one crucial way: there was a contractual relationship between the support agency and the producer association. This forced the producers to work together in a problem-driven way, to monitor each other's work, and to formulate focused and concrete requests for assistance to the service provider. The end result, among other things, was a strengthening of the capacity of such groups to transform themselves into civic associations providing benefits to the broader community. Just as important were the striking improvements in the performance of the support agencies themselves as a result of these contract-like relationships, given that the latter required that service to these groups be more customized and flexible. All this had nothing to do with decentralization, local government, or a strong and preexisting civil society.

In the drought relief program, the state government created the conditions for strengthening civil society in a different way. It insisted on the establishment of a new municipal council, and it set clear criteria for making decisions about projects and allocation of jobs and relief supplies. The council could choose only from projects and names of the eligible submitted by village assemblies, which were convened and coached by the agronomist-representative of the state government for this purpose. The new formal structure made it possible for civil society to act collectively to solve its own problems, as well as to articulate demands to local government. This would not have happened without the intervention of and constant monitoring by state government, and without the chairing of the new council by the agronomist-representative from a state-government service.

These new procedures of the drought program clearly advanced the development of the two-way dynamic between civil society and local government. As some critics from Ceará's civil society pointed out, however, the new local councils were often far less democratic than D&P enthusiasts reported. The makeup of the councils, with the exception of the two members representing the rural labor union and local churches, came from civic associations representing local elites—like the landowners' association, the chamber of commerce, and the Rotary Club or Masons. These latter representatives did not necessarily share the interests of the rural poor for whom the drought relief program was intended. If anything, they traditionally cooperated with local government to produce the clientelistic results of previous programs. Although this point may seem obvious, it bears stating because it is often lost in the enthusiasm for decentralization, which assumes that giving more power and responsibility to local government goes along with all other good things, including greater representation for the poor and servicing of their needs.[8] Those observers of Ceará who praised the 1987 drought relief program on D&P grounds, then, were not quite right about what was happening. But neither were the critics.

Whether or not the new councils truly represented the poor, they created the conditions for more than one elite position to emerge on how to manage public programs. Retail business associations, for example, worried that unemployed peasants begging for food would appear on the doorsteps of their establishments and disrupt their business. They therefore sided, sometimes, with the agronomist-chair of the council from state government and the small minority of members from the intended beneficiaries—the poorest—in arguing that drought relief should be run less clientelistically. Whereas in previous droughts these local business associations had not been called upon formally to think about where their interests might lie and how best to serve them, the extended debates of the new councils induced them into articulating a position.

To the extent that the decisions made by the local councils served the rural poor better, then, it was not necessarily because the poor were more significantly represented on the councils, or because civil society had held the feet of local officials to the fire. Rather, in that the formalization of new procedures and decision-making processes enabled more than one elite opinion to emerge, this also created the conditions for the emergence of a more public-serving elite vision of local governance. The new process, in addition, created opportunities for the genuine drought victims to increase their strength on the councils by making alliances with like-minded local elite members, whether from elite civic associations, central government, or local government itself.

D&P's simple two-way dynamic between local government and civil society does not account for, nor could it have produced, these kinds of results. D&P enthusiasts miss the point by describing processes like these as more representative and truly beneficiary-driven than they actually are. Those who criticize such programs for not being democratic enough, in turn, also miss the point. They do not understand that genuine representation of the poor is not always a prerequisite to their needs being better served.

D&P thinking also errs in focusing only on the wholesome effects of civil society on government at the local level, as opposed to higher levels. The error is based on the reasonable assumption that local government, being smaller and "closer" to citizens, is more vulnerable to citizens' expressions of their needs. These cases, however, revealed some powerful effects of civil society on central, and not only local, government. In the rural preventive health program, a handful of public health professionals masterminded this new initiative, the boldest and most successful of this set of cases. When the new government took over in 1987, the governor named one of these professionals, a public health physician, to enact his vision of the right preventive health program. He brought in a few others from outside government from this same circle of professionals. They joined with yet others already inside government who had similar visions of how to improve public health. The shared vision of this public-private informal network had been developed, in part, through their membership in associations of health professionals. For many years, and especially as part of the movement for democracy in Brazil, these professionals had engaged in long debates about how public health should work in a democratic country. The debates had taken place far away from the civil society of the communities where the health program was to operate, although many of the participants in the debates had led or worked in programs in such communities in the past. It was this common history in a movement of public health professionals with a reformist bent, rather than their location in civil society or government, that united the group. It allowed them to easily "take over" the state's Department of Health and "impose" a reform agenda on local government, involving no initial consultation with civil society in the communities where the program was to operate.

Professional associations like these, or reformist-minded fractions within them, are another important form of civic associationalism that can contribute toward reforming central, and not just local, government. Indeed, the new reformist state government in Ceará was itself the result of a long period of debate among the members of another civic association—the Ceará Society of Industrialists (CIC/Centro Industrial do Ceará). Going back as far as 20 years prior to the late 1986 election of Tasso Jereissati, a younger and reform-minded faction of the CIC began to sponsor public debates about what the state's role should be in promoting development and in bringing the state from backwardness into modernity. By the early 1980s, these "young turks"—among whom was Jereissati—came to dominate the CIC. They ultimately chose Jereissati from among them to run for governor, ending the grip that three clientelistic families had held on the governorship for more than 20 years and enacting their shared vision of development.[9]

CIC, of course, was an association of powerful businessmen rather than professionals. But its role as the crucible in which an agenda of reform was developed and then enacted was similar to that played by the reform-minded among the public health professionals. The importance of CIC in explaining at least part of the civic processes that led to "the Ceará story" has remained almost as little noticed by its admirers as the long associational history that gave rise to the state's internationally acclaimed preventive health program. The prior history of both these events seemed to get lost in the widespread public admiration for the two governors who ruled the state after 1986—lost, at least, in the renditions of these stories by the press, international donors, and other observers. Captivated by the images of two charismatic and highly effective governors, these commentators portrayed them as having burst suddenly and idiosyncratically onto an otherwise hopelessly clientelistic scene.

When professional associations appear at all in the D&P scenario, they are usually portrayed as obstructing reform rather than leading it. In this picture, teachers are always obstructing educational reforms, and physicians and nurses are always objecting to the hiring of paraprofessionals. In laying out the arguments for decentralization, then, D&P discourse portrays greater local power as a way of getting around professional and other employee associations, particularly in health and education.

No one, of course, would dispute the fact that professional and other associations of public-sector workers have made reform of government difficult on various occasions. But on other occasions they have also played the kind of role that appeared in our health case.[10] Their obstruction of sensible reforms by central government, moreover, has frequently been no less fierce than obstruction by elite civil society at the local level, when faced with the kinds of de-clientelizing reforms introduced by the drought relief program. There is no justification for assuming, in other words, that civic associations have a wholesome effect on governance at the local level but a retrograde effect—or, at least, no significant effect—at the central level.

In conclusion, these cases revealed a set of interactions leading to good civil society and to good local government. They differ markedly from that of the D&P scenario. Civil society was not a homogeneously virtuous institution, keeping wayward governments on the straight and narrow and working its magic best on local government. The causal relationships between good government and civil society were anything but unidirectional or strictly local, and central government played a more active role than the D&P scenario would lead us to expect.

Civil society, in turn, was not an unmitigated good. Important fractions of it perpetuated poor government, while others were pressuring effectively for better government. When local civil society played a role in bringing about better government, it was sometimes because central government had made it possible for alliances to form across the government-civil society divide. This enabled reformist fractions of civil society to unite with reformist fractions within government, sometimes at both the local and central levels. If one could discern something like a virtuous circle between local government and local citizens, then, it was set in motion and sustained by a three-way dynamic among local government, civil society, and central government. Central government was far from being the "third wheel" of an otherwise well-balanced local twosome.

The D&P scenario, in conclusion, has exaggerated the extent to which civil society can counteract the rent-seeking tendencies of government. It has not sufficiently appreciated the extent to which civic associations can contribute just as strongly toward reinforcing rent seeking in government as counteracting it. In rushing to embrace the nongovernment sector as a way of fixing some of the problems of government, moreover, D&P has also chosen to ignore the problem of self-seeking behavior, let alone incompetence, within the nongovernment sector itself. Improving government performance at the local or central level, then, requires having a clear idea of exactly what central government has to do in order for good institutions—both civic and government—to emerge at the local level.

The three-way dynamic I suggest may seem to complicate the already difficult task of improving local government or, at least, make it seem messier. At the same time, however, this revised interpretation does not pose the difficult prerequisite that decentralization policies do—namely, that central government first give up power to local governments. Indeed, the three-way dynamic works precisely because it takes strength from central government's distrust of local government—which takes the form of the resistance to decentralize that so frustrates experts.

The Comparative Advantages
of NGOs and Government

As noted in the first section of this chapter, the explanations for good performance in these cases were consistent with many of the best practices recommended for restructuring large firms by the IPWT literature. But these practices seem to require the kinds of organizational traits that are said to inhere in nongovernment organizations, as opposed to government. While the IPWT literature talks of the need for greater flexibility and innovativeness in organizational processes, that is, the development community says that flexibility and innovativeness are inherent in NGOs and not government. While IPWT talks of worker dedication to the job, the development community talks of how much more committed NGO staffs are than those of government agencies. While IPWT talks of work being tailored to client needs, the development community speaks of the greater capacity of NGO staffs for outreach to the poor—their ability to sympathize with them and understand their problems over against the government bureaucrat's distance and disdain. While IPWT points to the importance of job enlargement and multitask jobs, the development community talks of the greater versatility of the more "generalist" NGO staffs as opposed to the narrowness and rigidity of many specialist professionals in government—engineers, architects, agronomists, physicians. Whereas IPWT stresses the importance of decentralized management, the development literature stresses the bottom-up style of NGO operation over the hopelessly top-down style of government.

Both IPWT and the development literature put this all together in a package labeled "flexible," "innovative," and "experimental." The fit is not perfect, but it is remarkably close. Indeed, both donors and NGOs would probably agree on this characterization of their views—an unusual case of convergence in worldview between these two often antagonistic parties. Do the findings of this book, therefore, not simply reinforce the current view that some of the kinds of services reviewed here would be best transferred, at least in part, from government to NGOs? This section brings evidence to bear on this question from the Ceará cases and the literature.

Comparative perspectives on NGOs and government tend to attribute to government a set of shortcomings that mirror in negative terms the strengths of NGOs. Government agencies are doomed, in this mirror, to be more bureaucratized, standardized, top-down, and unsympathetic to citizens—especially to the poor. Phrased more positively by some researchers, government does best at delivering services of uniform quality to large numbers of people, and in accordance with political mandates that require "equal access" for all.[11] Some researchers have also pointed to a number of NGO shortcomings, though one hears less about them in the D&P discourse. A list of them would include the difficulty of most NGOs in reaching significant numbers of those in need of service, their tendency to pick and choose or to "cream" from the client population, their lack of technical expertise, their sometimes high unit costs despite low total budgets or overheads, their frequently poor accounting practices, and the absence of pressures from their funders or clients for accountability.[12]

Comparing government to NGOs as service providers in the Ceará case does not confirm the mirror image of advantages and disadvantages. For that matter, neither does much of the empirical research on the subject. Sometimes, as illustrated below, the public agencies of our cases behaved more like NGOs than the NGOs themselves. This is not to say that the government agencies were consistently more flexible, innovative, or close to the people than NGOs. Indeed, some agencies were distinctly inconsistent. The same agency behaved "like" NGOs in some parts of its programs, and like the stereotype of government service in others—as if it had a split personality. This suggests that it is something other than "inherent traits" that keeps governments from performing better.

Take the example of the agricultural extension services provided by the two NGOs to their farmer-members—the agricultural cooperatives of the municípios of Senador Pompeu and Piquet Carneiro. The style of extension of these two cooperatives, though a distinct improvement over that of the Extension Service, was still more top-down and standardized than in the case of the local office of that service in its assistance to the farmer group of Santana. To complicate things further, the "NGO-like" service of the public agency in the Santana case differed substantially from the service provided by the exact same public agency in surrounding municípios. The latter was more "typically" standardized, client-indifferent, and top-down—even more so than that of the two cooperatives. The business extension agencies of the public procurement program displayed the same dual personality. In the procurement program, they were strikingly customized, flexible, innovative, and close to their clients. In their other programs, they were just the opposite—standardized, centralized, and not designed to meet the needs of particular sets of producers.

In yet another example of such seeming confusion, each of the municipally based offices of the rural public health program behaved, in certain ways, like an "independent" NGO rather than the arm of a standardized public program run out of the state capital by the state Department of Health. Each municipal office had placed its own particular stamp on the program. Some stressed family planning and sex education while others offered nothing in this area; some became very involved in advocating environmental health issues vis-à-vis local government and private firms, while others limited themselves to visiting households and preaching preventive health practices to mothers. To be sure, some of this local variation was influenced by the role played by municipal governments in hiring and paying the supervising nurse. But the variation was also the result of the unusual discretion granted by the state's Department of Health to the supervising nurse. It was also due to interaction with local civil society, once the program got started.

The way the state Department of Health delivered preventive services, in turn, was more decentralized, flexible, and "client-sympathetic" than that of existing NGOs in the health sector of Ceará. Many of the well-established NGOs in preventive health delivered their messages and other services in a clinic to which mothers came, while the public service sent its workers into households. Many of the NGOs, moreover, couched their health messages in a religious language that inadvertently reinforced the paternalism of the existing social context and the fatalism about disease.

In an ironic twist on the vision of governments' adopting and "scaling up" models first developed by NGOs, the architects of the preventive health program—some of whom had previously worked in NGO programs themselves—explained how they learned from the "mistakes" of these latter programs. By operating centrally out of clinics, these now-public managers said, the NGOs had not been able to reach the significant number of mothers who did not come to the clinic because they lived too far away, or were too distrustful or busy to come in. These women, moreover, were from among the poorest—exactly those who needed to be reached the most by such programs. The architects of the new public service therefore decided upon a different model of service delivery. They would organize an "army" of low-paid paraprofessional health agents and send them out to find mothers in their homes. And they would couch their health messages in the language of human agency and of control over one's destiny—the language of "empowerment," a favorite NGO term.

Both these improvements, obviously, did not represent the fine-tuning of a basically good NGO model. They meant serving a much larger number of clients, with more time spent per client. This required a much larger, cheaper, and therefore generalist workforce, deployed in a significantly more decentralized way. The NGO experience had provided substantial learning to these public sector health reformers, then, but not in a way that confirms the assumed inherent traits of NGOs over against government. And it was the NGOs in this case that relied mainly on specialist rather than generalist staff, at least in comparison to the public program, whose specialists were dwarfed in number by the hundreds of untrained generalists hired by that program.

Evidence from a substantial body of case studies also raises questions about the assumed mirror image of advantages and disadvantages of government and NGOs. Vivian and Maseko's study (1994) of public and NGO agencies engaged in rural development in Zimbabwe shows no consistent differences between them with respect to organizational styles. In many instances, moreover, workers in the field offices of the public agencies were more informed than the NGOs about their clients' problems. Most of the NGOs studied had surprisingly top-down decision-making styles, at least in relation to their rhetoric of consultation with communities. If anything, Vivian concluded, these findings were a result of the small budgets that characterize NGO operation. Truly consultative decisions would have required much more staff time spent in traveling to the numerous dispersed communities and holding meetings with them. This was beyond the realm of possibility for NGOs which, by their very nature, are typically lean organizations with small staffs, few vehicles, and little funding for staff travel expenses. Van Wicklin's study (1987, 1990) of Caribbean NGOs also found a remarkably large number of NGOs with top-down styles of service delivery, despite their bottom-up rhetoric, alongside the truly consultative ones.

In a different vein, Kramer's study (1981) of NGOs in four industrialized countries found that the most innovative were those that were more centralized and bureaucratized, not less. (A similar finding emerged from Jain's much later study of 11 successful developmental organizations in Asia [1994], many of which were NGOs: a key trait that set these organizations off from the less successful, as noted previously, was the extent to which they "standardized" their operations.) Kramer also found that NGOs did better at extending already-existing models of service delivery developed by government or other NGOs to groups unserved, rather than at developing new and innovative ways of delivering service.

Fifteen years after Kramer's study, a review by the British Overseas Development Institute (ODI) of numerous evaluations of donor-financed NGO projects in developing countries came to remarkably similar conclusions. In a generally favorable but balanced report, the reviewers found that "[f]ew of the projects stood out as being particularly innovative or flexible."[13] As with Kramer, the review went on to report that "innovation" among these NGOs often turned out to be "merely" replicating other NGO efforts in areas or countries not yet serviced. The few striking examples of real innovation, moreover, were "frequently the result of years of costly research and experimentation"—certainly not the typical mode of operations, or within the financial reach, of most NGOs. When the review did find cases of the "flexibility" for which NGOs are said to have a comparative advantage, this appeared to be linked to the skills, strengths, and other attributes of these particular NGOs as distinct from the others. This suggests, again, that the assumed "traits" of NGOs are not really inherent to them as a group. When the studies reviewed by ODI did find flexibility, finally, this seemed to be the result of the "small size" of the project. This last finding shows how the comparison of NGOs to government is in certain ways irrelevant, given that government must operate on a much larger scale than NGOs.

Consistent with these reports, Salamon's writings on the role of NGOs in industrialized countries (1987, 1989) have pointed to the analytical difficulty of drawing the boundary between NGOs and government and of characterizing NGOs as independent of government. For example, he has stressed the large impact of government on NGO actions and goal setting through government's financing of NGO service providers, its setting of standards for service delivery, and its monitoring of performance. To capture the sense of this complex relationship between NGOs and government, he baptized NGO service providers—in the title of a widely cited article—as "third-party government" (1987). And he questioned the validity of describing the traits, style, and goals of NGOs as so distinct from government, let alone as government's polar opposite.

James, in a 50-country research project on NGOs, asked why NGOs were prominent in providing services in the same sector in particular countries and not in others. Looking at the education sector, she found that the presence of NGOs in one country or another varied with the religious or linguistic diversity of the country's population (1987, 1989, 1993). In the more religiously or linguistically diverse countries, or regions within countries, NGOs rather than government dominated service provision. This was because the divergent groups could not agree on a uniform standard of service to be delivered by a single provider—namely, government. In more homogeneous countries, public service tended to dominate because common values and traditions allowed for a consensus on the kind of education government should deliver. The presumed "inherent traits" of public as opposed to NGO service, in other words, were not the deciding factor as to whether NGO or public service made more sense in a particular country and sector.

Finally, recent studies in industrialized countries have chronicled numerous cases of improved service delivery in the public sector that involved customization, increased worker commitment, and greater responsiveness to client needs.[14] Many of these cases, of course, represent best practice rather than the norm. But their high visibility in the current thinking about public-sector reform in the United States and other industrialized countries suggests that it is not unreasonable to at least imagine striving toward this kind of service delivery in the public sector.

The cumulative impression of these studies, together with the findings, suggest that if one is looking for a way to characterize NGOs as distinct from governments in the provision of services, the empirical record does not help much. Despite the rhetoric to the contrary, these findings add up to a significant body of evidence against the argument that NGOs have a particular purchase on flexible and client-centric behavior, or that NGOs have desirable traits that are the mirror images of undesirable traits of government. If there are any patterns to be found in this evidence, they run *across* the public-private divide rather than along it. This means that the lessons drawn from the Ceará cases should be able to explain not only why some public agencies or programs do better than others, but why some NGOs do better than others.

More of the problems of government than we think, in conclusion, may actually be resolvable within the public sector itself. Switching to NGO providers, in turn, may not so easily cure the ills now viewed to be inherent in public provision.

Leadership, Inadvertency, and Advice

A final thread that ran through the Ceará cases had to do with the mixed nature of some of these achievements. Some of them were actually inadvertent. Some of the causes of the good results were not perceived. And some of the successes, or their significance, were not noticed. These kinds of lapses are familiar to evaluators of government programs. They crop up as much in tales of visionary leaders and good governments as in those of bad governments. Indeed, the fascinating presence of these lapses in Ceará is why, in part, I was not drawn to perceive that case as unique. I close with this subject in order to return to the matters of leadership and advice brought up in the opening of this book.

Some of the stories told above represented outstanding episodes embedded in otherwise quite pedestrian programs. The state's innovative program to redirect 30 percent of its purchases to small firms and tradesmen is an example. The program existed side by side in the same agencies with older, less impressive programs, and also seemed to have no transforming effect on them. Other achievements took place only in certain local offices of larger programs, the case of agricultural extension to the farmer association of Santana being an example. In yet other cases, the lessons of striking initial successes seemed not to be learned, because they were not repeated. The growth-pole success story of the woodworkers of São João do Aruaru was the most interesting example.

In a similar vein, it would be difficult to attribute some of the favorable impacts of these cases to intention. The profound impact on worker morale of the state's information campaigns and its boasting about its successes in the media are striking examples. Another example is the rich pattern of microregional growth induced by the state's procurement of school desks in the district of São João do Aruaru. This was not foreseen by the program's architects nor completely understood in terms of the lessons it signified for the program's purchases elsewhere in the state.

Even when parts of a program worked quite well, managers or workers did not necessarily understand what they had done right. The successful farmers' association in Santana is an example. Professionals from the state's agricultural agencies repeatedly named Santana as a striking case of small farmers collectively increasing their output and productivity. Yet few seemed to have noticed the unusual relation that Santana had with the state's Extension Service, or its obvious implications for thinking about how to improve that service. Indeed, Ceará's Extension Service, like many others elsewhere, opposed contractual relations with farmers like those of the Santana case and, in general, did not seem interested in moving toward a more client-driven style of organizing service delivery.

By 1992, similarly, few people in state government could remember how the 1987 drought relief program had worked then, their memory obscured by the passing years and similar efforts in response to a subsequent drought in 1990. People in the drought-prone communities remembered vividly, however, and complained that "it hadn't been the same" in subsequent droughts. This was because the state government had lost some of the ground gained in de-clientelizing the program's decisions. Only a handful of persons at middle levels of state government knew, finally, about the successful decentralization to public school principals of decisions about school maintenance, repair, and reconstruction. No one proclaimed these particular successes and, by 1995, the program had died.

These kinds of inadvertent lapses are difficult to notice when one is captivated by the kind of visionary public leadership that appeared in Ceará. Outstanding leadership, after all, seems to be the ultimate in intentionality. It saps the evaluator's ability to see inadvertency, which then makes it difficult to understand the very nature of the successes themselves. When stories of inadvertency like this *are* told, moreover, they are often pointed to as grist for the mill of despair about government: the moral of the story, in these interpretations, is that good government depends on the idiosyncratic appearance of outstanding leaders and is therefore doomed to not last. In revealing the lapses of the Ceará case, I had no such intentions. I was striving, rather, toward a more faithful representation of reality—to show what good government is really like beneath the mantle of hyperbole that comes to envelop it.

To interpret good government as a result of circumstances lying within the control of the typical agency manager or division chief, in sum, poses a particular challenge. It requires that such experiences be unearthed, pored over, and interpreted back accurately to those who invent advice. This will enable inadvertency to be turned into intention the next time around. To draw attention to achievements that governments are not noticing or not repeating, then, is not to dismiss them. To the contrary. It is a way of showing what governments are already capable of doing. This, after all, is how an edifice of good advice should be built.

Notes

Chapter 1. *Introduction*

1. This literature is now referred to as the "new political economy" or, more narrowly, the literature of rational choice and rent-seeking elites. The seminal work with respect to developing countries was Krueger (1974); with respect to government in general, Tullock (1965), Niskanen (1971), and Buchanan et al. (1980). Subsequent important works in this genre include Lal (1983), Colander (1984), Bates (1988), and Gelb et al. (1991). For a recent discussion and the literature cited therein, though mainly with respect to the industrialized countries, see Schwartz (1994). For critiques of the rational choice literature and its application to the thinking about government, see Samuels and Mercuro (1984), Grindle (1991), Fishlow (1991:1735–36), Moore (1989), and Streeten (1993); for critiques without a particular focus on developing countries, see Starr (1988) and Kelman (1988).

2. For reviews of the thinking about public management that has emerged from these concerns, see Hood's (1991) and Nunberg's (1995, 1996) discussions of the New Public Management. For a seminal study from the development literature of public management on the application of some of the concepts of pressures and incentives, see Israel (1987).

3. Williamson (1993) was one of the first to use the term in print and explain what it meant.

4. Some scholars have questioned the empirical evidence for the claim that developing country public sectors are overextended in comparison to other countries. See, for example, Colclough (1983) with respect to sub-Saharan Africa, and Schmitz and Cassiolato (1992) with respect to Brazil. Others argue that the downsizing of the state and the concomitant stripping away of prestige that public service previously had have contributed to an increase in corruption and a decrease in the quality of public services, rather than vice versa. See O'Donnell (1993) for Latin America, and Mkandawire (1995) for Africa.

5. Other researchers have made similar critiques, although often with respect to particular sectors. In a cross-country study of government interventions in the small-enterprise sector, for example, Levy (1994:3) notes the "surprisingly . . . ample documentation of failed attempts at interventions" in contrast to the "remarkably little empirical research" on successful interventions. In a study of Zimbabwe's Green Revolution in maize production, Eicher (1994:25) criticizes "generalized policy prescriptions . . . and standardized institutional models" that are not grounded in country-specific experiences. See also note 7 below.

6. See Nunberg (1995, 1996) for a statement of this particular problem, as well

as an excellent discussion of the experience in various industrialized countries and NICs with the New Public Management and Managerialism. Nunberg also notes that much more is known about best practice in the New Public Management in the industrialized countries and NICs than in developing and transitional countries, where evaluation work is thin and focused narrowly on outputs rather than outcomes and impacts (1996:4). She suggests relying less for an understanding of civil service problems in developing countries "on classic caricatures of the bloated bureaucracy and galloping wage bill syndrome" and more on careful empirical observation (p. 6). She also notes that many of the best-practice public-management reforms recommended to developing countries are "only now being tested" in the advanced countries from which they were taken, and "the jury is still out" on some of their more controversial elements—like widespread contractual employment in core civil services and market mechanisms like performance pay (p. 12). For comments and references on the East Asian models and the interpretation of them, see the next paragraph of the text and notes 9 and 10.

7. See Locke (1995) for an excellent critique of the "national models" perspective in the introduction to his book on Italian political economy. Granovetter (1994), picking up on Locke's critique, also objects to "quite a lot of analysis [that] adds up to saying that country X—Japan, South Korea, Taiwan are examples that come to mind—had something going as *countries*—at this national level—that mightily facilitated development."

8. Two of the earliest studies attempting to draw lessons from this comparison were Sachs (1985) and Fishlow (1989).

9. WB (1993b).

10. For this early evidence, see Amsden (1979), Jones and Sakong (1980), and the two widely read collections of the mid-1980s in which Amsden (1979) was reproduced (Evans et al. [1985] and Bates [1988]). See also Amsden (1989), Wade (1990), and the additional literature on these cases cited in World Bank (1993b). These studies all point to a combination of high intervention and, at the same time, high discipline by government of the institutions to which subsidies are given. Another similarly more plausible interpretation of these and other successful developmental states points to the combination of interventionism, autonomy, and "embeddedness" in the larger societies of which they are a part. See, for example, Evans (1992, 1995) for this argument with respect to developing and newly industrialized countries, and the literature cited therein.

The East Asian Miracle was a valiant attempt to adapt to the findings of this research on the East Asian cases. It characterizes the interventions as "market-friendly"—quite a step forward but still not as faithful to the realities of the cases, or as nuanced, as the studies noted above. For a critical comment in this same vein on the Bank's learning from the East Asian cases, see Moore (1993); see also Wade's interesting account (1996) of the evolution of the position taken by the World Bank in *The East Asian Miracle*—from a somewhat more to a less interventionist interpretation—and how this is revealed in the various drafts that led up to the final version of the report. Also on learning the wrong lesson from the East Asian experiences, see Singh (1995) and Mkandawire (1995).

11. See the excellent recent review of this literature, and citations therein, in

Appelbaum and Batt (1994). I am particularly thankful to Rose Batt for long discussions about the IPWT literature and its shortcomings, and for directing me to several quite useful readings.

12. See Batt (1995, 1996) for an example of the new research on the relevance of the new thinking about high-performance practices to the service industry in the case of telecommunications, as well as a critique of the paucity of IPWT research on services as compared to manufacturing.

13. See, for example, Altshuler and Zegans (1990), Barzelay (1992), Behn (1988, 1991), Osborne and Gaebler (1992), and Levine and Helper (1993).

14. In addition to Appelbaum and Batt (1994), see the seminal work of Piore and Sabel (1984) with respect to the positive effects of a more flexible organization of work involving multitask jobs; on trust between firms and between workers and clients, see Sabel (1992) and the literature cited therein; on shopfloor participation, see Thomas (1989). For a much earlier formulation of similar thinking about the relationship between job flexibility and so on and worker dedication to the job and productivity, see Mayo (1933). For an earlier generation of studies in manufacturing plants that produced findings that also linked increased performance to a more flexible organization of work, see Conant and Kilbridge (1965), Trist (1981), Davis and Taylor (1972:chap. 1), Thompson (1983), and Wood (1989).

With respect to the current popularity of flexible production models in business schools, restructuring corporations and their consultants, and the literature, it should be noted that some researchers have questioned the extent to which the link between more broadly defined jobs and productivity or job satisfaction has been empirically established, and have carried out research attempting to more carefully measure the relationship (Bailey [1992], Berg et al. [1996], Osterman [1994], Huselid [1995], Ichniowski et al. [1995], Batt [1995, 1996], Wever et al. [1996], and the recent special issue of *Industrial Relations,* with an overview article by Ichniowski et al. [1996]). Although these studies confirm the importance of one or more of these high-performance practices, they also indicate that there is still much to be understood through research, and that one cannot assume that these practices elicit greater worker commitment under all circumstances. Some workers, for example, may prefer more routine tasks, which do not require the more taxing demands for creativity that the broadly defined jobs do. As another example, Lincoln and Kalleberg (1992:225–28) found, in a study of U.S. firms, that workers indeed appreciated the greater autonomy, complexity, and skill demands of their jobs in independent small firms. At the same time, they preferred the better fringe benefits, career opportunities, job security, and prestige of working in larger firms, despite the disadvantages of more standardized and mechanized work in these latter firms.

15. See Nishiguchi (1989), Helper (1990), Dore (1987), and Cusumano (1985).

16. Sabel (1997) argues that much of late-twentieth-century social science is "a science of suspicion. It makes the pursuit of self interest and the fear of deception . . . the spring of individual action and the guiding motive of institutional construction." He starts by quoting Talleyrand's statement that "the most suspicious people make the biggest dupes."

17. Lindauer and Nunberg (1994) also note this greater preoccupation with down-

sizing as opposed to other issues of public management, particularly as guided by donors in the countries of sub-Saharan Africa, suggesting that this has to do with the prolonged fiscal crises of many developing countries during the 1980s and early 1990s. Nunberg (1996:6) criticizes pay-and-employment reforms in developing and transitional countries, as part of reform packages supported by the World Bank, for being "one-shot employment cuts—rather than longer-term sustainable rightsizing and performance improvements." She points out an additional problem of downsizing-only that is peculiar to the public sector: the subsequent rehiring of government personnel after a "purge" because of the same political pressures that led to the overexpansion of government in the first place, which she calls the "'bulimic' approach to civil service reform" (p. 6).

18. The most widely cited source for the negative effects on firm productivity of downsizing without instituting complementary practices is a 1993 survey of 531 U.S. companies by Wyatt Company (1993), as cited by Kettl and DiIulio (1995a: 31–34) in advising similar caution with respect to downsizing government in the United States (see also Kettl [1994:51–52] for a similar expression of this caution).

19. These views are presented in greater depth later in this chapter and at the beginning of chapter 2. For references, see notes 36 and 37 of this chapter. See chapter 6 for the fullest discussion of decentralization, local government, and participation.

20. See Kochan et al. (1986), Appelbaum and Batt (1994), United States (1994a, 1994b), Kochan and Osterman (1994), Locke et al. (1995), and Locke and Thelen (1996).

21. For example, although the World Bank commendably devoted its 1995 *World Development Report* exclusively to the subject of workers (1995b), only one of the 18 chapters treats labor unions, of which only a half page discusses public-sector unions explicitly. One of the main background papers commissioned for the report, on labor and economic development, devoted only a two-page section to public-sector unions, which limits itself to describing the "special problems" they pose because their product markets tend to be monopolistic (Pencavel 1995:21–22). Referring to private-sector unions, the *Report* confirms that there are "very few studies of the relationship between trade unions and productivity in low- and middle-income countries" (p. 80). It mentions one exception, an outside study on Malaysia comparing unionized and nonunionized firms in the private sector (Standing 1989), which "provided some evidence that unions can enhance productivity and efficiency" (p. 80), but makes no mention of similar case-study research on public-sector unions.

In another section of the *Report*, and in the same positive vein, the report cites another study of 18 large Brazilian firms (Fleury and Humphrey 1993) in which labor was said to cooperate with management in introducing total quality management and other high-performance practices (p. 83), and then concludes that in many countries, "labor and management get together to consider ways of increasing competitiveness" (p. 83). (Actually the Fleury and Humphrey study reported only that labor resisted these innovations much less than the authors expected, middle managers and supervisors being the most resistant [pp. 35–36]; with respect to unions in particular, moreover, Fleury and Humphrey reported that management actually kept "unions away from discussions of new working practices" [p. 36], and that "managements generally prefer to keep the union out of their factories [which is done] by a combination of persecution of union activitists and attempts to pre-empt union demands by offering wages and conditions which are attractive to workers" [p. 42].) The *Report* cites no similar case-study research on public-sector unions.

22. For example, the only reference to public-sector unions in a World Bank briefing document on Latin America (WB 1995a:A-5) dismisses them as "generally very powerful, put[ting] the producers' interests ahead of those of potential consumers." Another World Bank analysis of Latin America's problems and proposed reforms, in discussing the well-known poor quality of the education sector in many countries, points as a causal factor to teachers having "little motivation" and being "reluctant to use new techniques" and "resistant to becoming accountable to their communities" (Burki and Edwards 1996:21). In a study of Latin American poverty, Lustig (1995:chap. 1) suggests that the maintenance of social spending by Latin American governments after the crisis of the 1980s was probably less the result of government interest in protecting the poor than it was the resistance by "powerful public-sector unions to wage reductions attempted by government" (p. 32). Citing the chapter on Venezuela by Marquez (chap. 11), she reports that "pressure groups organized around unions, and the vocal university and medical personnel lobbies" ensured that wages could not be reduced, "to the detriment of primary education and medical services" (p. 26). The title of a World Bank two-page "development brief" (WB 1995c) on its 1995 *World Development Report* on workers (WB 1995b) announces that unions can be good as well as bad. But the "positive effects" of unions that it cites relate to private-sector unions—namely, some evidence of better results in productivity, equality, and discrimination for unionized as against nonunionized workers in the private sector. Public-sector unions appear, implicitly, mainly under "negative effects," in a subsection entitled "Opposition to Reform," where unions are criticized for "propping up the part of the economy most in need of reform" in India, and as opposing comprehensive reform programs in Brazil and Argentina.

23. Ames (1996:16–18). Among the Northeast states, Ames studied three in depth—Ceará, Maranhão, and Bahia.

24. With respect to such cooperation between public-sector unions and state and local governments in the United States, see Ginsburg (1994) and United States (1994c). For excellent illustrations of how lessons can be drawn from case studies of unions in the private sector that played constructive roles in restructuring and the adoption of high-performance practices, see Piore (1994), Locke and Frost (1994), and Wever et al. (1996) for U.S. cases, and Locke (1994, 1995) for an Italian case.

25. Among them, Denmark, Ireland, Jordan, Israel, El Salvador, Honduras, Nicaragua, Costa Rica, Burundi, and Benin. In area, Ceará is about the size of Portugal, Belgium, and the Netherlands combined. Of Brazil's 26 states or territories, Ceará is the eighth largest in population and the 16th largest in size (based on data from IBGE 1991).

26. The various sources in which these numbers are cited—the press reports on Ceará, speeches by the two governors, government documents, and other nar-

ratives—report quite different numbers for the data used in this paragraph. Many reports, for example, cited the share of personnel expenditures as 140 percent of total state receipts, but this refers only to the percentage of the state sales tax collected, the ICM (Imposto sôbre Circulação de Mercadorias). Although the ICM represented the largest source of internally generated revenue for the state, transfers from the federal government were also significant. Even the figure I report in the text for the total number of workers employed by the state when Jereissati took over (146,000) represents only one of various figures reported, which ranged from 140,000 (Botelho 1994) to 152,000 (Lobo et al. 1993). With respect to this total number for state employees, the discrepancies result from the fact that the record keeping of the state administration was such that it was not possible to determine how many persons were actually employed. (Botelho [1994] reports this, which was also confirmed by a high-level official involved in the reform, who told me that there were "no exact records" of those employed.) Given these discrepancies in the published numbers, I have mostly chosen the data reported by Botelho (1994) because it is the most serious and complete attempt to gather the data and analyze the fiscal experience and reform during these years. The data reported in this paragraph of the text, then, vary somewhat from the reports in the *Economist* and elsewhere. See also Rebouças et al. (1994:31–37).

27. Although much was made in the press and in public statements by the state government of the laying off of thousands of workers, this does not mean that 40,000 workers left the public service. The reduction of the payroll was accomplished by the stopping of payment to those who collected salary checks but never showed up at work, and to those who collected checks for two full-time jobs while working at only one. In addition, the reduction in state expenditures achieved by "dismissal" of ghost workers (11.4% of the reduction of expenditures over the 1987–91 period) was actually less than the reduction achieved by lowering the rate at which worker salaries were adjusted to inflation (13.1%). The latter created much more political difficulty for the new governors than the former, as well as compromising the quality of government service. As often happens when governments try to reduce their workforces, moreover, payments to outside contractors increased markedly, more than doubling in real terms between 1986 and 1990. (The data in this note are from Botelho [1994:73–80].)

28. The better performance of Ceará over the Northeast and Brazil had actually started several years before the advent of the subsequent Jereissati governorship. In fact, the growth rate of that earlier period (8.1% for 1980–86) was significantly higher than the 3.4 percent annual rate of the Jereissati-Gomes period (1987–96). It is important to note, however, that the lower growth of the later period for Ceará reflected a Brazil-wide phenomenon of fiscal crisis and stagnation, starting in the mid-1980s and lasting into the early 1990s. Ceará's growth rate in this later depressed period (1987–93) did not fall quite as much (from 8.1% to 3.4%) as that of the Northeast in general (from 5.4% to –0.04%) or of Brazil (from 2.7% to 0.87%).

I calculated these compound growth rates of output from data kindly supplied by the Ceará State Planning Institute (Instituto de Planejamento do Estado do Ceará/ IPLANCE), which are, in turn, based on data supplied by the Brazilian Institute of Geography and Statistics (Fundação Instituto de Geografia e Estatística/FIBGE) and the Northeast Regional Development Authority (Superintendência de Desenvolvimento do Nordeste/SUDENE). Data for Ceará are based on factor prices; data for the Northeast and Brazil are based on market prices *(preços do mercado)*, strictly comparable data not being available. This should not introduce too much distortion, in that I am drawing on the data only to compare variations between years, and not absolute magnitudes. Three-year moving averages were used for the end points of each period. Thanks to Mônica Amorim for help in obtaining the data and making the calculations. See also Ferreira (1995).

29. See *Newsweek* (1992), *Christian Science Monitor* (Blount 1993), *Washington Post* (Preston 1992), *New York Times* (Brooke 1993a, 1994), and a subsequent article in the *Economist* of London (1995). For examples of reports in the Brazilian press, see *Jornal do Brasil* (1992), the cover story in the weekly newsmagazine *Veja* (1993), and *Gazeta Mercantil* (1995). See also Lobo (1992:10–12).

30. Spain has a population of 39.3 million in comparison to the Northeast's 45 million.

31. A typical example of the portrayal of Northeast Brazil can be found in a *New York Times* article (Brooke 1993b) on the government of the Northeast's smallest state, Alagôas. That state was also home of the first Brazilian president (Fernando Collor) to be impeached (for corruption) in 1992. Collor was governor of Alagôas before becoming president.

32. The Brazilian *município* is the next smallest administrative unit after the state, followed by the *distrito* (district), which is smaller. I use the term *município* throughout, rather than *county* or *city*, because the Brazilian municipal government is responsible for both its main city and rural hinterlands and towns, is usually the seat of the most important city, and has more political and administrative expression than the U.S. county in that it has political and administrative autonomy and holds elections every four years for mayor and city council members. In 1992, the state of Ceará had 178 municípios.

33. The only exception being Fortaleza which, as the state's capital and largest city, already had health services.

34. During the same period, the share of industry grew from 26.8 percent to 35.8 percent (data from Ceará [1995a, 1995b]). Some of this change reflects the expected structural transformation of developing economies from agriculture to industry and services, which had already started in the late 1970s. But much of it reflects the low productivity of agriculture, declining international prices for cotton in the 1980s (the state's traditional export crop), and an infestation by the cotton boll weevil starting in the mid-1980s. Further details on these phenomena are provided in chapter 4.

35. Only shortly before this manuscript went to press did I run across the excellent research of Pankaj Jain (1994, 1996), who studied 11 successful nongovernment and semigovernment organizations (with at least 100 employees) in five Asian countries. One of his findings was just the opposite of mine on flexibility and customization—namely, that the tasks of workers in these successful organizations were highly standardized. (Other findings of his were quite consistent with mine—such as those having to do with the agency's creation of a sense of calling

and "brotherhood" among employees.) Jain's finding of greater standardization among the more successful of such organizations is interesting partly because of its counterintuitiveness with respect to the current debate about NGOs. NGOs, after all, are said to be best at being flexible, not standardized; my finding of greater flexibility among the more successful of government programs, in turn, mirrors Jain's in that it is the opposite of the conventional wisdom that governments do best at standardized work or, less charitably, that they are doomed to behaving in rigidly standardized ways, often inappropriate to the task. (For more discussion on these contrasts, see chap. 6.)

Part of the difference between Jain's and my findings, I would speculate, has to do with the fact that his organizations were non- and semigovernmental. Although large in terms of NGOs (greater than 100 employees), they were still smaller than most government service organizations. Another reason for the contrast between our findings with respect to standardization and flexibility may have to do with the nature of the task. In Jain's most outstanding cases of performance—irrigation, milk processing, bank credit—the activity is more amenable to standardization than are those involving agricultural extension, business extension, and the decentralized public works programs. My preventive health case would seem to be the most amenable to some standardization and hence more like Jain's cases, because of the repeated health messages about breastfeeding, diarrhea prevention and treatment, and so on. If I had read Jain's piece before writing the health case, I may have pointed to the mix of flexibility with standardization as key (together with the greater standardizability of preventive health programs as opposed to the others).

Even with respect to the more standardizable irrigation services, around which some of the most interesting recent thinking about developmental service bureaucracies has emerged (Wade [1988], Moore [1989], Lam [1996], Ostrom [1996], and Evans [1996]), many observers of successful public-sector systems are struggling to understand the exact nature of the combination of standardization and flexibility in public bureaucracies that has been found there. This works together, and is entangled with, the combination of two other sets of seeming opposites—central and local, and state autonomy and embeddedness. To genuinely integrate my findings with those of Jain represents an appealing challenge for my further thinking and field research.

36. For a fuller presentation of these issues, see the first section of chapter 2 and the large middle section of chapter 6 on decentralization. For statements of these views and reviews of the decentralization literature, see Rondinelli (1990), Rondinelli et al. (1984), Cohen and Lee (1993), and Dillinger (1993). For the classic public finance arguments in favor of decentralization, see Musgrave and Musgrave (1984). Peterson (1994) reviews the recent decentralization experience in Latin America, and Affonso and Silva's edited volume (1995) contains various entries on federalism and decentralization in Brazil, as well as in Latin America and other Western industrialized countries. For some cautionary statements about the current enthusiasm for decentralization and participation, see Peterson (1994:11), Oates (1994), Binswanger (1994), Dillinger (1995), Tanzi (1996), Prud'homme (1995), Lustig (1995: 32), and Hommes (1996). (For excellent earlier statements of some of these same concerns, see Montgomery [1979] and Colclough [1983:27–28].) A good number

of these cautionary statements about the decentralization "fever" are written by researchers working for the World Bank, or are found in papers commissioned by the Bank. In proposing that the Bank support research on decentralization within the context of rural development (RD) programs, for example, Binswanger (1994:viii) states that "it is not even possible to state whether greater decentralization . . . is associated with greater success in RD and rural service delivery or not, or whether it results in better targeting of the poor and reduced poverty levels [or] *causes* better RD outcomes." These cautionary statements of researchers, nevertheless, do not seem to have dampened the enthusiasm for decentralization, or the claims made for it, in the kinds of donor publications cited above, including those of the World Bank, or in the approach of these organizations to designing projects and giving advice.

37. See, for example, WB (1991), UNDP (1992, 1995), OECD (1991), and UNCDF (1995).

38. Social investment funds are now referred to commonly as SIFs or, in a more recent variant, as demand-driven social investment funds (DRIFs). For references on SIFs, see chapter 5, notes 12 and 20, and the surrounding text; also, this book's analysis of the employment-creating works program (chap. 3), the public procurement program (chap. 5), and the discussion of decentralization and participation (chap. 6) have findings of relevance to the SIFs.

39. The actual central government of Brazil was a minor actor in most of these programs in relation to state government, except for intergovernment transfers of funds, especially in the case of health. In addition, and as will become apparent later, my argument stresses the importance of there being on the scene *any* strong actor from a higher level of government. This can be a state, regional, or central government, or a strong parastatal. The arguments about central versus local in this text, then, have relevance for unitary governments as well as for federated governments like that of Brazil.

40. In a study of 11 successful development organizations in five Asian countries, for example, Jain (1994) also found that these agencies tended to centralize recruitment and training of field-workers. Jain explains that, on the one hand, agency managers realized the importance of the quality of manpower for services with field-based operations and, on the other hand, "the possibility of error in the selection and grooming process" (p. 1371). In order to train the new entrants, he explains, the organizations "deployed some of their best people and made heavy investments which in itself required centralized training." In another example, scholars looking into the successes of irrigation bureaucracies in Taiwan and South Korea, especially in comparison to India's less impressive performance in this area, have also come up with an explanation that involves the combination of a strong and controlling central bureaucracy together with effective local organizations. (See references at the end of note 35 above.) It is interesting to note that the Taiwanese and South Korean irrigation successes were originally misinterpreted, and continue to be, along the lines of the decentralizationist vision summarized in the text—namely, as examples of the importance, mainly, of local water-user associations in contrast to the "overcentralized" Indian model. See in particular Moore's critique of this misinterpretation (1995).

41. Robert Putnam's research on the factors explaining the presence of good regional governments in some parts of Italy and not others, particularly in the north as against the south, has made a seminal contribution to the view that good civil society leads to good government (Putnam 1993). Putnam's book has been widely read and cited by the development community, including both large international donors and NGOs, many of whom viewed his findings as consistent with their own thinking on government.

42. See, for example, Carvalho et al. (1990), Lobo et al. (1993:10–12), Melo et al. (1994), Rebouças et al. (1994), Botelho (1994), Gondim (1995), Beserra (1994), Ferreira (1995), Parente (1992), and the press reports cited above.

43. See the evaluation reports under my name in the References.

44. Israel (1987) was among the first in the donor community to draw attention to these factors with respect to the issue of "institution building," and has been frequently cited by those writing subsequently in the development literature about these matters.

45. See, for example, Tendler (1982a, 1989).

Chapter 2. *Preventive Health*

1. See Peterson (1994) and Afonso (1993). Navarro (1996:5) reports that between 1988, when the new constitution was enacted, and 1992, the share of total tax revenues collected by the federal government and returned to municipalities increased from 11.4 percent to 17.2 percent.

2. The only exception was Fortaleza which, as the state's capital and most populous city (1.5 million inhabitants), already had health services. See Freedheim (1993) for sources of this and any other unreferenced data in this chapter. For further information on the PAS program, see Freedheim (1994a, 1994b) and McAuliffe and Grangeiro (1994).

3. See Freedheim (1994a). Note 29 of chapter 1 references the various reports on Ceará's accomplishments in the Brazilian and international press, among which the health program figured prominently.

4. See UNICEF (1993) and Brooke (1993a).

5. The drought relief program gave temporary employment to 232,000 persons, of which 6,350 were the health agents of what would soon become the PAS program. The rest were employed in the construction of public works. Based on data from the state Department of Social Action (Secretaria de Ação Social).

6. See McGreevey (1988) for the $US80 per capita figure. Preventive care typically accounts for only a small fraction of curative care costs, even in countries with good preventive care service. The existing system in Brazil, in addition, is heavily biased toward curative care.

7. For some excellent and typically negative pictures of unhappy, self-seeking government workers in health programs in developing countries, see Aitken (1992) and Justice (1986) for Nepal, and the literature cited therein for other countries.

8. For example, see Lobo et al. (1993:11–12), which lauds Brazil's state government for having decentralized ("municipalized") health.

9. WB (1994b). Although this case, along with several others, was widely cir-

culated within and without the World Bank, it was later removed just before final publication because, unlike the other cases, the program was not funded by the World Bank.

10. For references to these views, see notes 36–38 of chapter 1 and the surrounding text, and the note following this one; for a fuller statement of them, see the middle section of chapter 6.

11. To take an example from Ostrom's study (1983) of the decentralization of police services in U.S. cities, the more central headquarters unit does best at running evidence labs, maintaining vehicles, and so on, while the decentralized precinct stations do best at managing police patrol and other activities requiring constant contact with the community—namely, "outreach."

12. The quote is from Peterson (1994:11). For other more cautionary or skeptical views on the current enthusiasm for decentralization, see note 36 of chapter 1.

13. These items varied from one município to the next, covering such things as transportation (bicycles, canoes, donkeys), nutritional supplements, meals for training sessions and other meetings, chlorine for cholera campaigns, and so on.

14. The state did see a certain advantage to the nurse-supervisors being hired by the municípios rather than by the state, somewhat counterbalancing their concern about patronage in hiring. If the Department of Health were to hire the nurse-supervisors, the program's architects reasoned, they (the supervisors) would see their professional futures as lying in the capital city and not in the communities where they worked. The nurse-supervisors did value the jobs in the municípios, but for more positive reasons than the absence of a career ladder to higher-level state jobs, as seen in the following section.

15. Each backpack contained oral rehydration packets, antiseptic cream, iodine, gauze, cotton, adhesive tape, thermometer, soap, comb, scissors to cut hair and fingernails, measuring tape to monitor babies and pregnant women, growth and immunization charts for children under five years, and cards to record information about the households (status of mother's breastfeeding, mother's prenatal care, number of deaths and illnesses in the household, family's access to clean water, and the vaccination status of domestic animals).

16. The vaccines were actually supplied by the federal government, but through the state government.

17. See, for example, Gelb et al. (1991), Hood (1991), and Lindauer and Nunberg (1994). Hood, as do Lindauer and Nunberg, identifies as problematic the "bottomheaviness" of employment in the public sector of developing countries—that is, the high ratio of unskilled, low-wage workers to skilled workers. Correspondingly, they are also concerned with "wage compression"—the low ratio of skilled wages to unskilled wages in the public sector.

18. See, for example, Osterman and Batt (1993). They also point out that this problem appears more in small than large firms, and hence recommend that public training programs focus special attention on developing programs with small firms.

19. Lipsky and Lounds (1976) reviewed the U.S. experience with preventive health and other community programs in the 1960s when, as in Ceará, large numbers of untrained workers from the community were hired—in the U.S. case, in the name

of "maximum feasible participation." They cite the eventual frustration these workers felt at their inability to move upward in the organizations where they worked or to obtain equivalent jobs elsewhere and the hostility they directed toward the very programs that hired them.

20. In the industrialized world, merit hiring and civil service norms for institutions have come to be taken for granted. Some development management experts argue that civil service institutions and the "Weberian" bureaucracies of which they are a part have come under so much criticism in the literature of organizations and management that they are now *too* taken for granted in the world of advice. One of the consequences is that donors are not paying enough attention to the basic and painstaking task in many developing countries of building these institutions from scratch. See, for example, Hood (1991), Blunt (1990:302ff.), and Moore (1992:74).

21. Although the wage for agricultural day labor was sometimes as little as half the minimum, agricultural workers often earned an additional income in kind, depending on their informal arrangements with their employers.

22. For a similar argument about the importance of protection—in this case, with respect to protecting technocrats carrying out macroeconomic policy reforms— see Grindle (1996:chap. 5) and Grindle and Thoumi (1993).

23. The Department of Health also raised financing in this way for the training of existing curative-care personnel in vaccination and oral rehydration therapy; and it successfully lobbied the medical schools operating in the state to require that medical students take courses in preventive health care as a requirement for board certification.

24. By the time of this writing, the first governor had been elected to a second term (1995–98), and both governors were being regarded as future presidential candidates.

25. See, for example, Gondim (1995) and Beserra (1994).

26. In a fascinating analysis of the impacts of public information campaigns and their deliberate use for these purposes, Weiss and Tschirhart (1994) point out how difficult it is to distinguish the "good" from the "bad" aspects of public information campaigns. They also point to the same kinds of positive impacts on users and the public that emerged in this case. They do not, however, include the impact on worker performance discussed here.

27. See Willis's study (1990) of the National Development Bank.

28. The sense of being an elite, of course, can cut both ways. Public services with this sense of eliteness are often criticized for being arrogant. For a recent example from developed countries, see Whitney (1995).

29. See, for example, Vaughan and Walt (1984), Walt (1988), Walt et al. (1990), Gilson et al. (1989), and WHO (1989).

30. Rosabeth Kanter (1982) of the Harvard Business School is one of the most important of those responsible for bringing this concern to prominence. See other works cited by her, as well as a critical review of her position by Fulop and others (1991) in the middle manager literature.

31. This resistance sometimes comes from previously trained paraprofessionals themselves. In a study of a similar program in India, Antia (1985:2259) tells of

how physicians and nurses "took every opportunity to undermine the working of the project." For other mentions of the resistance to the use of paraprofessionals, see Marchione (1984), Cumper and Vaughan (1985), WHO (1989), and Walt et al. (1990).

32. In Brazil and other Latin American countries, *doutor* or *doutora* is a form of address used not only with physicians, but with all those who are set off from others in a hierarchy of education, work, political, and economic power. Some of the health agents themselves, then, also came to be addressed as *doutora* by their clients.

33. In the case of physicians, the lack of resistance can be attributed to two factors. First, the program operated only in rural areas, avoiding the state's largest city, where most physicians were concentrated. It did not, therefore, impinge on their domains as professionals, which were mostly urban. Second, the first director of the Department of Health, who created the program, had previously come together with a group of 200 like-minded public health physicians in the state, and lobbied for the election of the gubernatorial candidate who, after winning the election, appointed him. The program started with the support, then, of an important group of physicians in the state.

34. See, for example, Underwood and Underwood (1981), Bannerman et al. (1983), Heggenhougen (1987), and Heggenhougen and Gilson (1992). Also, Heggenhougen and Shore (1986) cite WHO estimates that traditional medicine is the primary health service for up to 80 percent of the population in rural areas of many countries.

35. See Tendler (1979b) for the case of road maintenance versus road construction. Hirschman (1967:113–17) wrote about this tradeoff in roads earlier, although in the context of arguing that it was not such a bad thing. In explaining the neglect of labor-intensive techniques in construction as opposed to capital-intensive ones, Thomas (1974) also pointed to, among other things, the greater taste for the "wrong" approaches on the part of powerful professionals. In analyzing public works programs in South Asia that were meant to reduce unemployment by using labor-intensive construction techniques, Thomas showed how the lure of capital-intensive approaches to engineers and contractors caused them, through time, to edge out labor-intensive ones. With respect to electric power, I pointed to similar forces operating to cause the neglect of distribution versus generation (Tendler 1968).

36. See, for example, Heggenhougen (1984, 1987) and Berman et al. (1986).

37. The work environment of extension workers changes radically when they are faced with an epidemic of crop disease or pests. Often threatening the agricultural economy of a whole region—its income, employment, and tax base—an epidemic mobilizes high-level concern and support across the public sector. With respect to the reaction of extension services to epidemic infestations of the cotton boll weevil alone, see Hirschman (1981:215), citing Owen (1969:215) for the late-nineteenth-century British colonial administration in Egypt; Baker (1939) for the U.S. Extension Service in the early twentieth century; de Wilde (1967) for francophone West Africa; and Tendler (1993b) for the extension services of Northeast Brazil (including serious infestations of orange tree disease, potato blight, and black bean fungus, as well as the cotton boll weevil).

38. For a review of the large literature on the participatory and empowering aspects of health programs, see the first chapter of Morgan's (1993) study of a participatory preventive health program in Costa Rica.

39. As discussed in the following two chapters, extension experts worry about agents being "pulled away" from their "real" work to do nonessential things like drought relief, arranging for agricultural credit for their clients, or surveys. They also disagree frequently with the idea that extension workers should become "agents of change"—at least in the broader sense—because they (the agents) get themselves and the program in trouble with local elites when they side with small or landless farmers in contesting the power of larger farmers over access to land, credit, and farming inputs subsidized by the state.

40. See, for example, Sabel (1992) and Evans (1992, 1995), and the literature cited therein.

41. The cases of irrigation and water-user associations in South Korea and Taiwan, with their similar combination of trust and monitoring with strong central authority and highly locally embedded workers, have drawn the attention of several scholars. See Wade (1988), Moore (1989, 1995), and Lam (1996). For other such cases and an overview discussion, see the special section of *World Development* edited by Evans (1996).

Chapter 3. *The Emergency Employment Program and Its Unlikely Heroes*

1. In 1988, the closest year for which data were available, the economically active population (EAP) that was male and rural numbered 758,874. As in the other Northeast states, the Ceará emergency program employed only males—with the unusual exception of the 6,113 women employed under the drought relief program as health agents in the first year of the preventive health program, described in the previous chapter. In calculating the percentage of the male EAP employed by the drought relief program, I have excluded the 6,113 jobs for women.

2. For histories of the Northeast droughts and government efforts to mitigate their effects, see Magalhães (1991) and Carvalho (1988). For an excellent earlier history of these efforts in English, see Hirschman (1963).

3. See Magalhães (1991:67). In a study of the employment-creating works programs in various developing countries funded out of U.S. agricultural surpluses (Food for Work), Thomas (1986:26) reports an average 52 percent of total expenditures on labor, with a maximum of 77 percent; von Braun et al. (1992) stipulate at least 60 percent for labor expenditures as desirable for African programs. Studies of the Maharashtra Employment Guarantee Scheme in India (Costa 1978; D'Silva 1983), considered to be one of the best in the world, show how labor intensity varies with the kind of project, with water projects using the largest percentage (80%) and road projects the lowest (55%). More recently, the Maharashtra Scheme has required that at least 60 percent of total costs be spent on unskilled labor (Deolalikar and Gaiha 1996).

4. Issues related to the performance of these services in their capacity as agents of the transformation of agriculture are treated in the following chapter.

5. Respectively, the state Department of Planning (Secretaria de Planejamento/ SEPLAN), Department of Social Action (Secretaria de Ação Social), Department of Agriculture (Secretaria de Agricultura), Department of Roads (Departamento Autónomo de Estradas de Rodagem/DAER—now Departamento de Estradas de Rodagem e Transportes/DERT), Department of Waterworks (Superintendência de Óbras Hidráulicas/SOHIDRA), and Department of Health (Secretaria de Saúde); the state parastatals, the Agricultural Extension Service (Empresa de Extensão Agrícola/EMATERCE—now Emprêsa Cearense de Pesquisa e Extensão Rural/ EMCEP), the State Housing Company (Companhia de Habitação/COHAB), the Ceará State Mining Company (Companhia Estadual de Mineração/CEMINAS— now defunct), and the Industrial Technology Unit (Fundação Núcleo de Tecnologia Industrial do Ceará); and the federal Department of Public Health Campaigns of the Ministry of Health (Superintendência de Campanhas de Saúde Pública/SUCAM) and Federal Railways Company (Rêde Ferroviária Federal, Sociedade Anônima/ RFFSA). The bulk of employment under the 1987 program (93%) fell within the responsibility of only three of these agencies—the Extension Service (44%), the Department of Roads (32%), and the Ceará State Mining Company (17%).

6. In an assessment of the performance of Northeast Brazil in relation to the rest of Brazil during the "lost decade" of stagnation of the 1980s, Gomes points to the emergency employment programs as explaining, in part, why Northeast employment data show lower unemployment rates during this period of generally high unemployment throughout the rest of Brazil (Gomes et al. 1985; Gomes and Vergolino 1994).

Magalhães (1991) provides the data on numbers employed during the drought. The percentage of the economically active population (EAP) employed in the drought relief program was calculated in the following way (based on data from IBGE [1988:chap. 8]). The EAP of Northeast Brazil (urban and rural) was 15.1 million in 1986, the closest year to 1983 for which data were available. The EAP in rural areas was 44 percent of this total, which gives a 6.6 million EAP in rural areas. The percentage impact of the drought relief program on employment is underestimated by this figure in that the denominator includes men and women, and only men (who account for 68% of the EAP) are employed in the employment-creating programs, with rare exceptions.

7. In 1988, Ceará's Extension Service had 1,060 higher-level (university-trained agronomists) and 62 middle-level (agricultural vocational school) staff, in addition to 700 support staff. Data from Ceará (1988).

8. In previous droughts, there were no limits on the number employed per family and all adults over 15 in a particular family might be employed by the program, including children. Together with the clientelistic criteria that also determined the allocation of projects and jobs, this meant that employment was unequally distributed among families and communities. The 1987 drought relief program, in contrast, limited the jobs to one per family so as (1) to distribute the employment more equally across communities; (2) to keep children from being taken out of school; (3) to have enough resources to pay laborers the minimum wage (previous programs had paid less than one-quarter of the minimum wage); and (4) to cope with the relatively smaller amount of funds available from the federal gov-

ernment for the 1987 drought as compared to the 1983 drought (Magalhães [1991] and personal communication from Antônio Rocha Magalhães, Secretary of Planning of Ceará at the time of the 1987 drought). Items 3 and 4 are discussed further in the text below.

9. The 1987 program did allow a few large and labor-intensive projects in cases where large concentrations of unemployed workers already resided in the project area.

10. Thomas (1974) documents this tendency of works programs to become less labor-intensive over time—he calls it "mutation"—because of the pressures of equipment-based contractors, equipment manufacturers and dealers, and professional engineers in public agencies. Tendler (1979b) analyzes the dynamics of a similar phenomenon with respect to road maintenance as compared to road construction—the latter, which is more equipment-intensive, often crowding out the former.

11. These objections were the subject of an article in one of the major Ceará newspapers, *O Povo* (July 27, 1992), with respect to the administration of the emergency program during the subsequent 1991–93 drought.

12. The Department of Agriculture had been feuding for some time with the Department of Planning over which agency should house the state's Agriculture Planning Commission (CEPA/Comissão Estadual de Planejamento Agrícola). CEPA had first been in Agriculture, and then had been transferred to Planning. At the moment of the drought, CEPA was in a somewhat in-between, semiautonomous position. It was later transferred to Planning, a few years after the 1987 drought, confirming the suspicions of Agriculture; subsequently, it was abolished as a separate unit and absorbed into Planning. Given that the Department of Planning was also active in coordinating the drought relief effort, and given the historical distrust of Agriculture for Planning, the lending of the Extension Service to another agency would seem to have exacerbated the problems of interagency coordination during the drought.

13. A parastatal mining company was responsible for the only other significant share of employment generated by the drought relief program—17 percent (masonry, brickwork, mineral extraction, etc.); the Department of Water Resources had responsibility for only two percent, and the agents of the preventive health program for another three percent.

14. See Lipsky (1980) and Wilson (1989) for seminal studies on the subject of "street-level bureaucrats" or frontline workers. Lipsky and Wilson drew on case studies of police, teachers, and welfare workers in the United States.

15. The following works describe how these particular changes manifested themselves in the Northeast and in rural areas: Falcão Neto (1985), Guimarães Neto (1988), Lavaredo and Pereira de Sá (1986), Muda Nordeste (1985), Sales (1988), Santos (1988), and Carvalho (1994). For a work in English on the democratization process of the 1980s in Brazil, see Stepan (1988).

16. See WB (1983) and Tendler (1993a, 1993b) for a description and evaluation of these efforts.

17. Over the past two decades, a large literature has appeared that documents and analyzes this interlinking of markets in labor, credit, land, marketing of crops,

and input acquisition in the rural areas of developing countries, and its effect on agricultural performance and income distribution. For a review of this literature, see Bardhan (1984, 1989).

18. For a sense of the political turmoil that swirled around the job of an extension agent in this kind of context, and the highly political choice sometimes involved in taking seriously the seemingly technical mandate to "work with small farmers," see the studies of programs in particular municípios in Ceará by Costa (1993) and Beserra (1994).

19. One of the earliest documented examples of the difficulty of using local extension agents to de-clientelize programs comes from the United States, and the story of the U.S. Tennessee Valley Authority in the 1930s and 1940s, as told by Selznick (1966).

20. Another example of this blurring between agriculture and "other things" is the processing of credit applications for small farmers, a task that often falls to the extension agents because of disinterest on the part of the banks. Most agricultural extension experts, and many agents themselves, object to the inclusion of this "unrelated" and "paper-pushing" task among the extensionist's chores. Although many agents themselves complain about the paperwork associated with credit processing, however, they at the same time often report that farmers "would not give them the time of day" if they could not deliver credit. As in the case of drought relief, then, extension agents were uniquely suited to play the role of credit intermediary for farmers whose access to the bank was limited or came only with high transaction costs. As with the drought relief, moreover, this "unrelated" task also helped the agents to be effective in their direct agricultural assistance. Cutting out the credit work, although perhaps desirable for other reasons, could also reduce the service's effectiveness on matters of agricultural technique itself.

21. For example, in an otherwise favorable evaluation of an extension program in Kenya, Bindlish and Evenson (1993:sec. 3 and p. 9 of sec. 4) found that supervisors and field-workers pointed to fieldwork-related problems caused by funding shortfalls as constituting the most serious constraints on carrying out their jobs effectively. Among these problems, the worst was delays in reimbursements of claims for expenses incurred in field travel; the second most serious related to unavailability of vehicles and of funds for fuel, maintenance, and repair.

22. As cited by Behn (1988:650–52); this article also appears as chapter 7 in Behn (1991).

23. This resulted not only from poor management of drought relief, but from other factors like labor legislation or improved enforcement of existing legislation, which caused landowners to evict tenant farmers and replace crops with pasture.

24. See Stock (1996) for how this worked in a labor-promoting rural road construction program in Ghana, funded by the World Bank and the International Labour Organisation, and Tendler (1979a) for how it worked in food-for-work earthmoving programs in Bangladesh.

25. In past droughts, the Northeast state governments tended to allow Brazil's double-digit inflation to reduce the total real value of the cumulated wages received by any one worker over the several weeks or even months of relief employment. In past droughts, moreover, many farmers had failed to plant their crops

because, even when the drought ended, they still had to seek outside work in order to subsist, and had neither the time nor the capital to prepare the land and plant.

26. See Ravaillon (1991) and von Braun et al. (1992). These researchers argue that although policy makers often set wages at a higher level in these programs in order to meet certain subsistence needs or standards of "decency," their evidence suggests that the higher wage reduces the effectiveness of the programs at targeting the poorest—namely, those who need jobs most. This happens because (1) by making wage payments that are higher than a "market-clearing" wage, there is more demand for the jobs than there are jobs available, causing a rationing of jobs to those most able to bargain for them—namely, the least poor among the job seekers; and (2), to some extent the flip side of the foregoing, the better-off among the job seekers will, at the lower wage, not seek those jobs, thus reducing the market of job seekers to the poorest and accomplishing targeting more simply, through "self-targeting."

27. A sampling of news items from the bulletins circulated by the GAC in Tauá included the following: the GAC announced it had registered 3,220 people as eligible for drought employment to date; the state mining company had temporarily employed 22 groups of laborers working in the production of 190,000 bricks and 37,000 roofing tiles; a state agency was looking for a piece of land for herb production to employ six to 10 women; various civic groups were distributing 2,400 liters of milk daily to needy families in the municipal seat (including the Women's Union, the Residents' Association, the Methodist Church, the Masons' Service Club, and the Lions' Club); and the municipal government had contracted and was training 15 young people for a house-to-house campaign against malaria and Chagas' disease. These items are taken from two issues of the Tauá bulletin from 1987 and 1988 (Sherlock 1987, 1988).

Chapter 4. *Frontline Workers and Agricultural Productivity*

1. Data on agriculture in this and the following paragraph are based on Ceará (1995a, 1995b).

2. Small landowning farmers are 53 percent of this category, and tenants 47 percent. Tenants encompass sharecroppers (22%), renters (8%), and legally recognized squatters *(ocupantes)* (17%). In 1985, 63 percent of farm establishments were less than 10 hectares (6% of total area), with another 30 percent in the 10- to 100-hectare range (28% of area). Because of the aridity and poor soils of Ceará's agriculture, small farms are usually considered to be within the up to 50-hectare range. Based on data from Ceará (1995a).

3. Based on data from Tendler (1993a:2,65,67, tables 1.1, A3, A5). A fourth project is now being negotiated as of this writing, but considerably scaled down from the previous ones and more along the lines of a demand-driven social investment fund, with no formal role for agricultural extension.

4. See, for example, Homem de Melo (1983), Homem de Melo and Canton (1980), Alves (1988), Jatobá (1993), and Evenson (1989).

5. For a review of the evidence on the high returns to agricultural extension,

see Birkhaeuser *et al.* (1991) and WB (1994). For two recent country case studies (Kenya and Burkina Faso) showing high returns to agricultural extension, see Bindlish and Evenson (1993) and Evenson and Gbetibouo (1993).

6. In 1988, for example, the extension service had 1,060 "higher-level" professionals, in addition to 62 "middle-level." This excludes agricultural professionals in the state Department of Agriculture who, presumably, are concentrated in the state capital. Figures for teachers, health workers, and armed forces personnel are not exactly comparable, because they include personnel working in urban areas, including the state's capital. For the same year, there were 34,370 teachers, 3,439 in health (middle- and higher-level, mostly in urban areas), and 11,112 armed forces personnel (8,571 military police and 2,541 public security). Based on data from Ceará (1988).

7. Agricultural Cooperative of Senador Pompeu (Cooperativa Agropecuária de Senador Pompeu) and Agricultural Cooperative of Piquet Carneiro (Cooperativa Agropecuária de Piquet Carneiro).

8. As seen from the figures in the preceding text, Santana's membership was one-tenth that of each of the two other groups. At least as important, Santana farmers came to own and operate their land collectively, as explained further below, whereas the members of the two other groups were mainly sharecroppers and small-farm owners, working individually on lands that were not contiguous.

9. For an analysis of the exceptions, and their lessons for policy and program design, see Tendler (1993b). The narratives of the many World Bank Supervision reports on the Northeast rural development projects, starting in the late 1970s, also provide evidence of several striking exceptions.

10. See Ruttan (1994), Uphoff (1993), and WB (1993a). For an excellent earlier statement of the argument in favor of nongovernment provision—based on case material from Papua New Guinea and written before this thinking had come so clearly into vogue—see Hulme (1983).

The negative judgments about public-sector extension are grounded in various disappointing experiences with agricultural extension services, many documented in the evaluations of agricultural and rural development projects funded by international donors. See, for example, WB (1987, 1993a, 1994). In a comprehensive review of its support to agricultural extension throughout the world (WB 1994), the World Bank's Department of Operations Evaluation—though echoing the general disappointment about the past performance of public extension services—is less sanguine about the possibility for nonpublic solutions or, at least, argues that no particular model is preferable over another.

11. Tendler (1993).

12. Because sheep and goats consume less pasture than cattle, these smaller livestock count as 0.2 animal units per head, rather than one—in accordance with international conventions.

The previous owner of Santana's lands had grazed 400 head of cattle (no sheep or goats) on 3,000 hectares of land, not including 100 hectares in other uses. Santana grazed 418 cattle, 443 sheep, and 620 goats on 2,870 hectares, not including 230 hectares in other uses.

13. As in other sectors, agency managers give priority to paying personnel when

funds are short, thus skimping on complementary expenditures for other operating costs, let alone for investment. Salary payments themselves are often jeopardized. In Ceará, extension agents frequently received their monthly salary payments only after several weeks or even months of delay. For attendant problems related to agents' field trips, see note 21 of chapter 3. The World Bank (1994) points to the problem of shortfalls in operating funds as one of the major problems afflicting the quality of extension services in developing countries.

14. For other instances in Northeast Brazil, see Tendler (1993b); for instances in Kenya, see Tendler (1989). For Punjab state in India, Tewari (1996:chap. 3, p. 28, note 28) recounts how farmers made payments to public veterinary agents of their own volition, even though their services were offered for free.

15. See the note immediately preceding this one.

16. Field research on the cotton campaign was carried out by Damiani for Ceará (Damiani 1993), and by Tendler for the Northeast in general, part of which was reported in Tendler (1993a).

17. From an annual average of 1.2 million hectares to 0.3 million hectares, and from 200,000 tons to 62,000 tons. Based on data from IBGE (1975–91), Damiani (1993:29). These figures should be taken as rough orders of magnitude because they are not completely consistent with those reported by the state of Ceará (Ceará 1993), and also seem somewhat inconsistent with data reported in IBGE (1994). Figures for 1992–93 are excluded here because they were drought years.

18. For the annual variety, 86,932 hectares were planted and 17,614 harvested; for the perennial variety, 97,729 hectares were planted and 75,815 harvested. See IBGE (1994:T.3.17).

19. Some sources show the share of the new variety as ranging from 33 percent to 38 percent during the 1988–90 period (Ceará 1993), and lands planted with the new variety in 1994 as being 48 percent (IBGE 1994).

20. In the nondrought period (1988–90), lands planted with annual cotton declined from 172,000 hectares to 78,216 hectares (Ceará 1993). Planting went up in 1993 by 11 percent to 86,932 hectares, but only 20 percent or 17,614 hectares were actually harvested because of the drought of that year (IBGE 1994).

21. In contrast to the Northeast cotton-growing areas, the South was a region of small, landowning farmers. Their small holdings excluded the alternative of extensive livestock production or cultivation of cotton in conjunction with livestock grazing and subsistence crops. In addition, the South had always grown annual cotton, since the perennial variety grown in the Northeast flourishes in semi-arid conditions and therefore was never grown in the wetter South. Switching to the more weevil-resistant variety, then, did not involve such a radical change in the agricultural economy of the South as it did in the North. Unlike in the Northeast, finally and for reasons discussed further below in the text, the Southern farmers tended to adopt the entire technical package in its recommended form, including irrigation, and therefore obtained significantly higher yields and profits.

22. See Ranis and Stewart (1987), Hazell and Ramaswamy (1991), and Mellor and Johnston (1984).

23. For a description of the model, written by its originator, Daniel Benor, see Benor and Harrison (1977) and Benor et al. (1984).

24. A recent evaluation of agricultural extension by the Bank (1994), which involved Bank projects funded between 1977 and 1992 and drew from a sample of projects for which post hoc evaluations have been carried out, listed as involving T&V 30 of 33 freestanding extension projects and 26 of 74 projects with other components in addition to extension.

25. There is by now a substantial literature on the T&V experience, from which I cite only a few references, in addition to those of note 23: Feder and Slade (1986a, 1986b), Rivera and Gustafson (1991), Gustafson (1994), WB (1994), and the references in note 27. For the T&V experience in Africa, see the three chapters on T&V in Roberts (1989). For critical views of T&V, see note 26.

26. For critical views of T&V based on field research, see Goodell (1983), Moore (1984), Salmen (1995), Hulme (1992), and a set of exchanges in *Public Administration and Development,* starting with Hulme's critical article and a response by Venkatesan (1993) of the World Bank. More recently, the World Bank's evaluation department carried out an excellent review of the cons of T&V, as well as the pros (1994).

27. See Bindlish and Evenson (1993), Evenson and Gbetibouo (1993), and WB (1993a:9). WB (1994) reviews this evidence, along with similar econometric studies of the impact of agricultural extension on production and productivity.

28. WB (1994:vi). Italics mine.

29. Moore (1984:313). See also Goodell (1983).

30. Exactly 10 years after Moore's critique and suggestion, Jain (1994) found, in a study of 11 successful development organizations in Asia, that building a sense of calling and "brotherhood" among field agents was a common feature, among others, that explained their success and that set them off from similar organizations. (Only some of the organizations provided agricultural extension, but all programs required large field staffs.)

31. The case of drought relief, it should be noted, does partly qualify as a change in authority relations and supervisory styles à la Moore—albeit temporary—because of the takeover of the Extension Service during this period by a new director, his unusual informal contacts with the extension staff, and the role of the drought emergency activities themselves in changing superior-subordinate relations.

32. The above-cited evaluations by Bindlish and Evenson, as well as Evenson and Gbetibouou, used control groups, which would presumably eliminate such factors.

33. The Northern Branch included all states outside the U.S. South. Material on the U.S. case in this and the following paragraph is based on Baker (1939), Rasmussen (1989), and personal communication with Vernon Ruttan.

34. The Southern Branch did not have county farm bureaus. Writing in 1939, Baker actually considered the Southern Branch to have had a better start than the Northern Branch precisely *because* of crop campaigns. The Southern Branch, that is, originated in the first quarter of the twentieth century in a dramatic campaign against the cotton boll weevil. She contrasts the "homogeneous" nature of the cotton-based Southern agriculture, together with the "easiness" of crop campaigns, to the greater heterogeneity of Northern agriculture. As a result, she argues, the evolution of the Northern Branch was more difficult, and each state developed its own particular multifaceted work agenda.

Ironically, I cited this point about homogeneity in an earlier article as evidence of the relative "easiness" of crop campaigns like that mounted against the Northeast's cotton boll weevil, compared with other attempts of governments to disseminate improved agricultural techniques (Tendler 1993b). With respect to the Northeast, however, homogeneity did not prevent the wrong solution from being pressed on farmers. In addition, it was precisely the *assumption* of homogeneity that caused Ceará's boll weevil campaign to be problematic. The way out of the problems was to be found in the heterogeneity among cotton farmers: the weevil-resistant package did make sense for a minority of small, landowning farmers, and not for the majority of large landowners and sharecroppers, suggesting therefore that the minority should have been targeted.

35. For example, the World Bank–funded Northeast Brazil rural development programs noted earlier tried to experiment with a variation on performance contracting in some states: a farmers' association (or other nongovernment entity) was to draw up a contract with the local extension office to work on a particular set of problems for a certain period of time—sometimes even naming the agent it wanted assigned to them. But the state extension services disliked this and similar proposals that would have reorganized their work along more customized and client-driven lines, although they went along with the experiment unwillingly, because of World Bank insistence. Based on field interviews, 1989–90.

Chapter 5. *Small Firms and Large Buyers*

1. SIC is Secretaria de Indústria e Comércio, and SEBRAE is Serviço de Apoio à Micro e Pequenas Empresas.

2. See Schmitz (1982), Mead (1982), Boomgard et al. (1986, 1992), Liedholm and Mead (1987), and Levy (1993).

3. At the time of this research, credit terms were substantially less subsidized than in the past, mainly because loan principal was indexed to inflation, albeit not fully (70–80% of the increase in the price index), and interest rates were 3 to 12 percent annually.

4. This particular case involved a new trading center for 60 leather footwear firms in Ceará's second largest city, Juazeiro do Norte. See Dorado (1993).

5. Both Dorado (1993) and Schmitz (1995) draw attention to traders in the provision of demand-driven assistance to SFs and hence to the importance of supporting trade fairs.

6. See, for example, Best (1990), Dertouzos et al. (1989), Helper (1990, 1991), Sabel (1994), and Watanabe (1983). For the Japanese case, see Nishiguchi (1989), Helper (1990), Dore (1987), and Cusumano (1985).

7. See, for example, Piore and Sabel (1984), Sengenberger and Pyke (1992), Schmitz (1995), Mody (1991), and Humphrey (1995). For the "darker," exploitative potential of large-customer/small-supplier relations, see Harrison (1994), Portes et al. (1989), and Piore and Berger (1980). For a recent review of these literatures and their arguments, see Humphrey and Schmitz (1995), McCormick (1996), and Montoliu (1995).

8. See Cartier and Castañeda (1990), Souza et al. (1990); Perez-Aleman (1992),

Tewari (1994, 1996), and Tendler (1987, 1994). For exceptions to the general lack of interest in demand-driven assistance to small firms as provided by large sophisticated customers in the public or private sectors, see Mead and Kunjeku (1993) and Gierson and Mead (1995) with respect to Zimbabwe, Sabel (1995) with respect to the United States, and Fleury and Humphrey (1993:61) with respect to Brazil.

9. Saxenian (1994).

10. The quoted phrase comes from Porter et al. (1995) who, it should be noted, would not necessarily agree with my arguments for public procurement.

11. See ILO (1972), Watanabe (1971, 1974), and ILO and the Republic of Kenya (1988).

12. See Gopal and Marc (1994), Graham (1994), Fox and Aranda (1996), Haider and Reilly (1994), Mesa Lago (1993), Schmidt and Marc (1994), Stewart and van der Geest (1995), and Glaessner et al. (1995). See also note 38 of chapter 1.

13. Porter et al. (1995:8).

14. Kelley and Watkins (1995) researched this same set of concerns with respect to large defense contractor firms in the United States, and found that a large share of the business of these contractors was with private customers, even during the best years for defense contracting.

15. See Porter et al. (1995) for India and Bates (1995) for the United States.

16. The expression comes from Bates (1995).

17. Sabel (1995) describes a similar iterative problem-solving process as "discursive," a term used by some of the technology-and-business extension centers of the Manufacturing Extension Partnership Program in the United States.

18. The seminal work is Peters and Waterman (1982); see also Best (1990).

19. For developing countries, see Hood (1991), Murray (1992), and Blunt (1990). For the industrialized countries, see Behn (1988), Levine and Helper (1993), Osborne and Gaebler (1992), Altshuler and Zegans (1990), Barzelay (1992), Kettl (1994), and Kettl and DiIulio (1995a, 1995b).

20. In an evaluation of a social investment fund in Honduras, Watson (1994) found that although the construction contractors complied with the program's requirement that they hire "local" labor, they hired locally only for their most unskilled jobs and brought in outside workers already known to them for the skilled work, usually from urban areas. Goodman (1995:iv) made a similar critique for El Salvador, noting that the program used beneficiaries for nonskilled labor in construction activities "rather than training them in skills that might broaden their long-term job prospects."

21. For similar findings, see Gopal and Marc (1994), Biddle and Milor (1994: 55), Souza et al. (1990:53, 70), Stock (1996), and Stock and de Veen (1996).

22. Gopal and Marc (1994:15–16).

23. Souza et al. (1990:52–53, 92).

24. See Adams and von Pischke (1992) for a statement of this critique.

25. Available data did not make it possible to determine whether this commission fully covered the program's costs.

26. Stock (1996), Stock and de Veen (1996), and Gopal and Marc (1994) also stress the importance of an advance payment to SF contractors. Among the cases of social investment funds reviewed by Gopal and Marc in various countries, the

advance was nowhere near the 50 percent of the Ceará case, tending to range between 10 percent and 30 percent.

27. Piore and Sabel (1984) is the seminal work on small-firm clusters, mainly in the United States and Western Europe. For applications to developing countries, see Schmitz (1994).

28. Information on the Sobral case is taken from Dorado (1993), from personal communications with her, and from interviews conducted by Amorim.

29. The quotation is from Havers and Gibson (1994). For expression of this caution by cluster researchers, see Piore and Sabel (1984) and Schmitz (1994). In their more recent works, these researchers have become more interested in the role of government in supporting "embryonic clusters" (the term is from Schmitz's forthcoming work). See Schmitz (1995) and Sabel (1995).

30. For example, Watson (1995) found the same dynamic to be operating in repair and construction of water and sewerage systems in three cities in Brazil, and Tendler found it among contractors who bid for work in a large program of squatter upgrading and sites-and-services projects in South Africa, carried out by the Independent Development Trust (interviews carried out in Durban and Capetown, South Africa in 1993–94, as part of an evaluation of the program).

31. For the education sector in the Brazilian state of São Paulo, see Souza et al. (1990) and Oliveira (1993); for monitoring by village construction-watchers in a CARE program to build road structures in far-flung villages in Bangladesh, see Tendler (1979a).

32. Some time after the field research was carried out on this case, the program was temporarily suspended for more than a year as a result of being challenged in the courts on the grounds that it violated government procurement regulations requiring publicized tender announcements and competitive bidding. I did not incorporate this challenge in the text, because I was waiting for the case to be resolved. The outcome would alter my treatment of the case—namely, whether I would treat the legal challenge and its resolution (if resolved in the state's favor) as a reinforcement of the program's successful strategy of dealing with opposition, or as a sign of failure, weakness, and lack of commitment. Although program advocates alluded vaguely to "the opposition" as the source of the legal challenge, it was not possible to determine, without further research, whether this was the case. Even if political opposition were indeed to explain the challenge, it also was not clear whether this constituted opposition from bypassed suppliers and dealers, or more general opposition to the two politically salient reformist governors. As of this writing, program advocates were predicting resolution of the challenge shortly and favorably, and the state government was resolutely defending what it did.

Chapter 6. *Civil Servants and Civil Society*

1. Other countries with closed systems are Germany, the Netherlands, Korea, and Singapore. My understanding of the mandarin systems and their pitfalls is based on Nunberg's work (1995) on the lessons to be learned by developing countries from civil service reforms in advanced industrialized countries.

2. Hommes (1996:331).

3. For a discussion of this thinking earlier in the book, see the text surrounding notes 36–38 of chapter 1, and references in those notes, as well as notes 10–12 of chapter 2.

4. In chapter 1, note 39, and surrounding text.

5. See, for example, Dillinger (1993) and the chapters on Brazil in the edited volume of Affonso and Silva (1995).

6. UNDP (1995:5).

7. Moore (1995) makes a remarkably parallel point about three-way as against two-way dynamics, in criticizing the interpretation by the development community of the research on successful irrigator associations in Taiwan. He first objects to the popular interpretation of this story as one of "unambiguous, developmentally-positive synergy between state agency and civic action, of the kind [Robert] Putnam celebrates for Italy. . . . [T]he differences between two major levels of the state are such that to use the state-civic distinction is consistently misleading." He then suggests the "need to think instead of *three* levels: central state, IA [irrigation associations staffed by locally recruited government officers], and civic (farmers)" (p. 6) (italics mine).

8. This critique has also been made by others. Binswanger, for example, notes that it is assumed by many that political decentralization will extend representative democracy, but cautions that "[g]iving greater voice to lower-level political institutions . . . [also] run[s] the risk of entrenching further local, often highly unequal, power structures and worsening income inequalities" (1994:6).

9. Jereissati was actually the second candidate to be put up by the group. In the previous election, the CIC group had also decided to put forward a candidate who would carry out their vision of better government, a technocrat from outside the group who seemed to agree with their vision. Although the group succeeded in getting him elected, things did not work out as they had hoped and not much was accomplished in terms of reform.

10. See the examples, and the longer discussion of this issue, in note 24 of chapter 1 and the surrounding text.

11. See Smith and Lipsky (1993), and Salamon (1987, 1989).

12. In addition to the references of the previous note, see Kramer (1981), Tendler (1982b), Lipsky and Smith (1989), Vivian (1994), Vivian and Maseko (1994), and Van Wicklin (1987, 1990).

13. ODI (1996:2). The 11 donor countries that carried out the evaluation of their NGO projects were Australia, Canada, Denmark, European Union, Finland, Germany, the Netherlands, New Zealand, Norway, Sweden, and the United Kingdom. The ODI report does not name the number of evaluations it reviewed, but mentions that each country typically has funded hundreds of NGO projects in different countries over the past 10 to 15 years. The most common approach of each donor was to select a small number of countries (usually between four and nine) in which it funded a fairly large cluster of such projects and then choose a sample of projects for closer scrutiny.

14. Osborne and Gaebler (1992), Kettl (1994), Ginsburg (1994), and Kettl and DiIulio (1995a, 1995b).

References

Adams, Dale W., and J. D. von Pischke (1992). "Microenterprise Credit Programs: Déjà Vu." *World Development* 20 (10): 1463–70.

Affonso, Rui de Britto Álvares, and Pedro Luiz Barros Silva, eds. (1995). *A Federação em Perspectiva—ensaios selecionados.* São Paulo: Fundação do Desenvolvimento Administrativo—FUNDAP.

Afonso, José Roberto R. (1993). "Descentralização Fiscal e Financiamento da Saúde: Algumas Idéias ou Provocações." Texto para Discussão, no. 16, Centro de Estudos de Políticas Públicas, Rio de Janeiro, October.

Aitken, Jean-Marion (1992). "Conflict or Complicity? Different 'Cultures' within a [Health] Bureaucracy in Nepal." Liverpool School of Tropical Medicine.

Altshuler, Alan, and Marc Zegans (1990). "Innovation and Creativity: Comparisons between Public Management and Private Enterprise." *Cities* 7(1): 16–25.

Alves, Eliseu (1988). "The Challenges Facing Rural Extension in Brazil." Translation from the Portuguese, LATAC (Department of Latin America and the Caribbean), 88E0410, World Bank, February 12.

Ames, Barry (1996). "History Matters: The Interaction of Social Structure and Political Events." Part 1, chap. 4 of "Institutions and Politics in Brazil." Draft book manuscript.

Amorim, Mônica Alves (1993). "Lessons on Demand: Order and Progress for Small Firms in Ceará, Brazil." Master's thesis, Department of Urban Studies and Planning, Massachusetts Institute of Technology, May.

———. (1994). "Lessons on Demand." *Technology Review* 96 (1): 30–36.

Amsden, Alice H. (1979). "Taiwan's Economic History: A Case of Etatisme and a Challenge to Dependency Theory." *Modern China* 5 (3): 341–80.

———. (1989). *Asia's Next Giant: South Korea and Late Industrialization.* Oxford: Oxford University Press.

———. (1994). "Why Isn't the Whole World Experimenting with the East Asian Model to Develop? Review of *The East Asian Miracle.*" *World Development* 22(4): 645–54.

Antia, N. H. (1985). "An Alternative Strategy for Health Care? The Mandwa Project." *Economic and Political Weekly* 20(51–52): 2257–60.

Appelbaum, Eileen, and Rosemary Batt (1994). *The New American Workplace: Transforming Work Systems in the United States.* Ithaca: Cornell University Industrial and Labor Relations Press.

Bailey, Thomas, with Donna Merritt (1992). "Discretionary Effort and the Organization of Work: Employee Participation and Work Reform since Hawthorne." Teachers College and Conservation of Human Resources, Columbia University, August.

Baker, Gladys (1939). *The County Agent*. Chicago: University of Chicago Press.

Bannerman, R. H., J. Burto, and Ch'en Wen-Chieh, eds. (1983). *Traditional Medicine and Health Care Coverage: A Reader for Health Administrators and Practitioners*. Geneva: World Health Organization.

Bardhan, Pranab (1984). *Land, Labor and Rural Poverty*. New York: Columbia University Press.

Bardhan, Pranab, ed. (1989). *The Economic Theory of Agrarian Institutions*. Oxford: Oxford University Press.

Barzelay, Michael (1992). *Breaking Through Bureaucracy: A New Vision for Managing in Government*. Berkeley: University of California Press.

Bates, Robert, ed. (1988). *Toward a Political Economy of Development: A Rational Choice Perspective*. Berkeley: University of California Press.

Bates, Timothy (1995). "Why Do Minority Business Development Programs Generate So Little Minority Business Development?" *Economic Development Quarterly* 9 (1): 3–14.

Batt, Rosemary (1995). "Performance and Welfare Effects of Work Restructuring: Evidence from Telecommunications Services." Ph.D. dissertation, Sloan School of Management, Massachusetts Institute of Technology, July 13.

———. (1996). "The Outcomes of Self-directed Teams in Services." *Proceedings of the Forty-eighth Annual Meeting*, Industrial Relations Research Association (IRRA), January 5–7, San Francisco. Madison: IRRA Series.

Behn, Robert D. (1988). "Management by Groping Along." *Journal of Policy Analysis and Management* 7 (3): 643–63.

———. (1991). *Leadership Counts: Lessons for Public Managers from the Massachusetts Welfare, Training, and Employment Program*. Cambridge, Mass.: Harvard University Press.

Bell, David, William Clark, and Vernon W. Ruttan, eds. (1994). *Agriculture, Environment, and Health: Towards Sustainable Development in the 21st Century*. Minneapolis: University of Minnesota Press.

Benor, Daniel, and James Q. Harrison (1977). *Agricultural Extension: The Training and Visit System*. Washington, D.C.: World Bank.

Benor, Daniel, James Q. Harrison, and Michael Baxter (1984). "Agricultural Extension: The Training and Visit System." Washington, D.C.: World Bank.

Berg, Peter, et al. (1996). "The Performance Effects of Modular Production in the Apparel Industry." *Industrial Relations* 35 (no. 3): 356–73.

Berman, Peter, Gwatkin Davidson, and Susan Berger (1986). "Community-based Health Workers: Head Start or False Start towards Health for All?" Technical paper, Population, Health and Nutrition Department, World Bank, Washington, D.C.

Beserra, Bernadete Ramos (1994). "Clientelismo e Modernidade: O Caso do Programa de Reforma Agrária no Governo Tasso Jereissati." *Cadernos de Ciên-*

cias Sociais, Série Estudos e Pesquisa, no. 28. Dissertação de Mestrado. Fortaleza: Núcleo de Estudos e Pesquisas Sociais, Universidade Federal do Ceará.

Best, Michael (1990). *The New Competition*. Cambridge, Mass.: Harvard University Press.

Biddle, W. Jesse, and Vedat Milor (1994). "Institutional Influences on Economic Policy in Turkey: A Three-Industry Comparison." Department of Sociology, The American University, and Department of Sociology, Brown University.

Bindlish, Vishva, and Robert E. Evenson (1993). *Evaluation of the Performance of T&V Extension in Kenya*. Agriculture and Rural Development Series, no. 7. [Also issued as technical paper no. 208, 1993.] Washington, D.C.: World Bank.

Binswanger, Hans (1994). "Decentralization, Fiscal Systems and Rural Development: Description, Measurement and Impact." Request for Research Support Budget Funding, World Bank, September 19.

Birkhaeuser, Dean, Robert E. Evenson, and Gershon Feder (1991). "The Economic Impact of Agricultural Extension: A Review." *Economic Development and Cultural Change* 39 (3): 607–50.

Blount, Jeb (1993). "In Brazil's Ceará State: A Reversal of Fortune." *Christian Science Monitor*, March 18, 8.

Blunt, Peter (1990). "Strategies for Enhancing Organizational Effectiveness in the Third World." *Public Administration and Development* 10: 299–313.

Boomgard, James J., Stephen P. Davies, Steve Haggblade, and Donald C. Mead (1986). "Subsector Analysis: Its Nature, Conduct and Potential Contribution to Small Enterprise Development." MSU International Development Papers, working paper no. 26. East Lansing, Mich.: Department of Agricultural Economics, Michigan State University.

———. (1992). "A Subsector Approach to Small Enterprise Promotion." *World Development* 20 (2): 199–240.

Botelho, Demartone (1994). "Ajuste fiscal e reforma do Estado: o caso do Estado do Ceará, 1987 a 1991." Master's thesis, UFC/CAEN [Universidade Federal do Ceará/Centro de Aperfeiçoamento de Economistas do Nordeste], Fortaleza.

Brooke, James (1993a). "Brazilian State Leads Way in Saving Children." *New York Times*, May 14, A1.

———. (1993b). "Even Brazil Is Shocked: State Is One Family's Fief." *New York Times*, November 12, A3.

———. (1994). "The Flowering of Brazil's Dust Bowl." *New York Times*, April 14, A4.

Buchanan, J. M., Robert D. Tollison, and Gordon Tullock, eds. (1980). *Toward a Theory of the Rent-Seeking Society*. College Station: Texas A & M University Press.

Bucknall, Julia (1993). "Dual Habitats: Reconciling Nature Conservation with the Needs of Low-income Communities in Fortaleza, Brazil." Master's thesis, Department of Urban Studies and Planning, Massachusetts Institute of Technology, June.

Burki, Shahid Javed, and Sebastian Edwards (1996). *Dismantling the Populist State:*

The Unfinished Revolution in Latin America and the Caribbean. World Bank Latin American and Caribbean Studies—Viewpoints. Washington, D.C.: World Bank.

Callado, Antônio (1960). *Os industriais da sêca e os galileus de Pernambuco: aspectos da luta pela reforma agrária do Brasil.* Rio de Janeiro: Editora Civilização Brasileira.

Cartier, William J., and Alberto Castañeda (1990). "Una política de canalización de compras estatales hacia la micro-empresa: Estudio de caso de Manizales, Colombia." Chap. 3 in *Ventas informales: relaciones con el sector moderno.* Santiago, Chile: PME/Programa Mundial de Empleo [World Employment Program]—PREALC/Programa Regional de Empleo para América Latina e el Caribe [Regional Employment Program for Latin America and the Caribbean]—OIT/Organización Internacional de Trabajo [ILO/International Labour Organization].

Carvalho, Otamar de (1988). *A economia política do Nordeste: Secas, irrigação, e desenvolvimento.* Associação Brasileira de Irrigação e Drenagem (ABID). Rio de Janeiro: Editôra Campus, Ltda.

Carvalho, Rejane M. V. A., et al. (1990). "Voto Rural e Movimentos Sociais no Ceará: Sinais de Rupturas nas Formas Tradicionais de Dominação?" Relatório Final. Fortaleza, Ceará: NEPS [Núcleo de Estudos e Pesquisas Sociais], Departamento de Ciências Sociais e Filosofia, Universidade do Ceará, Fortaleza.

Ceará (1988). "Quadro de Cargos por Orgão." Governo do Estado, Secretaria de Administração, September, Fortaleza.

———. (1993). *Anuário Estatístico do Ceará, 1992.* Secretaria do Planejamento e Coordenação/SEPLAN, Fundação de Planejamento do Ceará/IPLANCE. Fortaleza: Fundação Instituto de Planejamento do Ceará/IPLANCE.

———. (1995a). *Anuário Estatístico do Ceará, 1994.* Secretaria do Planejamento e Coordenação/SEPLAN, Fundação de Planejamento do Ceará/IPLANCE. Fortaleza: Fundação Instituto de Planejamento do Ceará/IPLANCE.

———. (1995b). *Plano de Desenvolvimento Sustentável do Ceará, 1995–1998.* Projeto áridas/IPLANCE. Secretaria do Planejamento e Coordenação/SEPLAN, Fundação de Planejamento do Ceará/IPLANCE. Fortaleza: Fundação Instituto de Planejamento do Ceará/IPLANCE.

Cohen, Michael A., and Kyu Sik Lee (1993). "Urban Development Policies in the 1990s: A Summary of World Bank Urban Policy Paper and Research Update." Paper presented at the International Conference on Regional Science in Developing Countries, Beijing, China, October 11–14.

Colander, David C., ed. (1984). *Neoclassical Political Economy: The Analysis of Rent-Seeking and DUP Activities.* Cambridge, Mass.: Ballinger.

Colclough, Christopher (1983). "Are African Governments as Unproductive as the Accelerated Development Report Implies?" *IDS [Institute of Development Studies at Sussex] Bulletin* 14 (1): 24–29.

Conant, Eaton H., and Maurice D. Kilbridge (1965). "An Interdisciplinary Analysis of Job Enlargement: Technology, Costs, and Behavioral Implications." *Industrial and Labor Relations Review* 18 (3): 377–95.

Costa, E. (1978). "An Assessment of the Flows and Benefits Generated by Public Investment in the Employment Guarantee Scheme of Maharashtra." Working paper no. 12. Geneva: International Labour Organisation/World Employment Programme.

Costa, Liduina Farias Almeida da (1993). "Experiências Camponesas e 'Construção de Coletivos.'" *Cadernos de Ciências Sociais, Série Estudos e Pesquisa,* no. 23. Fortaleza, Ceará: Núcleo de Estudos e Pesquisas Sociais, Universidade Federal do Ceará, Mestrado em Sociologia.

Cumper, G., and Patrick Vaughan (1985). "Community Health Aids at the Crossroads." *World Health Forum* 6 (4): 5–7.

Cusumano, Michael (1985). *The Japanese Automobile Industry.* Cambridge, Mass.: Harvard University Press.

Damiani, Octavio (1993). "Learning from Collective Experience: Successful Small Farmer Associations in Northeast Brazil." Master's thesis, Department of Urban Studies and Planning, Massachusetts Institute of Technology, June.

Davis, Luis E., and James C. Taylor (1972). *Design of Jobs.* Santa Monica: Goodyear.

Deolalikar, Anil B., and Raghav Gaiha (1996). "What Determines Female Participation in Rural Public Works? The Case of India's Employment Guarantee Scheme." University of Washington and the University of Delhi, April.

Dertouzos, Michael, Richard Lester, and Robert Solow (1989). *Made in America.* Cambridge, Mass.: MIT.

de Wilde, John C. (1967). *Experiences with Agricultural Development in Tropical Africa.* Baltimore: Johns Hopkins University Press.

Dillinger, William (1993). "Decentralization and Its Implications for Urban Service Delivery." Draft paper, Urban Development Division, Transport, Water and Urban Development Department, Environmentally Sustainable Development Vice Presidency, World Bank, Washington, D.C., October 13.

———. (1995). "Decentralization, Politics and Public Services." Economic Notes, no. 2. Washington, D.C.: Country Department I, Latin America Region, World Bank.

Dorado Banacloche, Silvia (1993). "Fancy Footwork: Policies to Support Small Scale Footwear Enterprises in Ceará, Brazil, in the Light of Best-practice Firms' Strategies." Master's thesis, Department of Urban Studies and Planning, Massachusetts Institute of Technology, June.

Dore, Ronald (1987). *Taking Japan Seriously.* Stanford, Calif.: Stanford University Press.

D'Silva, E. H. (1983). "Effectiveness of Rural Public Works in Labor-surplus Economies: Case of the Maharashtra Employment Guarantee Scheme." Cornell International Agricultural mimeograph, no. 97. Ithaca: Cornell University.

Economist (1991). "Hope from the Northeast." 321 (7736): SS18–20.

———. (1995). "Leading by Example." 335 (7512): SS29, 32.

Eicher, Carl K. (1994). "Zimbabwe's Green Revolution: Preconditions for Replication in Africa." Staff paper no. 94–1, Department of Agricultural Economics, Michigan State University, East Lansing, Mich., January.

Enos, J. (1984). "Government Intervention in the Transfer of Technology: The Case of South Korea." *IDS Bulletin* 15 (2): 26–31.

Evans, Peter (1992). "The State as Problem and Solution: Predation, Embedded Autonomy, and Structural Change." Chap. 3 in *The Politics of Economic Adjustment: International Constraints, Distributive Conflicts, and the State*, ed. Stephan Haggard and Robert R. Kaufman. Princeton: Princeton University Press.

———. (1995). *Embedded Autonomy: States and Industrial Transformation*. Princeton: Princeton University Press.

———. (1996). "Introduction: Development Strategies across the Public-Private Divide," and "Government Action, Social Capital and Development: Reviewing the Evidence on Synergy." *World Development* 24 (6): 1033–37, 1119–32.

Evans, Peter, Dietrich Rueschemeyer, and Theda Skocpol, eds. (1985). *Bringing the State Back In*. New York: Cambridge University Press.

Evenson, Robert E. (1989). "Agricultural Technology and Market Failures: A Review of Issues with Reference to Brazil." Draft paper prepared for the World Bank Conference on Agricultural Development Policies and the Theory of Rural Organization, Yale University, New Haven, Conn., June 14–16.

Evenson, Robert E., and Mathurin Gbetibouo (1993). *An Economic Evaluation of the Impact of the T&V Extension System in Burkina Faso*. Washington, D.C.: Africa Technical Department, Environmentally Sustainable Development Division, World Bank.

Falcão Neto, Joaquim de Arruda, ed. (1985). *Nordeste: eleições*. Recife: Editora Massangana.

Feder, Gershon, and Roger Slade (1986a). "The Impact of Agricultural Extension: The Training and Visit System in India." *The World Bank Research Observer* 1 (2): 139–62.

———. (1986b). "A Comparative Analysis of Some Aspects of the Training and Visit System of Agricultural Extension in India." *The Journal of Development Studies* 22 (2): 407–28.

Ferreira, Assuéro (1995). "O Crescimento Recente da Economia Cearense." *Revista Econômica do Nordeste* 22 (2): 157–203.

Fishlow, Albert (1989). "Latin American Failure Against the Backdrop of Asian Success." *The Annals of the American Academy of Political and Social Science* 505: 117–28.

———. (1990). "The Latin American State." *Journal of Economic Perspectives* 4 (3): 61–74.

———. (1991). "Review of *Handbook of Development Economics*." *Journal of Economic Literature* 29: 1728–37.

Fleury, Alfonso, and John Humphrey (1993). *Human Resources and the Diffusion and Adaptation of New Quality Methods in Brazilian Manufacturing*. IDS Research Report, no. 24. Sussex, England: Institute of Development Studies.

Fox, Jonathan, and Josefina Aranda (1996). "Decentralization and Rural Development in Mexico: Community Participation in Oaxaca's Municipal Funds Program." Monograph Series, 42. San Diego: Center for U.S.-Mexican Studies, University of California at San Diego.

Frankenhoff, John (forthcoming, 1997). "A Few Good Apples—Some Lessons from Successful Educational Systems in Northeast Brazil." Master's thesis, Department of Urban Studies and Planning, Massachusetts Institute of Technology.

Freedheim, Sara Beth (1993). "Why Fewer Bells Toll in Ceará: Success of a Community Health Worker Program in Ceará, Brazil." Master's thesis, Department of Urban Studies and Planning, Massachusetts Institute of Technology, June.

———. (1994a). "Replicating a Successful Health Program Throughout Brazil." Unpublished paper prepared for LA1HR of the World Bank, October.

———. (1994b). "Toward Decentralized Health Care in Ceará, Brazil." Pp. 1–4 in *Decentralization to Local Government in LAC [Latin America and the Caribbean]: Sourcebook on Policies and Practices That Work.* Washington, D.C.: Latin America Technical Department, World Bank.

Fulop, Liz (1991). "Middle Managers: Victims or Vanguards of the Entrepreneurial Movement?" *Journal of Management Studies* 28 (1): 25–44.

Gazeta Mercantil (1995). *Balanço Anual—Ceará, 95/96,* 1 (1). São Paulo: Gazeta Mercantil, S.A.

Gelb, A., J. B. Knight, and R. H. Sabot (1991). "Public Sector Employment, Rent Seeking and Economic Growth." *The Economic Journal* 101 (408): 1186–99.

Ghanem, Hafez, and Michael Walton (1995). "Workers Need Open Markets and Active Governments." *Finance and Development,* pp. 3–6.

Gierson, John P., and Donald C. Mead (1995). "Business Linkage in Zimbabwe: Concept, Practice, and Strategies." Working paper no. 49, GEMINI (Growth and Equity through Microenterprise Investments and Institutions), U.S. Agency for International Development, Bureau for Private Enterprise Office of Small, Micro, and Informal Enterprises, May.

Gilson, Lucy, et al. (1989). "National Community Health Worker Programs: How Can They Be Strengthened?" *Journal of Public Health Policy* 10 (4): 518–32.

Ginsburg, Laura, ed. (1994). *Excellence in Public Service: Case Studies in Labor-Management Innovation.* Washington, D.C.: Public Employee Department, AFL-CIO.

Glaessner, Philip, et al. (1995). "Poverty Alleviation and Social Investment Funds: The Latin American Experience." World Bank Discussion Papers, no. 261. Washington, D.C.: World Bank.

Gomes, Gustavo Maia, Carlos Osório, and José Ferreira Irmão (1985). *Recessão e desemprêgo nas regiões brasileiras.* Com a colaboração da ANPEC e o apoio financeiro do PNPE. Recife: Programa de Pós-Graduação em Economia (PIMES/UFPE).

Gomes, Gustavo Maia, and José Raimundo Oliveira Vergolino (1994). "Macroeconomia do Desenvolvimento do Nordeste: Os Anos 1960–1994 e os Cenários

Para as Próximas Décadas." Versão preliminar, report prepared for Projeto Áridas, September, Recife.

Gondim, Linda M. P. (1995). *Os "Governos das Mudanças" no Ceará: Um Populismo Weberiano?* Caxambú, Minas Gerais: Universidade Federal do Ceará—Programa de Pós-Graduação em Sociologia—Núcleo de Estudos e Pesquisas Sociais.

Goodell, Grace E. (1983). "Improving Administrators' Feedback Concerning Extension, Training and Research Relevance at the Local Level: New Approaches and Findings from South East Asia." *Agricultural Administration* 13: 39–55.

Goodman, Margaret (1995). "*Ex-Post* Evaluation on Social Investment Fund—El Salvador Loan 861/SF-ES." Washington, D.C.: Evaluation Office (EVO), Inter-American Development Bank.

Gopal, Gita, and Alexandre Marc (1994). *Study of Procurement and Disbursement Issues in Projects with Community Participation.* AFTHR Technical Note, no. 17. Washington, D.C.: Advisory Committee on Procurement and Disbursement Issues in Bank-Financed Projects with Community Participation, Technical Department, Africa Region, World Bank.

Graham, Carol (1994). *Safety Nets, Politics, and the Poor: Transitions to Market Economies.* Washington, D.C.: Brookings Institution.

Granovetter, Mark (1994). "Memo on Social Capital and Economic Development." Wequasett Workshop, July 8–9, 1994. Department of Sociology, Northwestern University.

Grindle, Merilee (1991). "The New Political Economy: Positive Economics and Negative Politics." Chap. 3 in *Politics and Policy Making in Developing Countries: Perspectives on the New Political Economy,* ed. Gerald M. Meier. San Francisco: ICS.

———. (1996). *Challenging the State: Crisis and Innovation in Latin America and Africa.* Cambridge: Cambridge University Press.

Grindle, Merilee, and Francisco E. Thoumi (1993). "Muddling Toward Adjustment: The Political Economy of Economic Policy Change in Ecuador." Chap. 4 in *Political and Economic Interactions in Economic Policy Reform,* ed. Robert H. Bates and Anne O. Krueger. Oxford: Basil Blackwell.

Guimarães Neto, Leonardo (1988). "Notas sobre os Impactos Sociais da Evolução Econômica Recente do Nordeste." Recife, August.

Gustafson, Daniel J. (1994). "Developing Sustainable Institutions: Lessons from Cross-case Analysis of 24 Agricultural Extension Programmes." *Public Administration and Development* 14: 121–34.

Haider, Elinor, and Charles Reilly (1994). "Social Emergency and Investment Funds: Ten Country Profiles." Draft paper, Inter-American Foundation, Arlington, Va.

Harrison, Bennett (1994). *Lean and Mean: The Changing Landscape of Corporate Power in the Age of Flexibility.* New York: Basic Books.

Havers, Mark, and Alan Gibson (1994). "Supporting Small Business Membership Organizations." *Development Research Insights for Policy-makers* 14: 4.

[Published by the Overseas Development Administration and the Institute of Development Studies at Sussex.]

Hazell, Peter B. R., and C. Ramaswamy (1991). *The Green Revolution Reconsidered*. Baltimore: Johns Hopkins University Press.

Heggenhougen, Harald Kristian (1984). "Will Primary Health Care Efforts Be Allowed to Succeed?" *Social Science and Medicine* 19: 217–24.

———. (1987). *Community Health Workers: The Tanzania Experience*. Oxford: Oxford University Press.

Heggenhougen, Harald Kristian, and Lucy Gilson (1992). "Perceptions of Efficacy and the Use of Traditional Medicine with Examples from Tanzania." Department of Social Medicine, Harvard University. (Forthcoming in *Culture, Medicine, and Social Custom,* ed. Francis Zimmerman [n.p.: n.d.].)

Heggenhougen, Harald Kristian, and L. Shore (1986). "Cultural Components of Behavioral Epidemiology: Implications for Primary Health Care." *Social Science and Medicine* 22 (11): 1235–45.

Helper, Susan (1990). "Comparative Supplier Relations in the U.S. and Japanese Auto Industries: An Exit/Voice Approach." *Business and Economic History* 19:1–10.

———. (1991). "Strategy and Irreversibility in Supplier Relations: The Case of the U.S. Automobile Industry." *Business History Review* 65 (4): 781–824.

Hirschman, Albert O. (1958). *The Strategy of Economic Development*. New Haven: Yale University Press.

———. (1963). "Brazil's Northeast." Chap. 1 in *Journeys Toward Progress: Studies of Economic Policy-making in Latin America*. New York: Twentieth Century Fund.

———. (1967). *Development Projects Observed*. Washington, D.C.: Brookings Institution.

———. (1981). "Policymaking and Policy Analysis in Latin America—A Return Journey." Chap. 6 in *Essays in Trespassing: Economics to Politics and Beyond*. Cambridge: Cambridge University Press.

Homem de Melo, Fernando (1983). "Instabilidade de renda e estabilização de preços agrícolas." *Pesquisa e Planejamento Econômico* 13 (3): 829–62.

Homem de Melo, Fernando, and Adolpho Walter P. Canton (1980). "Risco na agricultura brasileira: Nordeste 'versus' Sul." *Revista Econômica do Nordeste* 11 (3): 471–83.

Hommes, Rudolf (1996). "Conflicts and Dilemmas of Decentralization." Pp. 331–50 in *Annual World Bank Conference on Development Economics, 1995,* ed. Michael Bruno and Boris Pleskovic. Washington, D.C.: World Bank.

Hood, Christopher (1991). "A Public Management for All Seasons?" *Public Administration* 69 (1): 3–19.

Hulme, David (1983). "Agricultural Extension: Public Service or Private Business?" *Agricultural Administration* 14: 65–79.

———. (1992). "Enhancing Organizational Effectiveness in Developing Countries:

The Training and Visit System Revisited." *Public Administration and Development* 12:433–45.

Humphrey, John, ed. (1995). "Industrial Organization and Manufacturing Competitiveness in Developing Countries." *World Development* 23 (1).

Humphrey, John, and Hubert Schmitz (1995). "Principles for Promoting Clusters and Networks of SMEs." Paper commissioned by Small and Medium Enterprise Branch of UNIDO, mimeo. Sussex, England: Institute of Development Studies.

Huselid, Mark (1995). "The Impact of Human Resource Management Practices on Turnover, Productivity, and Corporate Financial Performance." *Academy of Management Journal* 38 (3): 635–72.

IBGE [Fundação Instituto Brasileiro de Geografia e Estatística] [various years]. *Anuário Estatístico do Brasil*. Secretaria de Planejamento da Presidência da Republica. Rio de Janeiro: IBGE.

Ichniowski, Casey, Kathryn Shaw, and Giovanna Prennushi (1995). "The Effects of Human Resource Management Practices on Productivity." Working Paper Series, no. 5333. Cambridge: National Bureau of Economic Research.

Ichniowski, Casey, Thomas A. Kochan, David Levine, Craig Olson, and George Strauss (1996). "What Works at Work: Overview and Assessment." *Industrial Relations* 35 (3): 299–333.

ILO [International Labour Organisation] (1972). *Employment Incomes, and Equity—A Strategy for Increasing Productive Employment in Kenya*. Geneva: ILO.

ILO, and Republic of Kenya (1988). "A Strategy for Small Enterprise Development in Kenya: Towards the Year 2000."

Israel, Arturo (1987). *Institutional Development: Incentives to Performance*. Baltimore: Johns Hopkins University Press. [Published for the World Bank.]

Jain, Pankaj S. (1994). "Managing for Success: Lessons from Asian Development Programs." *World Development* 22 (9): 1363–77.

———. (1996). "Managing Credit for the Rural Poor: Lessons from the Grameen Bank." *World Development* 24 (1): 79–89.

James, Estelle (1987). "The Public/Private Division of Responsibility for Education: An International Comparison." *Economics of Education Review* 6 (1): 1–14.

———. (1989). "The Private Provision of Public Services: A Comparison of Sweden and Holland." Pp. 31–60 in *The Nonprofit Sector in International Perspective: Studies in Comparative Culture and Policy*, ed. Estelle James. Oxford: Oxford University Press.

———. (1993). "Why Do Different Countries Choose a Different Public-Private Mix of Educational Services?" *The Journal of Human Resources* 28 (3): 571–92.

Jatobá, Jorge (1993). "Rural Poverty in Brazil's Northeast: A Report for the World Bank." Federal University of Pernambuco, October, Recife.

Johnson, Chalmers (1982). *MITI and the Japanese Miracle: The Growth of Industrial Policy, 1929–1975*. Stanford: Stanford University Press.

Jones, Leroy P., and Il Sakong (1980). *Government, Business and Entrepreneurship in Economic Development: The Korean Case. Studies in Modernization of the Korean Republic, 1945–75.* Cambridge, Mass.: Harvard University Press.

Jornal do Brasil (1992). "Ceará vira novo modelo de desenvolvimento." Foco JB. December 11. Pp. 12–13.

Joshi, Anu (forthcoming, 1997). "Policy Reform: The Case of Joint Forest Management in India." Ph.D. dissertation, Department of Urban Studies and Planning, Massachusetts Institute of Technology.

Justice, Judith (1986). *Policies, Plans and People: Culture and Health Development in Nepal.* Berkeley: University of California Press.

Kanter, Rosabeth M. (1982). "The Middle Manager as Innovator." *Harvard Business Review* 60 (4): 95–105.

Kelley, Mary Ellen R., and Todd A. Watkins (1995). "The Myth of the Specialized Military Contractor." *Technology Review* 98 (3): 52–58.

Kelman, Steven (1988). "Why Public Ideas Matter." Pp. 31–54 in *The Power of Public Ideas,* ed. Robert B. Reich. Cambridge, Mass.: Ballinger.

Kettl, Donald (1994). *Reinventing Government: Appraising the National Performance Review: A Report of the Brookings Institution's Center for Public Management,* no. CPM 94–2, Washington, D.C., Brookings Institution, August.

Kettl, Donald F., and John J. DiIulio, Jr. (1995a). *Cutting Government: A Report of the Brookings Institution's Center for Public Management.* Washington, D.C.: Brookings Institution.

———. (1995b). *Inside the Reinvention Machine: Appraising Governmental Reform.* Washington, D.C.: Brookings Institution.

Kochan, Thomas A., Harry Katz, and Robert B. McKersie (1986). *The Transformation of American Industrial Relations.* New York: Basic Books.

Kochan, Thomas A., and Paul Osterman (1994). *The Mutual Gains Enterprise.* Boston: Harvard Business School Press.

Kramer, Ralph M. (1981). *Voluntary Agencies in the Welfare State.* Berkeley: University of California Press.

Krueger, Anne O. (1974). "The Political Economy of a Rent-Seeking Society." *American Economic Review* 64 (4): 291–303.

Lal, Deepak (1985). *The Poverty of "Development Economics."* Cambridge, Mass.: Harvard University Press.

Lam, Wai Fung (1996). "Institutional Design of Public Agencies and Coproduction: A Study of Irrigation Associations in Taiwan." *World Development* 24 (6): 1039–54.

Lavaredo, Antônio, and Constança Pereira de Sá (1986). *Poder e voto: luta política em Pernambuco.* Recife: Editora Massangana.

Levine, David I. (1995). *Reinventing the Workplace: How Business and Employees Can Both Win.* Washington, D.C.: Brookings Institution.

Levine, David, and Susan Helper (1993). "A Quality Policy for America." Organizational Behavior and Industrial Relations working paper no. OBIR-61, April.

Levy, Brian (1993). "Obstacles to Developing Indigenous Small and Medium Enterprises: An Empirical Assessment." *The World Bank Economic Review* 7 (1): 65–83.

———. (1994). "Successful Small and Medium Enterprises and Their Support Systems: A Comparative Analysis of Four Country Studies." Policy Research Department, Finance and Private Sector Development Division, World Bank, Washington, D.C., February 9.

Liedholm, Carl, and Donald Mead (1987). "Small Scale Industries in Developing Countries: Empirical Evidence and Policy Implications." *MSU International Development Papers,* no. 9. East Lansing, Mich.: Department of Agricultural Economics, Michigan State University.

Lincoln, James R., and Arne L. Kalleberg (1992). *Culture, Control, and Commitment: A Study of Work Organization in the United States and Japan.* Cambridge: Cambridge University Press.

Lindauer, David L., and Barbara Nunberg (1994). *Rehabilitating Government: Pay and Employment Reform in Developing Economies.* Washington, D.C.: World Bank.

Lipsky, Michael (1980). *Street Level Bureaucracy: Dilemmas of the Individual in Public Services.* New York: Russell Sage Foundation.

Lipsky, Michael, and Morris Lounds (1976). "Citizen Participation and Health Care: Problems of Government Induced Participation." *Journal of Health Politics, Policy and Law* 1 (1): 86–111.

Lipsky, Michael, and Steven Rathgeb Smith (1989). "Nonprofit Organizations, Government, and the Welfare State." *Political Science Quarterly* 104 (4): 625–49.

Lobo, Thereza (1992). "Decentralization as a Tool for Democratic Consolidation—The Brazilian Challenge." Paper presented at the "Extending the Public Policies Debate in Emerging Democracies" conference, Bellagio, Italy, December 1–3. [Centro de Estudo de Políticas Públicas, Texto para Discussão, no. 4, Rio de Janeiro.]

Lobo, Thereza, et al. (1993). "Descentralização—Cenário Brasileiro Pós-Constituição." Centro de Estudo de Políticas Públicas, Texto para Discussão, no. 18, Rio de Janeiro, August.

Locke, Richard M. (1996). "The Composite Economy: Local Politics and Industrial Change in Contemporary Italy." *Economy and Society* 25(4): 483–510.

———. (1995). *Remaking the Italian Economy.* Ithaca: Cornell University Press.

Locke, Richard M., and Ann C. Frost (1994). "The Paradox of Politics: Local Unions and Workplace Change in the U.S. Steel Industry." MIT IPC Working Paper 94–006WP. Cambridge, Mass.: MIT.

Locke, Richard M., Thomas A. Kochan, and Michael Piore, eds. (1995). *Employment Relations in a Changing World Economy.* Cambridge, Mass.: MIT.

Locke, Richard M., and Kathleen Thelen, eds. (1996). *The Shifting Boundaries of Labor Politics: New Directions for Comparative Research and Theory.* Cambridge, Mass.: MIT.

Lustig, Nora, ed. (1995). *Coping with Austerity: Poverty and Inequality in Latin America.* Washington, D.C.: Brookings Institution.

Magalhães, Antônio Rocha, ed. (1991). *Respostas Governamentais às Secas: A Experiência no Nordeste.* Fortaleza: Imprensa Oficial do Estado.

Marchione, T. (1984). "Evaluating Primary Health Care and Nutrition Programs in the Context of National Development." *Social Science and Medicine* 19 (3): 225–35.

Mayo, E. (1933). *The Human Problem of an Industrial Civilisation.* London: Macmillan.

McAuliffe, J., and G. Grangeiro (1994). "Análise Qualitativa do Programa de Agentes de Saúde do Ceará: Relatório Final." ISDS (Instituto de Saúde e Desenvolvimento Social), Fortaleza, August.

McCormick, Lynn (1996). "A Life-cycle Model of Manufacturing Networks and Chicago's Metalworking Industry," Ph.D. dissertation, Department of Urban Studies and Planning, Massachusetts Institute of Technology, June.

McGreevey, William (1988). *Brazil Public Spending on Social Programs: Issues and Options Report,* no. 7086-BR, Washington, D.C., World Bank, May 27.

Mead, Donald C. (1982). "Small Industries in Egypt: An Exploration of the Economics of Small Furniture Producers." *International Journal of Middle East Studies* 14: 159–71.

Mead, Donald C., and Petr Kunjeku (1993). "Business Linkages and Enterprise Development in Zimbabwe." Zimbabwe: Confederation of Zimbabwe Publishers.

Mellor, John W., and Bruce F. Johnston (1994). "The World Food Equation: Interrelation among Development, Employment, and Food Consumption." *Journal of Economic Literature* 22:531–56.

Melo, Marcus André B. C. de, Phil Gunn, Linda Gondim, and Catia Lubambo (1994). *Elites empresariais, processos de modernização e políticas públicas: o caso do Ceará.* Recife: IDEC [Instituto de Estudos da Cidadania].

Mesa Lago, Carmelo (1993). "Safety Nets and Social Funds to Alleviate Poverty: Performance, Problems, and Policy Options." Issues note for UNCTAD Standing Committee on Poverty Alleviation, Geneva, October.

Mkandawire, Thandika (1995). "The Adjustment Debacle and Democratic Consolidation in Africa." Paper presented at the Al-Atul conference on "Winners and Losers in Neo-Liberal Experiments: Towards More Equitable Development," Princeton University, December 8–9.

Mody, Ashoka (1991). "Learning through Alliances." Washington, D.C.: World Bank.

Montgomery, John D. (1979). "The Populist Front in Rural Development: Or Shall We Eliminate the Bureaucrats and Get On with The Job?" *Public Administration Review* 39 (1): 58–65.

Montoliu, Marisela (1995). "Blessing or Curse: Oil Riches, Economic Policy, and the Organizational Change of Venezuela's Plastics Manufacturing, 1983–1992." Ph.D. dissertation, Department of Urban Studies and Planning, Massachusetts Institute of Technology, June.

Moore, Mick (1984). "Institutional Development, the World Bank, and India's New Agricultural Extension Programme." *The Journal of Development Studies* 20 (4): 303–17.

———. (1989). "The Fruits and Fallacies of Neoliberalism: The Case of Irrigation Policy." *World Development* 17 (11): 1733–50.

———. (1992). "Competition and Pluralism in Public Bureaucracies." *IDS [Institute of Development Studies] Bulletin* 23 (4): 65–77.

———. (1993). "Declining to Learn from the East? The World Bank on 'Governance and Development.'" *IDS Bulletin* 24 (1): 39–50.

———. (1995). "Discussant's Comments on Paper by Lam Wai Fung 'Institutional Design and Collective Actions: A Study of Irrigation Associations in Taiwan.'" Paper presented at the "Government Action, Social Capital Formation, and Third World Development" conference, sponsored by the Economic Development Working Group, Social Capital and Public Affairs Project, American Academy of Arts and Sciences, Cambridge, Mass., May 5–6.

Morgan, Lynn M. (1993). *Community Participation in Health: The Politics of Primary Health Care in Costa Rica.* Cambridge: Cambridge University Press.

Muda Nordeste (1985). *Projeto Nordeste: Programa de Apoio ao Pequeno Produtor Rural—Debate Regional.* Convênio SUDENE/Clube de Engenharia de Pernambuco. Recife, Pernambuco: Movimento Muda Nordeste.

Murray, Robin (1992). "Introduction" and "Towards a Flexible State." In *New Forms of Public Administration,* ed. Robin Murray, *IDS [Institute of Development Studies] Bulletin* 23 (4): 1–5, 78–88.

Murillo, Maria Victoria (1996). "Latin American Unions and the Reform of Social Service Delivery Systems: Institutional Contraints and Policy Choice." Paper prepared for the Inter-American Development Bank Seminar on "Latin American Unions and the Reform of Social Service Delivery Systems."

Musgrave, Richard A., and Peggy B. Musgrave (1984). *Public Finance in Theory and Practice.* New York: McGraw Hill.

Navarro, Zander (1996). "'Participatory Budgeting'—The Case of Porto Alegre (Brazil)." Paper presented at the "Regional Workshop: Decentralization in Latin America—Innovations and Policy Implications," Caracas, May 23–24.

Newsweek (1992). "Working for the People: A Reformist State Government in Brazil." International edition. June 15, 17.

Nishiguchi, Toshihiro (1989). "Strategic Dualism: An Alternative in Industrial Societies." Ph.D. dissertation, Nuffield College.

Niskanen, William A. (1971). *Bureaucracy and Representative Government.* Chicago: Aldine.

Nunberg, Barbara (1995). *Managing the Civil Service: Reform Lessons from Advanced Industrialized Countries.* World Bank Discussion Papers, no. 204. Washington, D.C.: World Bank.

———. (1996). "Re-thinking Civil Service Reform: An Agenda for Smart Government." Draft, July 17.

Oates, Wallace (1994). "The Potentials and Perils of Fiscal Decentralization." unpublished ms, Department of Economics, University of Maryland, August.

ODI [Overseas Development Institute] (1996). "The Impact of NGO Development Projects." *ODI Briefing Paper* 2: 1–4.

O'Donnell, Guillermo (1993). "On the State, Democratization and Some Conceptual Problems: A Latin American View with Glances at Some Postcommunist Countries." *World Development* 21 (8): 1355–69.

OECD [Organisation for Economic Co-operation and Development] (1991). *Urban Infrastructure: Finance and Management*. Paris: OECD.

Oliveira, João Batista (1993). "Politics and Rationality in ED Reform." Washington, D.C.: World Bank.

Osborne, David, and Ted Gaebler (1992). *Reinventing Government: How the Entrepreneurial Spirit Is Transforming the Public Sector*. Reading, Mass.: Addison-Wesley.

Osterman, Paul (1994). "How Common Is Workplace Transformation and How Can We Explain Who Adopts It? Results from a National Survey." *Industrial and Labor Relations Review* 47 (2): 173–88.

Osterman, Paul, and Rosemary Batt (1993). "Employer-Centered Training for International Competitiveness: Lessons from State Programs." *Journal of Policy Analysis and Management* 12 (3): 456–77.

Ostrom, Elinor (1983). "A Public Choice Approach to Metropolitan Institutions: Structure, Incentives, and Performance." *Social Science Journal* 20: 79–96.

———. (1996). "Crossing the Great Divide: Coproduction, Synergy and Development." *World Development* 24 (6).

Owen, E. R. J. (1969). *Cotton and the Egyptian Economy, 1820–1914*. London: Oxford University Press.

Pacheco, Regina Silvia [n.d.]. "Gestão Metropolitana no Brasil: Arranjos Institucionais em Debate." Mimeo.

Parente, Josênio C. (1992). "Construindo a Hegemonia Burguesa: As Eleições Municipais de 1988 no Ceará." *Cadernos de Ciências Sociais, Série Estudos e Pesquisa*, no. 21. Fortaleza: Universidade Federal do Ceará/Núcleo de Estudos e Pesquisas Sociais/Mestrado em Sociologia.

Pencavel, John (1995). *The Role of Labor Unions in Fostering Economic Development*. Policy Research working paper, no. 1469. Washington, D.C.: Office of the Vice President, Development Economics, World Bank.

Perez-Aleman, Paola (1992). "Small Industry and State Policy in Nicaragua: Lessons from the Sandinista Experience." First-year doctoral paper, Department of Urban Studies and Planning, Massachusetts Institute of Technology.

Peters, Thomas J., and Robert H. Waterman, Jr. (1982). *In Search of Excellence*. New York: Harper & Row.

Peterson, George E. (1994). "Decentralization Experience in Latin America: An Overview of Lessons and Issues." Urban Institute, Washington, D.C., May.

Piore, Michael (1994). "Unions: A Reorientation to Survive." Chap. 19 in *Labor*

Economics and Industrial Relations: Markets and Institutions, ed. Clark Kerr and Paul Staudohar. Cambridge, Mass.: Harvard University Press.

Piore, Michael, and Suzanne Berger, eds. (1980). *Dualism and Discontinuity in Industrial Societies.* Cambridge: Cambridge University Press.

Piore, Michael J., and Charles F. Sabel (1984). *The Second Industrial Divide: Possibilities for Prosperity.* New York: Basic Books.

Porter, Michael E., Pankaj Ghemawat, and U. Srinivasa Rangan (1995). "A New Vision for Indian Economic Development." Working paper draft, Harvard Business School, Cambridge, Mass., March 9.

Portes, Alejandro, Manuel Castells, and Lauren A. Benton (1989). *The Informal Economy: Studies in Advanced and Less Developed Countries.* Baltimore: Johns Hopkins University Press.

O Povo [Fortaleza] (1992). July 27.

Preston, Julia (1992). "Brazil's Battle to Save Babies' Lives: Malnutrition and Preventable Childhood Diseases Are Being Conquered at the Grass Roots." *Washington Post,* February 25.

Prud'homme, Rémy (1995). "The Dangers of Decentralization." *World Bank Research Observer* 10 (2): 201–20.

Putnam, Robert D. (1993). *Making Democracy Work: Civic Traditions in Modern Italy.* Princeton: Princeton University Press.

Ranis, Gustav, and Frances Stewart (1987). "Rural Linkages in the Philippines and Taiwan." Pp. 140–91 in *Macro-policies for Appropriate Technology in Developing Countries,* ed. Frances Stewart. Boulder: Westview.

Rasmussen, Wayne (1989). *Taking the University to the People: Seventy-five Years of Cooperative Extension.* Ames: Iowa State University Press.

Ravallion, Martin (1991). "Reaching the Rural Poor Through Public Employment: Arguments, Evidence, and Lessons from South Asia." *World Bank Observer* 6 (2): 153–75.

Rebouças, Osmundo, Cláudio Ferreira Lima, Flávio Paiva, and João de Paula Monteiro (1994). *Gestão Compartilhada: O Pacto do Ceará.* Rio de Janeiro: Qualitymark Editora Ltda.

Rivera, William M., and Daniel J. Gustafson, eds. (1991). *Agricultural Extension: Worldwide Institutional Evolution and Forces for Change.* Amsterdam: Elsevier.

Roberts, Nigel, ed. (1989). *Agricultural Extension in Africa.* Washington, D.C.: World Bank.

Rondinelli, Dennis A. (1990). *Decentralizing Urban Development Programs: A Framework for Analyzing Policy.* Policy & Research Series (P&RS), no. PN-ABD-906. Washington, D.C.: Office of Housing and Urban Programs, U.S. Agency for International Development.

Rondinelli, Dennis, John R. Nellis, and G. Shabbir Cheema (1984). *Decentralization in Developing Countries: A Review of Recent Experience.* World Bank Staff working paper no. 581. Management and Development Series, no. 8. Washington, D.C.: World Bank.

Ruttan, Vernon W. (1994). "Global Research Systems for Sustainable Development: Health, Agriculture, and Environment." Chap. 14 in *Agriculture, Environment, and Health: Towards Sustainable Development in the 21st Century*, ed. Vernon W. Ruttan. Minneapolis: University of Minnesota Press.

Sabel, Charles F. (1992). "Studied Trust: Building New Forms of Cooperation in a Volatile Economy." Chap. 8 in *Industrial Districts and Local Economy Regeneration*, ed. Frank Pyke and Werner Sengenberger. Geneva: International Institute of Labor Studies.

———. (1994). "Learning by Monitoring: The Institutions of Economic Development." Pp. 231–74 in *Rethinking the Development Experience: Essays Provoked by the Work of Albert Hirschman*, ed. Lloyd Rodwin and Don Schön. Washington, D.C.: Brookings Institution.

———. (1995). "Bootstrapping Reform: Rebuilding Firms, the Welfare State, and Unions." *Politics and Society* 23 (1): 5–48.

———. (1997). "Constitutional Ordering in Historical Context." Chap. 2 in *Contemporary Capitalism: The Embeddedness of Institutions*, ed. Robert Boyer and Joseph Rogers. New York: Cambridge University Press.

Sachs, Jeffrey D. (1985). "External Debt and Macroeconomic Performance in Latin America and East Asia." *Brookings Papers on Economic Activity*, no. 2. Washington, D.C.: Brookings Institution.

Salamon, Lester M. (1987). "Of Market Failure, Voluntary Failure, and Third-Party Government: Toward a Theory of Government-Nonprofit Relations in the Modern Welfare State." Pp. 29–49 in *Shifting the Debate: Public/Private Sector Relations in the Modern Welfare State*, ed. Susan A. Ostrander and Stuart Langton. New Brunswick, N.J.: Transaction Books.

———. (1989). "The Changing Tools of Government." Pp. 3–49 in *Beyond Privatization: The Tools of Government Action*, ed. Lester M. Salamon. Washington, D.C.: Urban Institute Press.

Sales, Teresa (1988). "Movimentos sociais no campo frente à ação do Estado." Grupo de Trabalho: Estado e Agricultura. Trabalho apresentado ao XII Encontro Anual da ANPOCS. Águas de São Pedro.

Salmen, Lawrence (1995). "Listening to Farmers: Agricultural Extension in Senegal." Draft paper, Social Policy and Resettlement Division, World Bank, Washington, D.C., March 15.

Samuels, Warren J., and Nicholas Mercuro (1984). "A Critique of Rent-Seeking Theory." In *Neoclassical Political Economy: The Analysis of Rent-Seeking and DUP Activities*, ed. David C. Colander. Cambridge, Mass.: Ballinger.

Santos, José Maciel dos (1988). "Política Rural e Trabalho Assalariado: Uma análise a partir de POLONORDESTE." In *Congresso da Associação Nacional de Pós-Graduação em Economia (ANPEC)*. Belo Horizonte: ANPEC.

Saxenian, Anna Lee (1994). *Regional Advantage: Culture and Competition in Silicon Valley and Route 128*. Cambridge, Mass.: Harvard University Press.

Schmidt, Mary, and Alexandre Marc (1994). "Participation and Social Funds." Workshop on Participatory Development. Washington, D.C.: World Bank.

Schmitz, Hubert (1982). "Growth Constraints on Small-scale Manufacturing in Developing Countries: A Critical Review." *World Development* 10 (6): 429–50.

———. (1994). "Collective Efficiency: Growth Path for Small-Scale Industry." *The Journal of Development Studies* 31 (4): 1–38.

———. (1995). "Small Shoemakers and Fordist Giants: Tale of a Supercluster." *World Development* 23 (1): 9–28.

Schmitz, Hubert, and José Cassiolato, eds. (1992). *Hi-Tech for Industrial Development: Lessons from the Brazilian Experience in Electronics and Automation.* London: Routledge.

Schorr, Lisbeth B. (1988). "The Care and Education of Young Children: Inseparable Combination." Pp. 179–214 in *Within Our Reach: Breaking the Cycle of Disadvantage,* by Lisbeth B. Schorr with Daniel Schorr. New York: Doubleday/Anchor Books.

Schwartz, Herman M. (1994). "Public Choice Theory and Public Choices: Bureaucrats and State Reorganization in Australia, Denmark, New Zealand, and Sweden in the 1980s." *Administration and Society* 26 (1): 48–77.

Selznick, Philip (1966). *TVA and the Grass Roots: A Study in the Sociology of Formal Organization.* New York: Harper Torchbooks.

Sengenberger, Werner, and Frank Pyke (1992). "Industrial Districts and Local Economic Regeneration: Research and Policy Issues." Chap. 1 in *Industrial Districts and Local Economy Regeneration,* ed. Frank Pyke and Werner Sengenberger. Geneva: International Institute of Labor Studies.

Sherlock, Jorge Hauser (1987). *Boletim Informativo* (1, 2, and 3). Tauá, Ceará.

———. (1988). *Boletim Informativo* (4). Tauá, Ceará.

Singh, Ajit (1995). "Openness and the Market Friendly Approach to Development: Learning the Right Lessons from Development Experience." *World Development* 22 (12): 1811–23.

Smith, Steven Rathgeb, and Michael Lipsky (1993). *Nonprofits for Hire: The Welfare State in the Age of Contracting.* Cambridge, Mass.: Harvard University Press.

Souza, Paulo Renato, et al. (1990). "Efecto de la descentralización del gasto público sobre el empleo y los ingresos en el sector informal urbano." Chap. 2 in *Ventas informales: relaciones con el sector moderno.* Santiago, Chile: PME/ Programa Mundial de Empleo [World Employment Program]—PREALC/ Programa Regional de Empleo para América Latina e el Caribe [Regional Employment Program for Latin America and the Caribbean]—OIT/Organización Internacional de Trabajo [ILO/International Labour Organisation].

Standing, Guy (1989). "The Growth of External Labour Flexibility in a Nascent NIC: A Malaysian Labour Flexibility Survey." ILO Working Paper, no. 35. Geneva: International Labour Organisation.

Starr, Paul (1988). "The Meaning of Privatization." *Yale Law and Policy Review* 6: 6–41.

Stepan, Alfred, ed. (1988). *Democratizing Brazil: Problems of Transition and Consolidation.* London: Oxford University Press.

Stewart, Frances, and Willem van der Geest (1995). "Adjustment and Social Funds:

Political Panacea or Effective Poverty Reduction?" Chap. 5 in *Adjustment and Poverty: Options and Choices,* ed. Frances Stewart. London: Routledge.

Stock, Elisabeth (1996). "The Problems Facing Labor-based Road Programs and What to Do about Them: Evidence from Ghana." Sub-Saharan Africa Transport Policy Program working paper, no. 24. Washington, D.C.: Environmentally Sustainable Development Division, Africa Technical Department, World Bank.

Stock, Elisabeth, and Jan de Veen (1996). "Expanding Labor-based Methods in Road Programs: Approach Paper." Sub-Saharan Africa Transport Policy Program working paper, no. 18. Washington, D.C.: Environmentally Sustainable Development Division, Africa Technical Department, World Bank.

Streeten, Paul (1993). "Markets and States against Minimalism." *World Development* 21 (8): 1281–98.

Tanzi, Vito (1996). "Fiscal Federalism and Decentralization: A Review of Some Efficiency and Macroeconomic Aspects." Pp. 295–312 in *Annual World Bank Conference on Development Economics, 1995,* ed. Michael Bruno and Boris Pleskovic. Washington, D.C.: World Bank.

Tendler, Judith (1968). *Electric Power in Brazil: Entrepreneurship in the Public Sector.* Cambridge, Mass.: Harvard University Press.

————. (1976). *Inter-country Evaluation of Small Farmer Organizations.* Program Evaluation Study of the Agency for International Development, Latin America Bureau. Washington, D.C.: U.S. Agency for International Development.

————. (1977). "Case Study of a World Bank Livestock Program—Honduras." For the World Bank, April.

————. (1979a). "Rural Works Programs in Bangladesh: Community, Technology and Graft." Paper prepared for the Transport Department of the World Bank, June.

————. (1979b). *New Directions in Rural Roads.* U.S. Agency for International Development Program Evaluation Discussion Paper, no. 2, U.S. Agency for International Development, Washington, D.C., March.

————. (1980). *New Light on Rural Electrification: The Evidence from Bolivia.* Project on Managing Decentralization, Institute of International Studies, University of California–Berkeley, Publication no. R80.5, September.

————. (1981). "Fitting the Foundation Style: The Case of Rural Credit." For the Inter-American Foundation, February.

————. (1982a). *Rural Projects Through Urban Eyes: An Interpretation of the World Bank's New-style Rural Development Projects.* Staff Working Paper No. 532. Washington, D.C.: World Bank.

————. (1982b). *Turning Private Voluntary Organizations into Development Agencies: Questions for Evaluation.* AID Program Evaluation Discussion Paper, no. 12. Washington, D.C.: U.S. Agency for International Development.

————. (1983a). *Ventures in the Informal Sector, and How They Worked Out in Brazil.* AID Evaluation Special Study, no. 12. Washington, D.C.: U.S. Agency for International Development.

————. (1983b). *What to Think about Cooperatives: A Guide from Bolivia.* Rosslyn, Va.: Inter-American Foundation.

————. (1984). "Captive Donors and Captivating Clients: A Nicaraguan Saga." For the Inter-American Foundation, December.

————. (1987). *What Ever Happened to Poverty Alleviation?* Report prepared for the Mid-decade Review of the Ford Foundation's Programs on Livelihood, Employment and Income Generation, March. [A published summarized version appears in Tendler (1989).]

————. (1989). "What Ever Happened to Poverty Alleviation?" *World Development* 17 (7): 1033–44.

————. (1993a). *New Lessons from Old Projects: The Workings of Rural Development in Northeast Brazil.* Washington, D.C.: World Bank.

————. (1993b). "Tales of Dissemination in Small-farm Agriculture: Lessons for Institution Builders." *World Development* 21 (10): 1567–82.

————. (1994). "Support for Small Enterprises in South Africa: Impressions from Interviews with Firms, Their Corporate Customers, and Their Service Providers." Paper prepared for the Ministry of Trade and Industry of the South African Government, December.

Tendler, Judith, and Mônica Amorim (1996). "Small Firms and Their Helpers: Lessons on Demand." *World Development* 24 (3): 407–26.

Tendler, Judith, and Sara Freedheim (1994a). "Bringing Hirschman Back In: A Case of Bad Government Turned Good." Chap. 9 in *Rethinking the Development Experience: Essays Provoked by the Work of Albert Hirschman,* ed. Lloyd Rodwin and Don Schön. Washington, D.C.: Brookings Institution.

————. (1994b). "Trust in a Rent-seeking World: Health and Government Transformed in Northeast Brazil." *World Development* 22 (12): 1771–91.

Tewari, Meenu (1994). "Subcontracting Relations in the Age of Flexibility: Some Issues of Relevance from Indian Manufacturers." Draft paper prepared for the Employment and Strategies Branch, ILO, Geneva, Department of Urban Studies and Planning, Massachusetts Institute of Technology, April.

————. (1996). "When the Marginal Becomes Mainstream: Lessons From a Half-Century of Dynamic Small-firm Growth in Ludhiana, India." Ph.D. dissertation, Department of Urban Studies and Planning, Massachusetts Institute of Technology.

Thomas, John W. (1974). "Employment Creating Public Works Programs: Observations on Policy and Social Dimensions in Employment in Developing Nations." Pp. 297–311 in *Employment in Developing Nations: Report on a Ford Foundation Study,* ed. Edgar O. Edwards. New York: Columbia University Press.

————. (1986). "Food for Work: An Analysis of Current Experience and Recommendations for Future Performance." Development Discussion Paper, no. 213. Cambridge, Mass.: Harvard Institute for International Development, Harvard University.

Thomas, Robert J. (1989). "Participation and Control: A Shopfloor Perspective on Employee Participation." Pp. 117–43 in *Structuring Participation in Organizations,* vol. 7 of *Research in the Sociology of Organizations,* ed. Richard J. Magjuka. Greenwich, Conn.: JAI.

Thompson, Paul (1983). *The Nature of Work: An Introduction to Debates on the Labor Process.* New York: St. Martin's.

Trist, Eric (1981). "The Sociotechnical Perspective: The Evolution of Sociotechnical Systems as a Conceptual Framework and as an Action Research Program." Chap. 2 in *Perspectives on Organization Design and Behavior,* ed. Andrew H. Van der Ven and William F. Joyce. New York: John Wiley & Sons.

Tullock, Gordon (1965). *The Politics of Bureaucracy.* Washington, D.C.: Public Affairs Press.

Underwood, Peter, and Zdenka Underwood (1980). "New Spells for Old: Expectations and Realities of Western Medicine in a Remote Tribal Society in Yemen." Pp. 272–97 in *Changing Disease Patterns and Human Behaviour,* ed. N. F. Stanley and R. A. Joske. London: Academic Press.

UNCDF [United Nations Capital Development Fund] (1995a). *Poverty Reduction, Participation and Local Governance: The Role for UNCDF—A Fund for Community and Local Development.* UNCDF Policy Series, vol. 1. New York: United Nations Development Program (UNDP).

———. (1995). "Decentralized Governance Programme (DGP)." Draft, October.

UNDP [United Nations Development Program] (1992). *The Urban Environment in Developing Countries.* New York: UNDP.

UNICEF [United Nations Children's Fund] (1993). "Ceará Keeps Promise to Children." *First Call for Children* 4 (CF/DOI/FC/93–004): 7.

United States (1994a). "Commission on the Future of Worker-Management Relations: Report and Recommendations." Under the auspices of the U.S. Department of Labor and Department of Commerce. Washington, D.C.

———. (1994b). *Fact-Finding Report.* Departments of Commerce and Labor, Commission on the Future of Worker Management Relations, Washington, D.C., May.

———. (1994c). *The Seventh National Labor-Management Conference.* Sponsored by the Federal Mediation and Conciliation Service, the State and Local Government Labor-Management Committee, the National Labor-Management Association, and the U.S. Department of Labor, June 7–8. Washington, D.C.: Federal Mediation and Conciliation Service.

Uphoff, Norman (1993). "Grassroots Organizations and NGOs in Rural Development: Opportunities with Diminishing States and Expanding Markets." *World Development* 21 (4): 607–22.

Van Wicklin III, Warren A., (1987). "Challenging the Conventional Wisdom about Private Voluntary Organizations as Agents of Grassroots Development." Paper presented at the 28th annual convention, International Studies Association, Washington D.C., April 16.

———. (1990). "Private Voluntary Organizations as Agents of Alternative Development Strategies." Ph.D. dissertation, Department of Political Science, Massachusetts Institute of Technology.

Vaughan, Patrick, and Gill Walt (1984). "Implementing Primary Health Care." *Tropical Doctor* 14: 108–13.

Venkatesan, V. (1993). "Comments on 'Enhancing Organizational Effectiveness in Developing Countries: The Training and Visit System Revisited.'" *Public Administration and Development* 13: 515–29.

Veja (1993). "O agito cearense." 26 (48): 88–94.

Vivian, Jessica (1994). "NGOs and Sustainable Development in Zimbabwe: No Magic Bullets." *Development and Change* 25 (1): 167–93.

Vivian, Jessica, and Gladys Maseko (1994). "NGOs, Participation and Rural Development: Testing the Assumptions with Evidence from Zimbabwe." Discussion paper DP 49. Geneva: United Nations Research Institute for Social Development.

von Braun, Joachim, Tesfaye Teken, and Patrick Webb (1992). "Labor-intensive Public Works for Food Security in Africa: Past Experience and Future Potential." *International Labour Review* 131 (1): 19–34.

Wade, Robert (1988). "The Management of Irrigation Systems: How to Evoke Trust and Avoid the Prisoners' Dilemma." *World Development* 16 (4): 489–500.

———. (1990). *Governing the Market: Economic Theory and the Role of Government in East Asian Industrialization.* Princeton: Princeton University Press.

———. (1996). "Japan, the World Bank, and the Art of Paradigm Maintenance: *The East Asian Miracle* in Political Perspective." *New Left Review* 217: 3–36.

Wade, Ruth H. (1993). "Dry Solutions for Drought Relief: Institutional Innovation in Relief Delivery in Ceará, Brazil." Master's thesis, Department of Urban Studies and Planning, Massachusetts Institute of Technology, June.

Walt, Gill (1988). "CHW's: Are National Programmes in Crisis?" *Health Policy and Planning* 3 (1): 1–21.

Walt, Gill, et al. (1990). *Community Health Workers in National Programmes: Just Another Pair of Hands?* Philadelphia: Open University Press.

Watanabe, Susumu (1971). "Sub-contracting, Industrialization, and Employment Creation." *International Labour Review* 104 (1): 51–76.

———. (1974). "Reflections on Current Policies for Promoting Small Scale Enterprises and Subcontracting." *International Labour Review* 110 (5): 405–22.

———. (1983). *Technology, Marketing, and Industrialization: Linkages Between Small and Large Enterprises.* Delhi: Macmillan India Limited.

———. (1991). "The Japanese Quality Control Circle: Why It Works." *International Labour Review* 130 (1): 57–80.

Watson, Gabrielle (1994). "Targeted Interventions." Chap. 7 in *Honduras Country Economic Memorandum.* Washington, D.C.: World Bank. Also included in Webb et al. (1995).

———. (1995). *Good Sewers Cheap? Agency-customer Interactions in Low-cost Urban Sanitation in Brazil.* Washington, D.C.: World Bank.

WB [World Bank] (1983). *Brazil: An Interim Assessment of Rural Development Programs for the Northeast.* Washington, D.C.: World Bank.

———. (1987). *World Bank Experience with Rural Development, 1965–1986.* Operations Evaluation Department report no. 6883, World Bank, Washington, D.C., October 16.

———. (1991). *Urban Policy and Economic Development: An Agenda for the 1990s.* Washington, D.C.: World Bank.

———. (1993a). "Agriculture Sector Review." Agriculture and Natural Resources Department, World Bank, Washington, D.C., July.

———. (1993b). *The East Asian Miracle.* New York: Oxford University Press.

———. (1994). *Agricultural Extension: Lessons from Completed Projects.* Operations Evaluation Department report no. 13000, World Bank, Washington, D.C., April 29.

———. (1995a). "LAC in Brief." Department of Latin America and the Caribbean.

———. (1995b). *World Development Report 1995: Workers in an Integrating World.* New York: Oxford University Press.

———. (1995c). "Unions Can Be Bad—or Good." *Development Brief* 63.

Webb, Kathryn, Vandever Webb, Kye Woo Lee, and Anna Maria Sant'Anna (1995). *The Participation of Nongovernmental Organizations in Poverty Alleviation: A Case Study of the Honduras Social Investment Fund Project.* Discussion paper no. 295. Washington, D.C.: World Bank.

Weiss, Janet A., and Mary Tschirhart (1994). "Public Information Campaigns as Policy Instruments." *Journal of Policy Analysis and Management* 13 (1): 82–119.

Wever, Kirsten, Rosemary Batt, and Saul Rubenstein (1996). "Innovation in Isolation: Labor-Management Partnerships in the United States." *Economic and Labour Relations Review* (Summer).

Whitney, Craig R. (1995). "Where France's Bureaucratic Corps Gets Its Esprit." *New York Times,* December 28, 3.

WHO [World Health Organization] (1989). "Strengthening the Performance of Community Health Workers in Primary Health Care." *WHO Technical Report* 780: 1–46.

Wiesner, Eduardo (1995). "Fiscal Decentralization in Colombia: Advantages and Pitfalls." *Urban Age* 3 (3): 9.

Williamson, John (1993). "Democracy and the 'Washington Consensus.'" *World Development* 21 (8): 1329–36.

Willis, Eliza J. (1986). "The State as Banker: The Expansion of the Public Sector in Brazil." Ph.D. dissertation, University of Texas–Austin.

———. (1990). "The Politicized Bureaucracy: Regimes and Presidents in Brazilian Development." Boston College.

Wilson, James Q. (1989). *Bureaucracy: What Government Agencies Do and Why They Do It.* New York: Basic Books.

Wood, Stephen (1989). *The Transformation of Work? Skill, Flexibility and the Labour Process.* Boston: Unwin Hyman.

Wyatt Company (1994). *Best Practices in Corporate Restructuring: Wyatt's 1993 Survey of Corporate Restructuring.* Chicago: Wyatt Company.

Zarur, Sandra Beatriz (1993). "From Bad to Good Government: The Case of Three Local Governments in Ceará, Brazil." Master's thesis, Department of Urban Studies and Planning, Massachusetts Institute of Technology, June.

Index

Advertising. *See* Publicity and public information

Agricultural extension agents, 76; in boll weevil campaign, 84, 87, 88, 90; and customized approach, 95–96; in emergency drought-relief program, 47, 52–53, 54, 56–63, 73, 76, 94; during epidemics, 40, 179n. 37; and Santana cooperative, 76, 81–84, 93–94, 152; self-enlarging jobs of, 59–62, 138, 139, 183n. 20 and standardized messages, 94–95, 97, 140; and Training-and-Visit model, 56, 91–92, 93–94, 96–97, 139

Agricultural extension agents, U.S., 100

Agricultural extension program for small farmers, 12–13, 75–76; boll weevil campaign, 84–91; —and standardized messages, 95; and civil society, 152; and client-driven approach, 100–101; explanations for work performance of, 135–42; standardization vs. customization in, 73, 93–99 (*see also* Training-and-Visit model of agricultural extension)

Agricultural extension program for small farmers with Santana cooperative, 76–80, 101; and agents' motivation, 96–97; and boll weevil campaign, 90; as client-driven, 77–78, 81–84, 88; as customized, 77–78, 81–84, 93–94; as informal performance contracting, 83–84, 101; vs. larger associations, 76–77; lessons from, unnoticed, 164; as NGO-like, 159

Agricultural reforms, and Ceará, 10

Aruaru Association of Furniture-Makers (Associação dos Moveleiros de Aruaru), 118

Associationalism, worker associations vs. other forms of, 7

Autonomy, 5, 14

Boll weevil campaign, 84–91; and standardized messages, 95

Business extension service: and civil society, 152; and customized vs. standardized jobs, 73; demand-driven, 141; (*see also* Demand-driven approach to small-firm assistance); and public procurement from small firms program, 12, 102 (*see also* Public procurement program for small firms)

"Calling" or "chosenness," 14, 137. *See also* Worker dedication and morale

Ceará (state), 9–11, 17, 74–75; drought and drought relief in, 46, 48–49, 55; health and health-service access indicators for, 21; municípios in, 11, 173n. 32; and Northeast, 10 (*see also* Northeast Brazil)

Ceará (state), successful programs in, 11–13; mixed nature of, 163–64; themes prominent in, 13–16 (*see also* Agricultural extension program for small farmers; Emergency drought-relief program; Preventive health program; Public procurement program for small firms)

"Ceará fatigue," 17

Ceará Society of Industrialists (CIC/Centro Industrial de Ceará), 155–56

Change agents, preventive health workers as, 40, 180n. 39

Charismatic leader, 18. *See also* Leadership

"Chosenness" or "calling," 14, 137. *See also* Worker dedication and morale

Civil servants: "chosenness" of, 137; "good," 57; and public disasters, 53; unfavorable assumptions about, 5. *See also* Worker(s) in government

Civil society, 5–6; and good government, 15–16, 144–45, 146, 151–57; in three-way dynamic, 15–16, 146–50, 157. *See also* Nongovernmental organizations

Client-driven approaches, 5–6, 99–101, 138; in agricultural extension program, 77–78, 81–84, 88; demand-driven assistance as, 112; in industri-

Library of Congress Cataloging-in-Publication Data

Tendler, Judith.
    Good government in the tropics / Judith Tendler.
      p. cm. — (The Johns Hopkins studies in development)
    Includes bibliographical references and index.
    ISBN 0-8018-5452-0 (alk. paper)
    1. Ceará (Brazil : State)—Politics and government. 2. Government
productivity—Brazil—Ceará (State)—Case studies. I. Title.
II. Series.
JL2499.C43T46 1997
320.8'3'098131—dc21
                                            96-39215
                                          CIP